Richard Rorty

Education, Philosophy, and Politics

Edited by Michael A. Peters
and Paulo Ghiraldelli Jr.

ROWMAN & LITTLEFIELD PUBLISHERS, INC.
Lanham • Boulder • New York • Oxford

ROWMAN & LITTLEFIELD PUBLISHERS, INC.

Published in the United States of America
by Rowman & Littlefield Publishers, Inc.
4720 Boston Way, Lanham, Maryland 20706
www.rowmanlittlefield.com

12 Hid's Copse Road
Cumnor Hill, Oxford OX2 9JJ, England

British Library Cataloguing in Publication Information Available

Library of Congress Cataloging-in-Publication Data

Richard Rorty : education, philosophy, and politics / edited by Michael A. Peters and
Paulo Ghiraldelli Jr.
    p. cm.
    Includes bibliographical references and index.
    ISBN 0-7425-0905-2 (alk. paper)—ISBN 0-7425-0906-0 (pbk. : alk. paper)
    1. Rorty, Richard. 2. Philosophy. 3. Education—Philosophy. 4. Political
science—Philosophy. I. Peters, Michael (Michael A.), 1948– II. Ghiraldelli Jr., Paulo
(Ghiraldelli Junior)

B945 .R524 R554 2001
191—dc21

2001048441

Printed in the United States of America

♾™ The paper used in this publication meets the minimum requirements of
American National Standard for Information Sciences—Permanence of Paper for
Printed Library Materials, ANSI/NISO Z39.48-1992.

Contents

Introduction

Rorty's Neopragmatism: Nietzsche, Culture, and Education

Michael A. Peters and Paulo Ghiraldelli Jr.

All the beauty and sublimity we have bestowed upon real and imaginary things I will reclaim them as the property and product of man: as his fairest apology. Man as poet, as thinker, as God, as love, as power: with what regal liberality he has lavished gifts upon things so as to impoverish himself and make himself feel wretched! His most unselfish act hitherto has been to admire and worship and to know how to conceal from himself that it was he who created what he admired.

—Friedrich Nietzsche, *The Will to Power*, trans. Walter Kaufmann and R. J. Hollingdale, ed., with commentary, by Walter Kaufmann

Richard Rorty is undoubtedly one of the leading philosophers of our time and his reputation is well deserved, even if it is the case that one can find little on which to agree with him. He has written on a vast range of topics and engaged in the most pressing of contemporary philosophical debates with a variety of conversational friends and adversaries who are among the most influential thinkers of their age: Davidson, Quine, Derrida, Gadamer, Lyotard, Rawls, Habermas, Geertz, to name a few. In addition, he has engaged with some of the major philosophers of the twentieth century: not only the 'classic' pragmatists and especially John Dewey, but also Wittgenstein, Heidegger, Davidson and others in the analytic tradition. Rorty has distinguished himself as an original thinker in his contributions to these 'conversations' and debates over a considerable period of time—from his early analysis of the 'linguistic turn' in the 1960s to his more recent essays on politics, democracy, and social hope. Over this period Rorty's intellectual trajectory has become more obvious and it is clear that he has moved a considerable distance.

In a rare autobiographical piece he charts his own set of changing philosophical commitments: his Trotskyist family background, his early flirtation with Platonism during his teenage years, the turn to Hegel (and Proust) after leaving Chicago for Harvard, and his rediscovery of Dewey which coincided with his initial encounters with Derrida and Heidegger. As he writes: "I was struck by the resemblances between Dewey's, Wittgenstein's and Heidegger's criticisms of Cartesianism" (Rorty, "Trotsky and the Wild Orchids" 1999, 12), resemblances that became the theme for the now classic *Philosophy and the Mirror of Nature* (Rorty 1980). By contrast, *Contingency, Irony, and Solidarity* was a book that attempted to describe "what intellectual life might be like if one could manage to give up the Platonic attempt to hold reality and justice in a single vision" (Rorty 1979, 13). The result, at least in Rorty's own perception of how he has been received, is that he is attacked "with equal vigor from the political right and the political left" (Rorty 1979, 3)—a sign to him of being in good shape. He writes: "I am often cited by conservative culture warriors as one of the relativistic, irrationalist, deconstructing, sneering, smirking intellectuals whose writings are weakening the moral fibre of the young" (3). At the same time representatives of the political left (as he says) have described his position as complacent—in the words of Richard Bernstein "ideological *apologia*" (cited in Rorty 1979, 4). In contrast to the description of America as a "disciplinary society" (using Foucault's term) based upon the ideology of liberal individualism, Rorty sees America, pretty much as Whitman and Dewey did, as opening a prospect on "illimitable democratic vistas." "I think our country—despite its past and present atrocities and vices, and despite its continuing eagerness to elect fools and knaves to high office—is a good example of the best kind of society so far invented" (Rorty 1979, 4).

It is this kind of generalization on the part of Rorty that most annoys the political left. Our guess is that those on the left not only find the claim nauseous in terms of its "flag-waving" aspects but also its deliberate left-baiting qualities. This kind of remark for which Rorty is well known is like the taunts of a naughty child who wants to provoke and make themselves the center of attention. Rorty, having initiated a reaction, then often scales down the original provocation and takes the middle ground, reinterpreting the original issue. It is a characteristic Rortyan conversational tactical set of moves and, on the whole, it works perfectly well. We might consider this strategy part of the classical genre of the essayist. What distinguished Rorty's essays, however, is that they are not simply occasional; they rest on clear, coherent, and well thought out philosophical positions so that what looks like an offhand and inflated remark often turns out to be part of a well-considered position that has been strongly developed over a period of time. We might characterize this position not just as a form of neopragmatism, but also as a form of *naturalism* taken to its logical conclusion. Rorty's naturalism, for instance, denies that science has any special method to which we can attribute its success by virtue of its capacity to represent reality or how things really are in themselves. The vocabularies of natural science have no unique cultural significance for Rorty; they are of a piece with other vocabularies—moral and aesthetic—*tools* that equip us with beliefs for coping with our environment. His naturalism, thus, robs philosophy of its role in the analytic tradition as a sort of superscience given over to adjudicating truth claims or narrowly specialized as the discipline responsible for epistemology and the logic of justification. On Rorty's account once we rid ourselves of representationalism—the idea that knowledge is to be understood in terms of its relation to the world depicted in an accurate description of what there is and how things are—we also rid ourselves of a series of misleading metaphors that have governed modern philosophy. This realization frees us from thinking that there must be something outside history or the human community which can act as an independent check on the veracity of our beliefs, in much the same way that our forebears believed that we need and have an extrahuman external authority that shores up the truths of our moral universe. This Rortyan naturalism, while springing more immediately from Sellars and Quine, is quintessentially summed up by Nietzsche in the quotation we have taken from *The Will to Power* to open and orient this introduction. Yet if Rorty is Nietzschean in his naturalism, he is less than Nietzschean in his political beliefs.

Neopragmatism and Social Hope

In *Philosophy and Social Hope* Rorty (1999) restates one of the guiding themes of his work during the last decade: post-Nietzschean European philosophy and American pragmatism agree in attempting to jettison a set of philosophical distinctions—appearance/reality, mind/body, scheme/content, finding/making, morality/prudence—and the vocabularies built around them, vocabularies that since Plato have dominated the history of Western philosophy, culture, and education. Post-Nietzscheans and pragmatists are alike, Rorty suggests, in wanting to put aside this set of binary dualism or oppositions; they are alike in wanting to skew the language of metaphysics. To give up this language is to give up truth as correspondence and science as accurate representation of the world as it really is. It is to put science and philosophy on a par with the rest of culture and to emphasize a hermeneutic model of conversation as constituting the limits and possibilities of discourse and agreement. It is also to give up on the notion of morality that springs from the notion of the essence of human nature. Indeed, it is to give up once and for all, all versions of foundationalism—linguistic, moral, and epistemological—and all forms of representationalism. Like Nietzsche and Heidegger, Rorty is antagonistic to Platonism considered as the philosophical embodiment of these metaphysical dualisms and, like Dewey, he thinks, "the vocabulary built around these traditional distinctions has become an obstacle to our social hopes" (Rorty 1999, xii). The *only* substantial difference between Nietzsche and Dewey (taken by Rorty to be emblematic of the differences that separate European post-Nietzscheans and American neopragmatists) concerns the values of egalitarian ideas and of the ideal of democracy (Rorty 1999, 23).

Rorty's neopragmatism is based upon readings of both the "classic pragmatists"—James, Pierce, and Dewey—and the neopragmatists—Quine, Goodman, Putnam, and Davidson. While Rorty believes that philosophy and politics are not tightly linked, pragmatism, nevertheless, is the distinctive American "philosophy of democracy" (24), as Dewey himself claimed. Rorty reworks this line of thought to suggest that America and pragmatism share the same "hopeful, melioristic, experimental frame of mind" (24) and, after Dewey, he characterizes his own brand of neopragmatism as the attempt to substitute social hope for knowledge or for the attempt to penetrate behind appearances to reality. This substitution he regards as the most distinctive and praiseworthy capacity of humanity. Social hope is characterized by "our ability to trust and cooperate with other people" so as to work together to improve the future (xiii). This utopian vision is inspired by Dewey's notion of a classless, egalitarian society.

Rorty's neopragmatism has proved both powerful and controversial. It has propelled him into a series of debates both with analytic philosophers and with Continental philosophers. At the same time his work has acted as an intellectual bridge between them. His neopragmatism, starting with his challenge to the notion of analysis in analytic philosophy, first championed the hermeneutical conversation as the model of philosophy and culture. His heroes were Wittgenstein, Heidegger, and Dewey. As his writing career progressed the division between Nietzschean-inspired Continental thought and "American" neopragmatism became clearer. We might contrast Rorty as an American living at the end of the millennium, and Nietzsche, a German (who wanted to write for a French audience), living in fin de siècle Europe: the one full of social hope, imbued with a Deweyan utopian scientific attitude, and wanting to spread American democracy to the rest of the world; the other, also a "futurist" but of a different temperament—at the same time skeptical, cynical, and caustic—a witness to the fragmentation of the old world order, the breakup of the Habsburg empire and the dissolution of the old culture. Nietzsche is both more pessimistic and antiliberal than Rorty but also more hopeful that something *different* might still emerge. Both want to cash out the cognitivism that has dominated Western intellectual life since Plato, but, Rorty says he wishes to do so in terms of the interests of an egalitarian society rather than in the interests of Nietzschean individualism. Rorty, who links up to his American philosophical roots, epitomizes the New World pragmatist utopian philosophy that rejects foundationalism and representationalism, and yet tries to hold on to the promise of the Enlightenment's political project. In this he agrees with Habermas and Rawls against the so-called Nietzschean Left. Rorty still has faith in the cosmopolitan ideal and the universalism that supports it. Whether this cosmopolitanism is merely a cover for the universalizing tendencies of an ethnocentrism accompanying contemporary American "liberal culture" is a question that needs a great deal more discussion and analysis. Rorty's analysis of "the politics of identity" as "the result of a loss of hope . . . of an inability to construct a plausible narrative of progress" (Rorty 1999, 232)—a turn away from utopian dreams to philosophy which signals despair—is both too easy and convenient a description.

Richard Rorty (1999) maintains that the terms "identity" and "difference" have become popular in recent philosophy for two reasons. First, he writes:

> The Nietzsche-Heidegger-Derrida criticism of the Greek metaphysical tradition has insisted that sameness and difference are relative to the choice of description— that there is no such thing as the 'intrinsic' nature or the 'essential' attributes of anything. There is nothing which is vital to the self-identity of a being, independent of the descriptions we give of it. This insistence is found also in the work of philosophers like Wittgenstein, Quine, Davidson, and I am happy to join in the resulting chorus. (235)

He continues:

> The second reason why you hear a lot about identity and difference these days is that 'preservation of cultural identity' and 'identification with the oppressed group of which one is a member' have become political watchwords. Attempts to help native tributes threatened by economic development are run together with attempts to raise the consciousness of migrants or racial or sexual minorities. Out of this situation, the terms 'politics of identity' or 'politics of difference' have emerged, as descriptions of movements which are distinct from the familiar struggle of the poor against the rich. (235)

Rorty thinks we should abandon the last vestiges of eighteenth-century rationalism in favor of twentieth-century pragmatism and he believes that abandoning Western rationalism has no discouraging political implications. Rorty (1998) complains that the "cultural left"—a term he uses to describe the constellation of left academics who have chosen to embrace "apocalyptic French and German philosophy"—by focusing upon issues of race, ethnicity, and gender has steered towards identity politics and away from economic politics, thus fragmenting the Left and destroying the possibility of a progressive alliance. Based upon a "resigned," "pessimistic," "spectatorial," "abstract," "over-theorized" and "over-philosophized" system-critique, the cultural Left allegedly has substituted philosophy for political economy, sadism (Freud) for selfishness (Marx), Otherness for economic inequality, and collaborated with the Right in replacing real politics with cultural politics (see Peters, this volume). Accordingly, it has "no vision of a country to be achieved by building a consensus on the need for specific reforms" (15) and it has no program that can deal effectively with the immiseration produced by the globalization of the labor market.

As Peters notes in this volume, Rorty's philosophy is bedevilled with dualisms that perform a political service: two stories of the Enlightenment—political and intellectual; two selves, two "cultures"—public and private; two politics, two lefts—academic vs. activist, utopian vs dystopian. Ultimately, these dualisms artificially separate identity from economic politics, belying the way in which otherness is economically reproduced, as well as being socially and culturally reproduced, at a variety of sites.

Alternative accounts might want to embrace specific *historical narratives* of the growth of a kind of cultural pluralism that signifies an emerging complex of events: the revitalization of traditional ethnic cultures and languages as a result of struggles against imperialism and the liberal state; the growth of movements for cultural rights and sovereignty, increasingly against the economic exploitation of world multinationals; the diaspora of the modern world; the reassertion of the cultures of the major civilizations, including China, India, and the Islamic states; the growing separatist and regionalist movements within existing states; the Hispanicization of the United States; the growth and proliferation of postwar youth cultures that follow a logic of internal cultural differentiation; and so on. The turn toward "difference" and "identity" in this context might be seen more as the embrace of a Wittgensteinian philosophy of multiplicity and family resemblance focused upon hybridization and miscegenation, together with an emphasis, in certain cases, upon what Lyotard calls the *differend*. While these cultural processes might stand against each other, nevertheless, they simultaneously exist together, often in the same territory.

In rejecting foundationalism, Rorty also does away with any essence of the moral self, substituting a local, historical, and contingent self for the transhistorical metaphysical subject of philosophical liberalism. As Rorty (1999) writes:

> Dewey and Nietzsche of course agreed about a lot of things. Nietzsche thought of the happy, prosperous masses who would inhabit Dewey's social democratic utopia as 'the last men', worthless creatures incapable of greatness. Nietzsche was as instinctively antidemocratic in his politics as Dewey was instinctively democratic. But the two men agree not only on the nature of knowledge but on the nature of moral choice. (xxviii)

This means that the lesson Rorty takes from both Dewey and Nietzsche is the rejection of the idea that there is "a legitimating principle lurking behind every right action" (xxx) or the similar idea that "there must be a sort of invisible tribunal of reason administering laws which we all, somewhere deep down inside, recognize as binding upon us" (xxxi). Rorty puts the idea even more forcefully when he writes:

> The idea of a universally shared source of truth called 'reason' or 'human nature' is, for us pragmatists, just the idea that such discussion ought to be capable of being made conclusive. We see this idea as a misleading way of expressing the hope, which we share, that the human race as a whole should gradually come together in a global community, a community which incorporates most of the thick morality of the European industrialized democracies. (xxxii)

Perhaps therein is contained the difference between Dewey and Rorty, as his self-conscious heir, and the post-Nietzscheans (if we can really call them by that moniker)—Derrida, Deleuze, Foucault—for they, taking their inspiration from Nietzsche, engage in what Nietzsche called the "critique of modernity," precisely on the understanding of what might emerge is the creation of something new or something different. In texts like *Beyond Good and Evil* and also in Book II of *The Will to Power* Nietzsche embarks on the "Critique of the highest values hitherto," a threefold critique—of religion, of morality, and of philosophy—as a preliminary to establishing principles of a new evaluation.

In *Ecce Homo* (1992, orig. 1888), Nietzsche turns to *Beyond Good and Evil*, which he says belongs to the "No-saying and *No-doing* part: the revaluation of existing values themselves"—"*the work of destruction*" (82) and he comments:

> This book (1886) [*Beyond Good and Evil*] is in all essentials a *critique of modernity*, the modern sciences, the modern arts, not even excluding modern politics, together with signposts to an antithetical type who is as little modern as possible, a

noble, an affirmative type. In the latter sense the book is a *school for gentlemen*, that concept taken more spiritually *and radically* than it has ever been taken. (emphasis in the original, EH, 82)

In *The Genealogy of Morals* and *Twilight of the Idols* Nietzsche continues the work of critique, first, through exposing the psychology of Christianity, based upon the spirit of *ressentiment* in a preliminary study for the revaluation of all values, and, second, through an analysis of "modern ideas"—as he says, "the old truth is coming to an end" (86). In the essay "Expeditions of an Untimely Man" (*Twilight of the Idols*) he writes a section entitled *"Criticism of modernity"* beginning:

> Our institutions are no longer fit for anything: everyone is unanimous about that. But the fault lies not with them but in *us*. Having lost all instincts out of which institutions grow, we are losing the institutions themselves, because *we* are no longer fit for them. . . . For institutions to exist there must exist the kind of will, instinct, imperative which is anti-liberal to the point of malice: the will to tradition, to authority, to centuries-long responsibility, to *solidarity* between succeeding generations backwards and forwards *in infinitum*. . . . The entire West has lost those instincts out of which institutions grow, out of which the future grows: perhaps nothing goes so much against the grain of its 'modern' spirit as this. One lives for today, one lives very fast—one lives very irresponsibly: it is precisely this which one calls 'freedom'. (TI, 93–94)

The critique of modernity, for Nietzsche, then, involves a critique of "modern" ideas and institutions: democracy, liberalism, humanism, freedom, truth, equality, modern marriage, modern education, and science. The critique of modernity above all involves crucially the critique of modern philosophy based on these concepts and its respect for their founding institutions. In opposition to modern philosophy Nietzsche advocates an overcoming of the concepts of the "will" and the "soul" and, ultimately, of the morality that presupposes such notions.

Nietzsche, in passages like the one above in *Twilight of the Idols*, and in *Beyond Good and Evil* and *The Will to Power*, identifies the break with tradition as the defining feature of modernity, and, underscores its accompanying recognition that the sources of its values can no longer be based upon appeals to the authority of the past. It is a situation which Nietzsche understands brings about a kind of value reversal to traditionalism: traditionalism is understood in terms of the veneration of things past, crudely speaking, "the older the better," because the further back in time we go the closer we get to mystical first causes or origins and the closer we get to the sacred books of revelation in the religious tradition. By contrast, modernity understood as a break with the past—an aesthetic, moral, political, and epistemological break—encourages a self-consciousness of the present and an orientation to the future based on notions of change, progress, experiment, innovation, and newness. Most importantly, modernity involves that myth it constructs about itself that it is able to create its own values and normative orientations somehow out of its own historical force, movement, and trajectory. Nietzsche rejects any simple-minded opposition and refuses to embrace one option or the other unreservedly; rather, we might see him contemplating how and why "we moderns" want to draw up the historical stakes in terms of such an exhaustive dichotomy.

Not surprisingly Rorty's work has generated applications of his neopragmatism for many fields and disciplines strictly outside the world of philosophy: jurisprudence, literature, science, religion, and education.

Rorty's Neopragmatist Philosophy of Education

The main text on philosophy of education written by Rorty is "Education without Dogmas" published in *Dissent* (Rorty 1989a). It is available again in a new book by Rorty, *Philosophy and Social Hope* (1999), under the new title, "Education as Socialization and Individualization."

In this essay Rorty suggests that the Right and the Left are largely in agreement in that at the abstract level they both accept "the identification of truth and freedom with the essentially human" (115) yet "both tend to ignore the fact that the word 'education' covers two entirely distinct, and equally necessary, processes—socialization and individualization" (117). In contradistinction, for Rorty "there is only the shaping of an animal into a human being by a process of socialization, followed (with luck) by the self-individualization and self-creation of that human being through his or her own later revolt against that very process" (118).

Rorty's (1994) second most important text for philosophers of education is "Feminism and Pragmatism," originally delivered as a Tanner Lecture. Finally, the third article of major significance for the philosophy of education is "The Contingency of Language" which can be found in the now famous book *Contingency, Irony, and Solidarity* (Rorty 1989b). The first article tells us what education is from a neopragmatist perspective. It tells us about the past and present. The second and third texts describe neopragmatist strategies to change the world. They speculate about the future—what education could be and what education should do.

"Education as Socialization and Individualization" develops the following idea: given a choice between freedom and truth, the Left is right in seeking freedom. But the Left should not assume that freedom is an element of "human essence." If education is socialization and individualization, and socialization is the moment of acceptance of consensus, and if individualization is the moment of freedom and skepticism based on such consensus, then teachers could use the first moment to help the second moment. A neopragmatist teacher can say to students that the United States is not just the United States, but that there is an "America." It is a dream. Whitman's and Dewey's dream. They wanted the utopian metaphor of "America" to live in the minds of the first immigrants: a place of liberty, tolerance, social justice, and equal cultural and economic opportunity for all. A place without wars, intolerance, and the old hierarchies and oppressions. Socialization need not be carried out only according to the values of the Right. The Civil Rights Movement, for example, might provide American heroes about whom we can write appropriate sentimental stories designed to move the people. Individualization need not be pursued only with authors and theorists adopted by the Cultural Left—Foucault or Lacan or Marx. But it could be done with the dreamers and poets.

The second article is about strategy. Marx thought that we should change the world rather than simply interpreting it. Rorty, by contrast, believes that the transformations of the world happen as we make new interpretations and invent new vocabularies. Rorty doesn't believe in "the world" and "language" as separate things. Linguistic behavior is a behavior of the featherless biped. This is a *holistic view* of the relations between interpretation as a linguistic happening and physical or social happening. So, the power of education to change the world is linked to our power of interpretation or our redescriptions, as Rorty says. How? He explains:

> One way to change instinctive emotional reactions is to provide new language, which will facilitate new reactions. By "new language" I mean not just new words but also creative misuses of language—familiar words used in ways which initially sound crazy. Something traditionally regarded as a moral abomination can become an object of general satisfaction, or conversely, as a result of the increased popularity of an alternative description of what is happening. Such popularity extends logical space by making descriptions of situations, which used to seem crazy seem sane. Once, for example, it would have sounded crazy to describe homosexual sodomy as a touching expression of devotion, or to describe a woman manipulating the elements of the Eucharist as a figuration of the relations of the Virgin to her son. But such descriptions are now acquiring popularity. At most times, it sounds crazy to describe the degradation and extirpation of helpless minorities as a purification of the moral and spiritual life of Europe. But at certain periods and places—under the Inquisition, during the Wars of Religion, under the Nazis—it did not. (Rorty 1995, 126–27)

As we read Rorty, there are three ways to change the behavior of the featherless biped. First, by telling emotional stories in which different peoples develop a sense of unity because they have developed relationships with one another—they married across ethnic and 'racial' divisions. Second, by telling pragmatic stories in which one can choose a new way because this will produce better results for his or her life. Third, like in the case above, we invent new expressions that seek not just the guarantee of old rights but also new rights—democratic rights, of course. This is a future role of the philosophy of education on Rorty's account. In this case, Rorty is encouraging the creation of new metaphors and the development of our imaginations.

But now we have entered the field of the third text, "The Contingency of the Language." In it, Rorty shows his approach to Davidson's theory of metaphor. A new role for philosophy of education is the creation of metaphors. But these metaphors cannot be understood as different forms of literal expressions. They must be understood as creative expressions that make people stop their old conversations and begin new ones. With luck, these novel expressions and new vocabularies will encourage in us a form of political maturity defined by the fact that it does not require anything external to us—the moral authority of a god—to secure our democratic institutions or to anchor our democratic practices.

Organization of This Book

Bjørn Ramberg begins this collection of essays by developing a distinctive reading of Rorty, which differs from both deflationist and demonizing accounts. On Ramberg's view Rorty is exercising a pragmatist metaphysical critique on philosophy and, thereby, Rorty is involved in a kind of renewing practice. This practice is governed by Rorty's styles—his choice of instruments (in Plato's terms)—that together mark him out as a radical philosopher.

In chapter 2 Jim Garrison takes issue with Rorty's reading of Dewey in relation to metaphysics and what he calls the "education of human potential." Specifically, Garrison contra Rorty accepts Dewey's naturalistic metaphysics, not as a "contradiction in terms," but rather as a basis for a deconstruction of the metaphysics of presence. Together with Dewey's reconstruction of Aristotle's theory of potentiality, Garrison believes "we will have to rethink completely the ideas of human development and education." At any rate, Garrison explicitly rejects Rorty's account of Dewey's metaphysics.

Paulo Ghiraldelli Jr. embraces Rorty's philosophy wholeheartedly, defending him against both Habermasian and Deleuzean criticisms. Central to Ghiraldelli's argument is an account of metaphor that Rorty takes from Davidson.

It is an account, so Ghiraldelli maintains, that is central both to alternative vocabularies—to telling new stories—and to inventing our democratic future through the creation of new rights. These two aspects govern the way in which Ghiraldelli thinks we should do philosophy of education.

In chapter 4 James D. Marshall takes Rorty to task for his comparison of Dewey and Foucault who differ only in terms of "what we may hope." By contrast, Marshall finds a positive message in Foucault though not a "Deweyan progressive and optimistic message of hope." Marshall explores the Rortyan differences between Dewey and Foucault on methodology, arguing that Rorty downplays Dewey's notion of scientific method while at the same time elevating Foucault to a methodologist. He concludes that Rorty's argument for the superiority of post-Darwinian American philosophy, insofar as it depends upon an alleged difference between Dewey and Foucault, does not hold.

Steven Best and Douglas Kellner in chapter 5 examine Rorty's postmodern assault on theory and metatheory, not only the idea that theory can provide foundations, but also the notion that philosophy plays any political role at all. Their position from the tradition of critical theory is to argue against Rorty that theory provides the tools for social critique that can make a palpable difference to the goal of human emancipation. By contrast, they outline a role for public intellectuals where theory helps to provide social maps and historical narratives that together contextualize the present age.

Alberto Tosi Rodrigues focuses upon Rorty's anti-Marxism in his chapter on Rorty's political liberalism. Rodrigues first describes the differences between Marxism and Rorty's own account of political change, focusing on Marx's essentialism and Rorty's antilogocentrism. Next he uses both Castoriadis and Dewey to illuminate Rorty's position. Finally, he takes up the question of Rorty's anti-Marxism in relation to "really extistent liberalism."

In chapter 7, Peter McLaren, Ramin Farahmandpur, and Juha Suoranta take the position that the inherent limitations in Rorty's voluntarist philosophy and attendant (essentially reformist) political work precludes it from offering anything of substantial importance to the project of critical pedagogy. "From the context of the Marxist model of revolutionary praxis that we are attempting to develop, we believe that Rorty's politics seriously undermines the revolutionary basis of critical pedagogy. In so doing, it offers progressive educators little room to maneuver in creating a socialist approach to educational reform that is able to overcome the perils of neoliberalism."

In chapter 8 Kenneth Wain also turns to Rorty's remark that there is no more a relationship between philosophy and education than there is between philosophy and politics, to show that it is, in part, a consequence of his general rejection of the politics of the French poststructuralists and, in part, a consequence of his own problems with harmonizing the liberal and post-modernist elements in his thinking. Wain shows that Rorty has changed his view somewhat and has come to recognize a link between philosophy and politics and, by extension, education, of a particular kind. Drawing upon Dewey, Rorty comes to write about education and politics in a way which is in tune with his continuing rejection of 'philosophy of education' as a discipline.

In the final chapter (chapter 9), Michael Peters addresses the question of Rorty's critique of the cultural Left, focusing on one of his most recent texts, *Achieving America: Leftist Thought in Twentieth-Century America* (Rorty 1998). Peters wants to drive a wedge between Rorty's New World American utopian pragmatism and European Nietzscheanism. Rorty wants to jettison the metaphysical baggage of the Enlightenment (its foundationalism and its representationalism) but not the promise of the Enlightenment's political project, whereas on the basis of their critique and reevaluation of the Enlightenment (and modernity), the Nietzscheans wish to call into question the fundamental commitments of political liberalism.

Notes

1. M. A. Peters. (1998) "Wittgenstein and Post-Analytic Philosophy of Education: Rorty or Lyotard?" *Educational Theory and Philosophy* 29 (2), 1–32. Revised as "Rorty, Wittgenstein, and Postmodernism: Neopragmatism and the Politics of the *Ethnos*" (chapter 8) in M. A. Peters and J. D. Marshall. (1999) *Wittgenstein: Philosophy, Postmodernism, Pedagogy* (Westport, Conn.: Bergin & Garvey).

2. M. A. Peters. (1999) "*Achieving Our Country*: Postmodernism and Rorty's Critique of the Cultural Left," *The End of Postmodernism?* Invited paper presented at the Colloquium to Host Richard Rorty, Australian National University, August 21–22. Published as "*Achieving America*: Rorty, Postmodernism, and the Critique of the Cultural Left," *The Review of Education/Pedagogy/Cultural Studies* 22 (3): 223–41 (2001).

Bibliography

Nietzsche, F. (1968) *The Will to Power*, trans. Walter Kaufmann and R. J. Hollingdale, (ed.) with commentary, by W. Kaufmann. New York: Vintage Books.

Rorty, R. (1980) *Philosophy and the Mirror of Nature*. Oxford: Blackwell.

———. (1989a) "Education without Dogmas," *Dissent*, Spring: 198–204.

———. (1989b) *Contingency, Irony, and Solidarity*. Cambridge: Cambridge University Press.

———. (1990) "The Dangers of Over-Philosophication—Reply to Arcilla and Nicholson," *Educational Theory* 40 (1): 41–44.

———. (1991a) *Objectivity, Relativism, and Truth, Philosophical Papers*, Vol. 1. Cambridge: Cambridge University Press.

———. (1991b) *Essays on Heidegger and Others: Philosophical Papers*, Vol. 2. Cambridge: Cambridge University Press.

———. (1996) "Remarks on Deconstruction and Pragmatism." In Chantal Mouffe (ed.), *Deconstruction and Pragmatism*, London: Routledge, 3–18.

———. (1998) *Achieving Our Country: Leftist Thought in Twentieth-Century America*. Cambridge, Mass.: Harvard University Press.

———. (1999) *Philosophy and Social Hope*. Harmondsworth: Penguin.

———. (1994) "Feminism and Pragmatism," *The Tanner Lectures on Human Values*, Vol. 13, Salt Lake City: University of Utah Press.

CHAPTER ONE

Rorty and the Instruments of Philosophy

Bjørn Ramberg

And argument is a philosopher's instrument most of all.

(Republic, Book 9, 582d)

Three Readings of Rorty

In a response to Putnam's charge of relativism (Putnam 1990, 18–26), Rorty gives us the following pithy characterization of his philosophical strategy:

> In short, my strategy for escaping the self-referential difficulties into which "the Relativist" keeps getting himself is to move everything over from epistemology and metaphysics to cultural politics. (Rorty 1993, 457)

Construing traditional epistemology as unselfconscious sociology, and metaphysics, with Nietzsche, as an oddly alienated species of literature of self-creation, Rorty suggests that there are no deeper terms of assessment for philosophical theorizing than those expressing moral and political values. Rorty thereby challenges commitments that are deeply embedded in the self-understanding of Anglophone philosophy. Here I shall consider some of those commitments, and, in particular, the form of Rorty's opposition to them. I will suggest that Rorty's execution of his metaphilosophical critique is itself a distinctively philosophical activity. It embodies a conception of what it is to be a rational creature, and thereby offers us a possibility for the kind of self-renewing interpretation that philosophy has been performing on itself since Plato opened the chasm between appearance and reality by distinguishing lovers of truth from lovers of the spectacles of the sensory realm. Taking Rorty this way, I will be exploiting his work to articulate a pragmatist view of what philosophy is. This may be a form of co-option; for by the very attempt to say what philosophy is, I engage in a project towards which Rorty's laudably antiessentialist historicism makes him suspicious.

My reading of Rorty differs from two common perceptions, which we might call the deflationist view and the demonizing view. Deflationists tend to be sympathetic to Rorty's positions on particular issues. On their reading, neither the aim of Rorty's critique of modern epistemology and metaphysics, nor the reasoning behind it, situates Rorty in opposition to philosophy as a historical enterprise. Deflationists regard the appearance of end-of-philosophy radicality as largely a result of Rorty's rhetorical style—his Nietzschean penchant for tropes of provocation and exaggeration. According to the deflationist, Rorty emerges as the serious professional philosopher he is once we liberate him from the hyperbole in which he habitually wraps himself.

With the deflationists I regard Rorty as belonging to philosophy, indeed as offering a contribution to the continuation and development of the practice. Against the deflationist view, however, I will argue that Rorty's style, his rhetoric—that is, in Plato's metaphor, his instruments—are at the heart of that contribution. Rorty's particular choice of instruments and the way he conceives of their purpose makes Rorty, as the demonizers correctly perceive, a radical thinker, deeply opposed to certain still prevalent conceptions of the tasks of philosophy. But this radicality, this opposition, is a movement of a form inherent to philosophy; as philosophers we would do well to regard ourselves as participating in a practice which depends on just the sort of confrontation with itself that Rorty engages us in. Deflationists, reading Rorty through a filter designed to purify philosophical assertion of the obscuring particulates of rhetoric, are prone to underestimation of Rorty's opposition to current self-understandings of philosophy. They thereby distract themselves from Rorty's key contribution to philosophical thought.

Demonizers, by contrast, take that opposition very seriously indeed, but tend, whether they fear it or cheer it, to see it as an attack on the practice of philosophy itself. According to the demonizers, Rorty levels an assault against the core of the discipline, standing forth as an usherer-in of the post-philosophical era.

Deflationists and demonizers are both wrong about Rorty, though in different ways. Both kinds of misperceptions, however, may be encouraged by Rorty's reluctance to offer what we might call a first-order characterization of the practice of philosophical reflection. The suggestion I make in this chapter is that Rorty's scepticism toward the very idea of philosophy as a distinctive kind of intellectual activity inhibits his pragmatic reinterpretation of that activity. However, the tension that affects the relation between Rorty's antiessentialism and his positive view of philosophical reflection can be resolved once we see our way past the dualistic elements that inform some of Rorty's writings on argument and rationality.

Rorty's Rhetoric: The Relaxed View

When deflationists criticize Rorty, it is often for doing disservice to a quite plausible brief against a certain conception of metaphysics and epistemology by exercising too vigorously his penchant for dramatic rhetorical effect.[1] This claim is typically made by pragmatically inclined philosophers who are not without sympathy for Rorty's views, but much of whose work is directed toward an audience constituted in significant measure by philosophers who are.[2] Deflationist sentiments may thus serve as a kind of apologia for the deflationist's own Rortyan tendencies; Rorty, the deflationist says, doesn't really want to end philosophy, or usher in the postphilosophical era. He merely seeks to inoculate us against the view—and the not entirely eradicated assumptions behind the view—that it is a mandate of philosophy to settle on legitimating criteria for various forms of human conduct.

The deflationist may point out that Rorty himself is quite explicit on the matter; he does not want to extinguish philosophy. What Rorty recommends—the point, as he says in the last sentence of *Philosophy and the Mirror of Nature*, upon which he insists, is "that philosophers' moral concern should be with continuing the conversation of the West, rather than with insisting upon a place for the traditional problems of modern philosophy within that tradition" (394). A few pages earlier, he suggests that "we can continue the conversation Plato began without discussing the topics Plato wanted discussed" (391).

This is, the deflationist urges, on the face of it not implausible—it is far from obvious how such relative innocuousness could give rise to the vehement and passionate end-of-philosophy exchanges that followed in the wake of *Philosophy and the Mirror of Nature*. Surely, we can carry on philosophy while addressing topics or problems other than those given center stage by the founding fathers. Isn't it terribly conservative, conceptually and otherwise, to insist that philosophy is defined by just the problems addressed in Athens 2,500 years ago, and therefore not terribly radical to question such insistence? As human practices and their context evolve—in particular, as we

come to view the activity of philosophical reflection itself in increasingly naturalistic, secularized terms—we should expect that the substantive questions
of philosophy will change as well.[3] Rorty's basic claim, says the deflationist, is
that if we want to be naturalists, we must altogether cease to think in terms
of natures or essences characterizable from a timeless perspective. The
metaphilosophical corollary is that we must give up the idea that philosophy
is determined by some particular content or subject matter, that there are
questions or topics that are intrinsically philosophical in nature.

Rorty's Nihilism
(What Deflationists Don't Seem to Appreciate)

This deflationist version of Rorty is plausible enough, as far as it goes. If this
were the whole story on Rorty, however, it would make it difficult to escape
the conclusion that demonizers are a disastrously disadvantaged lot; either
die-hard Platonists, or (nonexclusive) fear-mongers with chips on their
shoulders and beams in their eyes. Certainly it would be surprising if there
were no such to be found amongst the many who have if not exactly read
Rorty, than at least written about him. But, patently, there are prominent demonizers who fall into neither category. This suggests that the deflationist
reading may be leaving out ingredients essential to the incendiary quality of
Rorty's views.

The persistence among sensible philosophers of the demonizing view of
Rorty is striking, not least to Rorty. Fourteen years after *Philosophy and the Mirror of Nature*, in a footnote to the response to Putnam from which I quoted at
the beginning of this chapter, Rorty finds it necessary to point out that "[t]here
is a difference between hoping for the end of "Philosophy 101" and hoping for
the end of philosophy" (Rorty 1993, 446fn). Rorty wishes to restrict himself to
the former hope, yet finds that Putnam saddles him with the latter:

> I am still thought of [as by Putnam, RHF (1990), 19] as recommending "the end of
> philosophy," despite my explicit rejection of this label on the last page of *Philoso-
> phy and the Mirror of Nature*, and my attempts in subsequent writings to scrape it
> off. Perhaps it may clarify matters if I say that I hope that we never stop reading,
> e.g., Plato, Aristotle, Kant, Hegel, Dewey, and Heidegger, but also hope that we
> may, sooner or later, stop trying to sucker the freshmen into taking an interest in
> "the problem of the external world" and "the problem of other minds." (1993,
> 446–47fn)

Putnam, we should bear in mind, is someone whose views on a number of
points are so close to Rorty's own that people have trouble telling the two

apart.[4] But even to him, Rorty's remonstrations continue to ring distressingly hollow. Putnam continues to insist that the philosophical positions he and Rorty occupy are importantly different, and that Rorty's is disastrous for philosophy. Concluding his recent *Pragmatism*, Putnam complains of Rorty: "telling us again and again that . . . all our thought is simply 'marks and noises' which we are 'caused to produce' by a blind material world to which we cannot so much as *refer*, is . . . a fruitless oscillation between a linguistic idealism which is largely a fashionable 'put on' and a self-refuting scientism"[5] (Putnam 1995, 75).

One may, like Putnam, agree with many of Rorty's views regarding the assumptions behind the agendas of modern philosophy; one may identify with his aspirations for a secularized or "de-divinized" philosophical self-image, an image which no longer hypostatizes theoretical knowledge as the paradigmatically human capacity, the one which connects us with the way things in themselves are; one may share his urge to get out from under the spell of the conceptual oppositions that pit realists against antirealists, objectivists against relativists, and everybody against the sceptic. Still, it seems, one may find oneself thinking that Rorty is undermining philosophy as a discipline. We might concede to the deflationist that Rorty does not *want* to think of himself as putting an end to philosophy—but this is not to concede very much; we know what we know of human intention. What is it, then, that the deflationist leaves out of account?

Consider again Rorty's suggestion that we should not think of philosophy as defined by the problems raised in Athens 2,500 years ago, or those debated in Continental Europe 300 years ago, or indeed by any set of questions at all. This is to give up the idea that philosophy commands a distinctive subject matter, something which other forms of inquiry cannot illuminate for us. A relatively painless way for professional philosophy to achieve this liberation goes via the assumption that there is a distinctively philosophical way of addressing problems, something like a form which identifies the enquiry in question as philosophical, independently of its topic, its subject matter. In "Philosophy in America Today" (1981), an essay written just after the publication of *Philosophy and the Mirror of Nature*, Rorty considers this transition:

> If a discipline has no well-defined subject matter, and no inter-university paradigms of achievement, then it will have to have *stylistic* paradigms. This, I think, is what has happened to analytic philosophy as it moved from its positivistic to its post-positivistic stage, in the course of the last thirty years [1950–80]. (1982, 220)

This shift—Rorty diagnoses it as a shift in the meaning of "scientific" as applied to philosophy by Reichenbach and as applied by analytic philosophers of the next generation, after the destruction of positivist metaphysics—gives us a way to fix philosophy independently of the particulars of any philosopher's material concern. It allows us to see preoccupation with any specific question or topic, on the grounds that it is a paradigmatically philosophical question or topic, as a socihistorically deconstructible hang-up. To identify the activity of philosophy as such with particular topics or questions appears, from this enlightened standpoint, as a manifestation of parochial presumption and prejudice.

But could this be Rorty's way of breaking the connection between philosophy and Plato's topics? Would Rorty have more truck with the idea of a defining Subject Form of philosophy than a Subject Matter? No more, but no less, either; neither approach can be said to fail to capture what philosophy really is: "Believing as I do," Rorty continues (just after his remark about the transition to stylistically construed paradigms),

> that philosophy is not the sort of thing that has an historical essence or mission, I am not saying that the analytic movement has somehow wandered off the true path. 'Philosophy,' in the narrow and professional sense, is just what we philosophy professors do (1982, 220).

A little later he puts his point differently: "'Philosophy' is not the name of a natural kind," Rorty tells us, "but just the name of one of the pigeonholes into which humanistic culture is divided for administrative and bibliographical purposes" (1982, 227). "We should," he accordingly recommends, "just drop the question of what philosophy really is, or who really counts as a philosopher" (1982, 225).

For Rorty, the critique developed in *Philosophy and the Mirror of Nature* has gradually come to serve as illustrative, as a demonstration of what might be done to any set of assumptions, to any philosophical perspective that history may bring us to. In his writings after the seminal critique of the mirror-paradigm, Rorty has been increasingly concerned to make this general, historicist, metacritical point, and to draw out increasingly explicitly the consequences of it for our conception of philosophical reflection as a project. This central strand of Rorty's thought, in which his own attack on representationalist epistemology and metaphysics plays a role which is ostensive as much as anything, is downplayed or ignored as the deflationist reads Rorty into a dialectical story of the progress of modern philosophy toward enlightened, science-oriented, pragmatic naturalism.[6]

Demonizers, by contrast, perceive in Rorty's dismissal of the question of the nature of philosophy a metaphilosophical nihilism. In their eyes, Rorty's own professed desire to see philosophy continue does little to bolster deflationist sangfroid; for this desire, the demonizers perceive, would be satisfied as long as we go on, in some way, reading and talking about the writings of those whom we want to count as philosophers. The attitude expressed in the metaphilosophical papers in *Consequences of Pragmatism* has, one is tempted to say, satisfaction conditions set far too generously for it to count as a desire for philosophy. When we are talking about the continuation or development of the intellectual practice we are professionally engaged in, everything depends on *how* one reads the texts. All Rorty explicitly means by his declarations of allegiance to philosophy is that he would like us to go on reading and talking about the texts of the tradition. This is just too weak a commitment to be reassuring, for although we may stipulate that as long as people read Plato, etc., there is philosophy, this is to ensure the survival of philosophy by an act of stipulation.

Rorty may say he does not want philosophy to end, and the deflationist—assuming that Rorty is in some identifiable sense doing what the target of his criticisms were doing—may believe him. But for the demonizer, Rorty's openness to different styles of philosophy is no grounds for praise; his tolerance arises from the realization that no such paradigm can be wrong, because there is nothing there to get right.

I believe the demonizers do latch on to a tension in Rorty's thought—though it is not the point they think they are making when they accuse Rorty of philosophical nihilism. In the remainder of this chapter, I will try to illuminate this tension. In section 4, I will canvas the criticisms of three demonizers, in an effort to focus more sharply the nature of their complaint against Rorty. I will then, in section 5, briefly summarize Rorty's attitude to their critical point, expressed in his disavowal of argument. In section 6, I argue that the demonizers do not come to grips with the heart of Rorty's pragmatic metaphilosophy. The reason is, I think, that they are still under the spell of the notion of philosophical method. I present in this section a view of philosophical argument, which dissociates it from the notion of method. On the basis of this view, however, I also press the point that we need not think—indeed, that we should not think—as Rorty at times appears to think, that the spell of the notion of philosophical method can only be broken if we abandon the attempt to provide normative characterizations of philosophy. I believe it is Rorty's fear of essentialism which drives him to this thought. This fear is well motivated. Nevertheless, the thought is at odds with, and sometimes obscures, what is Rorty's greatest contribution to pragmatism and to philosophy: namely, that he makes vivid a particularly illuminating and conversationally fruitful conception of what philosophers have been, and are, doing.

Haack, Putnam, and McDowell versus Rorty

Demonizers, I have just suggested, are in the grips of the notion of philosophical method. But that seems an implausible claim. Surely, the idea that philosophy can be defined in terms of methodological commitments has not much greater appeal than the thought that philosophy consists of a set of questions with a particular—philosophical—quality. I think the right response to this objection is, "that depends." What it depends on is the conception of method. The commitment at issue between Rorty and his demonizing critics is so general, so basic, it seems to its adherents hardly to be optional at all, which is exactly why it appears to them not as a particular methodological commitment, but as a minimal requirement for the practice of philosophy by any means or method whatsoever. To demonizers, Rorty is a metaphilosophical nihilist because he flouts this minimal requirement.

Haack, McDowell, and Putnam are three philosophers whose appreciation of Rorty is not of a piece, and precisely because of the differences between their respective assessments their convergence on a fundamental critical point stands out in sharp relief. Although the point takes three interestingly different forms, the briskly dismissive Haack, the sympathetically engaged McDowell, and the morally concerned Putnam all agree on what is the defining contention of the demonist view of Rorty: Rorty's choice of instruments constitutes a farewell to philosophy.

Haack (1995)—in what might be termed a "spirited polemic"—determines that Rorty, along with Stich, her "secondary target" (126), is a "vulgar pragmatist." Haack's "major theme is that neither Rorty nor Stich has any good argument that the familiar epistemological projects are misconceived" (126). Her "secondary theme" is

> that both Rorty and Stich fail to grasp that to believe that p is to accept p as true; with the result that the "edifying" philosophy into which Rorty wants the ex-epistemologist to put his energies masks a cynicism which would undermine not only epistemology, not only "systematic" philosophy, but enquiry generally. (126–27)

Haack is clear on the stakes; she is taking on men who threaten to seduce us into a premature end of enquiry. They are, she suggests, men with really quite preposterous views on truth and rationality and the nature of enquiry, views that they try by means of clever rhetorical strategies to foist on the unwary. Though perceptibly chagrined at the need for such a deployment of time and other resources, Haack nevertheless devotes eight or so pages to a reconstruction of Rorty's critique of the "epistemological enterprise," succinctly concluding that "since he has no arguments against pragmatist, minimally realist, strongly realist, or even grandly transcendental views of truth, he has, *a fortiori*, no good arguments against them, nor, therefore, against foundationalism ['the thesis that criteria of justification are not purely conventional but stand in need of objective grounding, being satisfactory only if truth-indicative'(130)], nor, therefore, against epistemology" (134).[7]

Haack responds to Rorty by providing distinctions in the light of which Rorty's claims about truth are vague, or ambiguous. She then sharpens these claims into contestable theses, structured by Haack's own spectrum of ontological attitudes to truth, and then diagnoses these theses to be without argumentative support. On her picture, we Rortyan pragmatists are failing to observe distinctions between various attitudes to truth, rather than denying their significance, the fruitfulness of the very axis along which these positions are plotted. This failure to observe the distinctions that on Haack's approach to philosophy are evidently significant stems from a damning error; we have "failed to grasp" a critical conceptual connection, and thus remain insensitive to the reassuring inferences that may be drawn from the fact that to believe that p is to accept p as true.

From the perspective to which Haack gives voice, Rorty appears as a dangerous distraction, someone whose regrettable influence can only be due to a widespread lack of discernment and stands as a symptom of a general withering of the ability to distinguish between rhetoric and genuine argument. Haack's view is that Rorty has advanced some dangerous theses, theses which would, if they were true, put in jeopardy the very point of philosophizing. Fortunately, Haack concludes, these theses are entirely free of the sort of support which would require us to take account of them: since Rorty's "arguments for abandoning epistemology rests, at bottom, on nothing more than a manifestly false dichotomy of extreme realism versus extreme irrealism about truth, the legitimacy of epistemology seems pretty secure" (139).

McDowell (1994) has a very different relationship to Rorty's project. He thinks Rorty is looking for a way to take the attitude toward the traditional problems of epistemology that McDowell, too, wants to take.[8] "Rorty," McDowell observes, "is very strong in his conviction that the supposed obligations of traditional philosophy are illusory," and McDowell has "every sympathy with that" (147). McDowell thinks, however, that "Rorty deprives himself of the right to take that attitude" (151); Rorty is not entitled to it; he "gives expression to the conviction in a way that spoils the point" (147). Rorty's pragmatism is "half-baked" (155), McDowell thinks, because his "thinking is organized around the dualism of reason and nature" (154). While it "is true that Rorty resists the blandishments of traditional philosophy . . .

the effect of the framework he assumes is that he can do that only by plugging his ears, like Odysseus sailing past the Sirens" (147).

Rorty appears to McDowell as someone who is simply refusing to listen, ignoring the temptations of traditional philosophy by an act of resolve rather than disarming them by an act of reason. What needs to be done, the task McDowell himself engages in, is to address those temptations in such a way that they "stand revealed as illusory" (151) before philosophical reason, and thus loose their power over us. If Rorty were a real captain of philosophy, McDowell implies, not only good at criticism, but also at providing a vision of something new, what he would do is take his fingers out of his ears, listen carefully, and then explain to all us mariners why those wicked, sweet-voiced sea-nymphs—Scepticism and Problem of Other Minds, as we may call them—sing as they do, and why their singing thus is not good or right or reasonable. The fatal temptation to seek out the lethal source of the song might thus be rationally eradicated. With an intended audience that hears, but does not respond, the Sirens might eventually just shut up.

Notice, however, that McDowell's image doesn't resolve quite straightforwardly. For Odysseus precisely did not want to miss the Song of the Sirens, and so, having stopped the ears of his faithful rowers, after instructing them to ignore all his signs and gestures until they were out of earshot of temptation, had them tie him, ears unplugged, to the mast. Indeed, I suspect Rorty would actually embrace the image that McDowell offers in criticism. We know, Rorty might point out, that Odysseus's rough suspension of his own authority stood him in good stead in exactly the relevant regard; he heard the songs, but suffered none of the dreaded consequences, and after their abject failure to entice Odysseus and his crew, the good singers were not heard from again. We can learn something about the difference between Rorty's conception of the progression of thought and McDowell's from the fact that Rorty, but not McDowell, would be perfectly content with an analogous neutralization of scepticism and the problem of other minds. Indeed, Rorty might be tempted to exploit the image further by insisting on a closer analogy between the siren-song and the temptations of philosophy than McDowell should want to allow; like the songs heard, the problems entertained are compelling—they result in an urge that reflection cannot curb. Rorty's view is that these sorts of problems set parameters for argumentative reflection, and are not themselves to be argued to resolution. McDowell, for all his sympathy with Rorty's assaults on the edifices of modern epistemology and metaphysics, thinks Rorty is blind, or deaf, or mastbound, with respect to the legitimate intellectual questions which lie at the root of the familiar problem matrices of these fields. He thinks that Rorty for that reason has failed to reflect himself into a position which renders him rationally inoculated to the Sirens of Modern Philosophy, and hence that Rorty, as a philosopher, has not earned the intellectual right to dismiss them. For Rorty, however, ignoring those Sirens is not something which requires that sort of entitlement at all. Rorty's attitude, rather, is just do it (if you can). But, of course, it is difficult to do. So Rorty offers help, casting about for ways to redescribe us talkers, thinkers, and knowers in ways that foreclose on the possibility of the Cartesian questions.[9] Once again, however, the advice Rorty offers and the tools he relies on do not constitute the kind of help which McDowell believes that a *philosopher* must administer. In non-Rortyan language, we might say that for Rorty the liberating movement that successful redescription makes is not—by Rorty's own admission—a movement described by reason; hence, for McDowell, Rorty is not advancing a *philosophical* move at all.

Putnam's recurring charge is that Rorty is an emotivist about truth; Rorty thereby jettisons the idea of substantial correctness that for Putnam gives meaning to our conception of ourselves as thinkers. Now "argument" and the notion of substantial correctness, or truth, that Putnam defends against Rorty, are buddy-notions. They swim or drown together. This is apparent both in the ordinary definition of logical validity in terms of truth-preservation, and in the broader, common claim that the very notion of justification carries with it a commitment to a distinct norm of truth. Putnam, like Haack and McDowell, is charging Rorty with failure to meet an obligation that he ought, as a member of the profession and practitioner of the discipline, to shoulder. We should note, though, that while all three critics fall into the demonizing category, they articulate their complaints against Rorty in ascending degrees of proximity and openness to Rorty's claims.

Haack, suggesting that Rorty is taken care of once one points out that he has failed to make the necessary distinctions between kinds of foundationalism and has simply missed the conceptual connection between belief (and the epistemic notions it carries in tow) and truth, reveals a determined lack of willingness to entertain the sort of question about her activity that Rorty seeks to raise. Content to point out what appears to her as rhetorical ploys devoid of argumentative force, Haack simply does not engage the suggestion that a case is being mounted against the presumed point of the question to which the various ontological attitudes to truth that she distinguishes yield distinct answers. Or perhaps it is fairer to say this: in engaging this suggestion, Haack refuses to distinguish a questioning of the idea that we have a concept of truth of a sort that can be relied on to provide a substantive measure of our argumentative and epistemic practices from a nihilistic assault on philosophy itself.

Unlike Haack, McDowell has sympathy with a great deal, perhaps most, of Rorty's critical diagnosis of the epistemological enterprise. McDowell's (1994) use of Kant and Aristotle is a self-consciously historicist attempt to modify our present sense of what is philosophically pressing in our understanding of ourselves as natural creatures. The chief aim of this attempt has close and acknowledged affinities with Rorty's purposes: to uncover—and liberate us from—the philosophical compulsions that make reductive analyses of the concepts of thought and agency appear attractive or even necessary. Still, McDowell is unwilling to put Rorty's Odyssean strategy with the Sirens of epistemology in the context of Rorty's account of intellectual and philosophical evolution—and it is no wonder that the resulting impoverished mix bakes slowly, since this account, pitched in terms of nonrational succession of vocabularies, is a critical factor in any reconstruction of Rorty's attitude to the question of the nature of philosophy. This account is the explicit target of Putnam's complaint. In this particular context it is therefore Putnam who is closest to finding terms with which to consider and assess the kind of view of philosophy that Rorty presents us with. Putnam attacks that view directly; his claim is that by abandoning any notion of substantial correctness, Rorty is left without any leverage to motivate a rational change in view. Rejecting truth, as Putnam thinks, Rorty must face the consequence that nothing he says could really be an argument. This is the clearest statement of the demonizers' complaint against Rorty. From her more remote perspective, Haack makes what is substantively the same point when she depicts Rorty as a cynical rhetorician: not only does Rorty, by giving up on truth, deprive himself of the very means of persuasion that is the hallmark of real philosophy; what is worse, he knows that he does, and yet is in no way impeded by this knowledge.

A Man without Arguments?

In "Philosophy as a Kind of Writing" (1978), Rorty makes the claim that "Non-Kantian philosophers like Heidegger and Derrida are emblematic figures who not only do not solve problems, they do not have arguments or theses" (1978, 93). Nor is this, Rorty believes, something that we should hold against them. As he explains in "Philosophy in America Today,"

> Analytic philosophers, because they identify philosophical ability with argumentative skill and notice that there isn't anything they would consider an argument in a carload of Heidegger and Foucault, suggest that these must be people who tried to be philosophers and failed, incompetent philosophers. This is as silly as saying

that Plato was an incompetent Sophist, or that a hedgehog is an incompetent fox. (1982a, 225)

Rorty concludes this passage with the remark I quoted earlier, that "we should just drop the question of what philosophy really is, or who really counts as a philosopher." His point here appears, bluntly, to be that we have no business expecting arguments of philosophers, because we have no business expecting anything in particular of philosophers—save that they talk about writers we agree are philosophers. So if Rorty has no arguments, then perhaps this is just because he, too, is a hedgehog; and since philosophy has no essence, nobody has any business saying hedgehogs are not philosophers.

I think this is a weak response to the worries of the demonizers, a response which simply reflects the absence of a normative description of the practice of philosophy; by affirming brute difference, it precludes engagement. But Rorty's case against argument isn't confined to the claim that it is parochial always to look for arguments in a philosopher, because, hey, philosophy is whatever we make of it. It turns out that Rorty has quite specific misgivings about arguments as instruments of philosophical reflection. "Hobbes," Rorty points out,

> did not have theological arguments against Dante's world picture; Kant had only a very bad scientific argument for the phenomenal character of science; Nietzsche and James did not have epistemological arguments for pragmatism. Each of these thinkers presented us with a new form of intellectual life, and asked us to compare its advantages with the old. (1981, 156)

Arguments simply are not responsible for the great shifts in cultural and intellectual history that have resulted in the possibility of an enlightened, liberal secularism. Furthermore, there is good reason why this should be so. Arguments, as philosophers deploy them, are symptomatic of "[t]he desire to harmonize pre-existent intuitions," which, according to Rorty, "has replaced the task of asking whether the vocabulary in which these intuitions are stated is a useful one" (1995a, 202). Arguments tie us to the very structures of thinking that we should be questioning. By contrast, in Rorty's view, "interesting philosophy is rarely an examination of the pros and cons of a thesis. Usually it is, implicitly or explicitly, a contrast between an entrenched vocabulary which has become a nuisance and a half-formed new vocabulary which vaguely promises great things" (1989, 8–9). The shifts Rorty surveys, the sort of shifts that "interesting philosophy" is involved in bringing about, are shifts of a sort, and on a scale, such that our concept of rationality and argument can play no illuminating role.

Here is the view of philosophy that Rorty recommends, attributed to his greatest hero. For Dewey, Rorty says,

> philosophy is always parasitic on, always a reaction to, developments elsewhere in culture and society. Dewey construed Hegel's insistence on historicity as the claim that philosophers should not try to be the avant-garde of society and culture, but should be content to mediate between the past and the future. Their job is to weave together old beliefs and new beliefs, so that these beliefs can cooperate rather than interfere with one another. Like the engineer and the lawyer, the philosopher is useful in solving particular problems that arise in particular situations—situations in which the language of the past is in conflict with the needs of the future. (1995a, 199)

Now, if by "argument" we mean the sort of intellectual engagement that takes at face value the terms of the vocabulary in which it is formulated, it is clear why Rorty cannot regard them as the tools of intellectual progress, given this vision of the task of philosophy. An argument, for Rorty, takes its compelling force from the vocabulary in which it is pitched—it requires a confidence in, and commitment to, that vocabulary. But philosophy ought to be an attempt to redraw, reinvent vocabularies. To do philosophy as Rorty conceives of it, is to endeavor to contribute to "the creation of a new form of cultural life, of a new vocabulary" (1989, 55), motivated by a sense that a current vocabulary is letting us down in some respect, or that vocabularies are getting in each other's way. Hence, Rorty urges,

> On the view of philosophy which I am offering, philosophers should not be asked for arguments against, for example, the correspondence theory of truth or the idea of "intrinsic nature of reality." The trouble with arguments against the use of a familiar and time-honoured vocabulary is that they are expected to be phrased in that very vocabulary. (1989, 8–9)

It turns out, then, that Rorty has a positive case against argument—a case, specifically, against the idea that philosophy should be conceived of as intrinsically and basically argumentative. That case is rooted in romanticism, which Rorty defines as "the thesis that what is more important for human life is not what propositions we believe but what vocabulary we use" (1981, 142). Because arguments tend to retard the emergence of new modes of description, new patterns of salience, they are for Rorty regressive instruments.

Notice, however, that Rorty's specific complaints against argument-based philosophy is allowed to emerge only against the backdrop of a more assertive metaphilosophical stance than the one he often takes in *Consequences of*

Pragmatism. It is only by risking a positive characterization of philosophy, a job description, that he has a way to go beyond the vacuous pluralism I parodied above, and state quite specifically what it is he finds troublesome and counterproductive with the idea that philosophy is by its nature argumentative. I think that this points to a tension in Rorty's attitude to reflection, and it is an element of this tension that demonizing critics have latched on to. Rorty's attempt to redescribe philosophy, to make us reconceive what we are doing when we philosophize, is at odds with the empty tolerance that arises from the thought that there is no right or wrong way to characterize philosophy. Rorty could, and ought to, resolve this tension by assertively staking a pragmatist claim about what philosophy is. Would such a move resurrect the essentialism that Rorty is trying to wean us from, degenerating into yet another demarcation campaign? I don't think it has to, provided we flush out the residual essentialism regarding argument and rationality that reveals itself in the dualistic elements in Rorty's account of intellectual progress.

Argument: Method, Technique, Dialectic

When Rorty disowns "argument," he portrays it quite deliberately as an impoverished notion, a kind of straightjacket for thought. But Rorty himself does argue, in a sense of the word that we should ingenuously want to preserve, in the sense of attempting to rationally persuade. In doing so, he seeks just that resistance of dialectic which takes thought beyond its starting point and leads to new understanding. In that sense, the sense I should like to attribute to Plato, the sense in which it is the philosopher's instrument, argument is something which, like philosophy, is dialogical, and thereby transcends methodology. Severing argument and rationality from the idea of method, however, threatens to deprive these notions of any interesting content. Indeed, that it does so deprive them is exactly Rorty's conclusion. My main task in this section is therefore to suggest a way to think about these notions which averts the threat.

As we have seen, Rorty's demonizing critics see his chosen discursive instruments as not being *philosophical* at all; Rorty, by disowning argument, concedes their basic claim, but then initially deflects it by being blandly pluralistic about the nature of philosophy. Now the demonizers are certainly right that Rorty's instruments, persuasion by redescription, differ from generally accepted methods of disciplinary progress in professionalized philosophy. And they are right, too, to be sceptical of the deflection; to assume a blandly pluralistic stance with regard to philosophy is simply to give up on the effort to conceive of philosophy as a living tradition, as a project. However, there is no compelling reason to accept the shared view that Rorty's instruments are not argumentative ones. This matters. If we can construe Rorty's self-consciously historicist and antiessentialist characterizations of his own rhetorical strategies as bona fide forms of philosophical argumentation, then we can avoid the methodology-based, reductive conceptions of the subject that Rorty warns against—the sort that give rise precisely to principles of demarcation and related futilities—without finding ourselves forced to assume a dismissive attitude toward efforts to give substantive characterizations of philosophy. That is important, because an intellectual tradition which ceases to try to understand its own nature—to say what it is—in terms of its past, by redescribing itself in ways which reveal a teleological unity across diachronic as well as synchronic differences, loses the impetus that makes it a going concern, a continuity, and hence something capable of having a future. I shall elaborate this crucial point in the last paragraphs of the chapter. First, however, it is necessary to suggest a conception of philosophical argumentation that will support the claim I just made: that both Rorty and his demonizing critics are wrong to conceive of Rortyan redescription as a form of rhetoric which stands in opposition to philosophical argumentation.

When Rorty casts his strategy as an *alternative* to argumentative philosophy, this move has its roots in the opposition he poses between the intravocabularic movement of rational thought and the dynamics of vocabulary change. This opposition, in turn, arises from a fundamental Rortyan claim: There is, he says, no "skyhook with which to escape from the ethnocentrism produced by acculturation" (1991, 2).[10] Rorty takes this to have important implications for how we construe intellectual change:

> To accept the claim that there is no standpoint outside the particular historically conditioned and temporary vocabulary we are presently using from which to judge this vocabulary is to give up on the idea that there can be reasons for using languages as well as reasons within languages for believing statements. This amounts to giving up the idea that intellectual or political progress is rational, in any sense of "rational" which is neutral between vocabularies. (1989, 48)

His point here is not that "the great moral and intellectual advances of European history . . . were fortunate falls into temporary irrationality." Rather, "the moral to be drawn is that the rational-irrational distinction is less useful than it once appeared." We should limit this opposition, Rorty thinks, "to the interior of a language game" (1989, 47).

Let us take it with Rorty that there is no skyhook. We should agree also that the idea of neutrality between vocabularies cannot serve as a norm for philosophical discourse. But the reason for this is not simply that argument *pro et contra* always presupposes an antecedent commitment to some vocabulary or other. Indeed, there is something problematical about this way of putting the point, because cultural and intellectual vocabularies of the sort that Rorty invokes in his account of intellectual evolution are, in a pretty strong sense, artifices of intellectual history. In a current field of active philosophical thought any disagreement about any statement, any disharmony of interlocutors' linguistic perceptions, may be the root or symptom of a sedimentation, or signs of fault lines presaging, in the hindsight of future historians, the emergence of distinct vocabularies. Vocabularies of active philosophical discourse are dynamically evolving processes, changing as we work our way through them; they are therefore not the sorts of things we stand over against and select between, nor are they, a fortiori, the sorts of things to which we may be antecedently committed. As fully thematized, conventional linguistic structures, vocabularies can only emerge clearly before us as objects of reflective deliberation and decision once we have a clear sense of the experience they make possible, when we know, that is to say, how to delineate and leave them behind. At that point, they will also be philosophically unproblematic—or infertile. It follows that the opposition between concepts that apply to our treatment of statements within "language games" and concepts that apply to supposed intervocabularic shifts can have little useful application in the midst of our struggles to think clearly and innovatively about philosophical issues. That distinction simply cannot figure in our conception of a norm for philosophical thought. This precludes our thinking of neutrality between vocabularies as a discursive aim, but it also undermines the suggestion that argument and rationality are concepts with clear application only *within* vocabularies.

It is the observation that the idea of neutrality across vocabularies is a figment, and not a genuine norm, that leads Rorty to suspect that the concept of rationality cannot be employed to capture the idea of philosophical virtue. It should be clear, however, that we need not draw this moral from the historicist rearticulation I have just offered of Rorty's claim about neutrality. For now the problem is no longer the uselessness of the concept of rationality and the regressiveness of argument with respect to vocabulary-innovative thinking. Rather, the problem now appears as the inadequacy of any elaboration of rationality in terms which presuppose that the distinction between cross-vocabularic (abnormal) and intravocabularic (normal) discourse can have significant guiding application in situ. To be sure, this compels us to follow Rorty and give up on the conception of substantive neutrality as an ideal for philosophical discourse, and also on the collateral idea that this neutrality gives us a way to understand the objectivity that argument achieves. How-ever, the historicist point cuts equally against the thought that the notions of argument and rationality can be usefully applied only to moves within vo-cabularies. Indeed, the natural further inference from the historicist concep-tion of vocabularies is that the issue of possible neutrality between dynami-cally evolving discursive structures has scant bearing on questions regarding the rationality of contributions to philosophical discourse.

The question is, why does Rorty infer in the opposite direction, to the philosophical uselessness of the concept of rationality? Making his point about the nonrationality of intellectual progress, Rorty says:

> Europe did not *decide* to accept the idiom of Romantic poetry, or of socialist poli-tics, or of Galilean mechanics. That sort of shift was no more an act of will than it was a result of argument. Rather, Europe gradually lost the habit of using certain words and gradually acquired the habit of using others. (1989, 6)

We may agree that these changes are not well described as decisions, as acts of will. Still, these shifts of vocabulary, these changes in linguistic habits, clearly have emerged through the conduct of a discourse where efforts to ar-ticulate features of human experience and ends engage with, and are shaped by, one another. That is how new ways of describing the world and our place in it come to be, new modes of description which allow us to see new possi-bilities for experience, which in turn provide us with new reference points for evaluations of those very descriptive strategies. What can Rorty's point be when he contrasts this conception of intellectual change with the sort of change in outlook that is caused by argument and assessable as rational?

What is lacking from intellectual discourse through the kind of funda-mental change that Rorty has in mind, as I have depicted it, is anything like a formula; there is no general method to be found here, no specification *in abstracto* of intellectual technique that can mitigate the sheer contingency of the kind of intellectual movement that led us from a teleological to a Galilean view of the world. That, I take it, is Rorty's central historicist metaphilosophical point. When Rorty couches this point as an attack on the utility of the notions of rationality and argument, I suspect that this is be-cause he conceives of argument as an instrument of method, and rationality as a methodologically governed notion.

In this Rorty is far from alone. On the contrary, Rorty's dismissal of ra-tionality expresses in a negative way some pretty gripping intuitions. To pro-fessionally prefer a view over another is, for a philosopher, just to express an opinion as to which view is, under the circumstances, more rationally held.

That question just is the question of which view is best supported by arguments. Insofar as we have available general characterizations of good argument, we have the means for articulating a notion of philosophical method; we are able to conduct, or at least to recognize, responsible philosophy as thought that conforms to certain abstract characteristics. However, for such general characterizations to play a methodological role—to yield anything like rules we may endeavor to follow—it is necessary that we are able to express them by using concepts of a different order than those captured by terms such as "rational," "reasonable," "justified," or, indeed, "truth-tracking" or "truth-indicating." Unless we can express our general account of good argument without relying fundamentally on terms that refer back to an unexplicated notion of cognitive goodness, we cannot expect our characterizations to function as constraints; they will not tell us what to do in order to argue well, how to go about realizing our aim of being rational in our preferences, of holding the justified view, of uncovering the truth—or even how to tell when we are presented with virtuous philosophical thinking. Moreover, if our rules are to have methodological import for philosophy, we cannot discharge the terms that threaten circularity in favor of appeals to particular substantive views or results without preempting the very questions we are looking for a way to grapple rationally with. For just as the idea of a philosophical method presupposes characterizations of our aim that have content that is applicable independently (more or less) of our concept of the aim itself (to arrive at a rationally held description of our subject matter), so it presupposes characterizations that possess a significant degree of autonomy with regard to particular applications or instances of philosophical thought. Without such (relative) autonomy, the notion of philosophical method will be of no use in cases of real controversy, where there is a conflict of fundamental views, because it cannot be construed as neutral in the required sense. The notion of neutrality at stake here does not, of course, imply that the issue between alternative views must be left undecided. Rather it is a notion of objective impartiality; it indicates that our methodological commitments must allow us to formulate the issue and evaluate it in terms that are detachable from a prior commitment to one side or the other.

We have, then, two fundamental requirements on a methodological conception of rationality, which we might call the substance-condition and the autonomy-condition. If we recognize these conditions, a tempting course is to narrow the scope of the concept of argument to the point where we are able to give formalized accounts of certain desirable features of the items in its extension, and then to rely on this concept to prop up our sense that we are able to say something about what it is to produce a sound argument that is both noncircular (i.e., genuinely constraining) and neutral (in the sense specified above) with regard to the questions we as philosophers seek to address. Now, Rorty's point against argument and rationality might then be put this way: a notion of argument that is sufficiently emasculated and regimented to meet the two requirements entailed by a methodological conception is thereby also impoverished to the point where it can no longer be used as a device for tracking good philosophical thought. As soon as we try to beef up the notion of argument to make it rich enough to settle what is or isn't genuine philosophy through methodological considerations, we find ourselves shuttling once again between characterizations of good argument whose terminological circularity renders them toothless, empties them of content, and conceptions that turn out to beg substantive questions at issue between opposed views, and so have significantly more bite than we are bargaining for. The kinds of examples that Rorty uses as his paradigm cases of intellectual change are exactly occasions where the substance-condition and the autonomy-condition cannot be simultaneously met. In such cases, the price of neutrality is lack of adjudicating power. (One can of course trade either way.)

It is important to see that we can make this point against a methodological conception of philosophical rationality while still holding that both the substance-condition and the autonomy-condition have important roles to play in intellectual exchange, and even that they will often both appear to have been satisfied. The critical point is that the successful resolution of particular intellectual conflicts by application of method rests on a certain kind of agreement or convergence, a convergence which itself cannot be contained or constructed in methodological terms. The discursive basis for the satisfaction of the substance-condition and the autonomy-condition remains contingent; it is altered, produced, and undermined as vocabularies evolve.

This way of putting the point of Rorty's criticism leaves us free claim that philosophical thought is a distinctively rational activity, and that its means of progress is argumentation, provided we are willing to give up on the thought that the concepts of rationality and argument in this context have methodological utility. One may wonder, however, whether this is a freedom worth having. For if the concept of argument can no longer be relied on to bolster an account of what characterizes the formation of rational philosophical views, what could the point possibly be of calling philosophy an argumentative, rational activity?

Clearly, the point is to characterize a certain kind of discursive virtue, to lay claim to and submit to a certain kind of ideal. But the question then becomes this: is there a way to say, in other than methodological terms, something about that ideal which will reveal salient characteristics of a practice defined in relation to it? If not, those of us who want to take up and preserve the historicism that Rorty articulates are left with no genuine alternative to his recommendation that we put these terms out to philosophical pasture. Perhaps we could approach the question by saying a little more about what we have in fact excluded by abjuring methodological characterizations.

The methodological conception of reason and of argument defines itself in opposition to the idea of the inherent contingency of thought; on the methodological conception, genuine intellectual progress, virtuous preference of view, is to be diagnosed as particular manifestation of general schema, as application of rules. Method underwrites its conclusions exactly because it does not depend on particular results for its validation, but indeed in large measure drives our assessment of the derivation of particular results. It allows us to transcend what may well not be in dispute, namely, what we might call the empirical contingency of human thinking, and see ourselves as manifesting, through that empirical contingency, a teleological form of necessity embodied in the idea of points of convergence; conclusions to which all well-thinking enquirers will, given a set of epistemic circumstances, be led.

But the idea of a teleological necessity conferred on our views by virtue of conformity to abstractable rules or guidelines is not the only possible way to conceive of discursive virtue. What might we say about the ideal of rationality if we conceive of the discursive virtue of philosophical discourse as in large measure conditioned by—indeed, as a response to—the contingency of thought, rather than as a transcendence or denial of it?

Let us consider the kind of discursive exchange we have in mind. When I present you with an argument of mine, sincerely and in good faith, I aim to persuade you of what I take to be a truth. An argument is thus a tool which aims at agreement. But we also speak of argument, by contrast, as an exchange, conceived now as a dialogical activity, which aims not primarily at agreement but at understanding. Let us call this process argumentation. Yet as we deploy our tools—arguments, aimed at producing agreement—this activity, argumentation, can succeed even without ending in agreement—even, that is, if the tools we use in the process each fails to realize its implicit aim.

If argumentation can bring about understanding without securing agreement, this suggests that our aim in using the particular tools by which argumentation is conducted is not just to produce in the interlocutor a sincere assent to the claim in support of which we are advancing our considerations. Of course, an argument is exactly not just a primitive stand-in for the belief-changing cerebrators of a neuro-technological future. Giving arguments as part of argumentation, our aim is also to have illuminated what we are saying, in particular, to have illuminated the nature of such persuasiveness as our thoughts may have. For this we need the resistance of genuine interlocution; we need, in Habermas's terminology, to be guided by communicative rather than by strategic rationality. Why? Because illumination, rather than strategic success, is a matter of having what one says or believes situated in relation to alternative thoughts. It is a matter of working one's way into a better—that is, a larger, more nuanced and detailed and imaginatively elaborated—space of discursive options. Clearly interlocutors may succeed in this endeavor without also being able to come to rest in a common location within that space.

In dialogue, argument and counterargument stand mutually illuminated in just this way. This, as Gadamer persuasively argues, is the essence of Platonic dialectic; it aims for just this illumination. Indeed, a way to think of Plato's complaint against the sophists is to see him as accusing them of treating arguments instrumentally. The sophists err, stray from philosophy, because they mistake the purpose of argumentation for the purpose of arguments, and they take the purpose of arguments, in turn, to be simply that of the belief-changing cerebrator.

Rhetoric, in Plato's slightly jaundiced eye, is just the art of shaping, by hook or by crook, the layout of people's propositional attitudes. Argumentation, by contrast, aims at dialectical illumination.

Could we not, however, still conceive of this latter activity as a basis for and object of methodological abstraction? If we think of philosophical thought as I here suggest, as thought aiming for dialectical illumination, then it clearly will not do for us to tie the notion of argumentation, even of an argument, to a particular sort of persuasive power, or a particular method of persuasion. For this would block a critical dimension of reflexiveness which this endeavor requires; philosophical argumentation, expanding and elaborating the space of discursive options, will always also be an exploration of the value of the terms in which a subject matter is initially characterized and critically assessed. If that reflexive dimension is lacking, we proceed as if philosophy were done with, and we were simply applying our wisdom to areas. This is why there is something profoundly antiphilosophical about methodological conceptions of philosophical rationality.

Note that on this picture we ought not to say that what is distinctive of philosophical argumentation is that it attempts to secure assent by logic rather than, say, by appeal to the sentiments. Going in this direction can only lead us into a futile oscillation between restrictive, antiphilosophical hypostatizations of particular ways of providing dialectical resistance on one side, and a nihilistic dismissal of all distinction between argumentation and manipulation or technique—force—on the other. Rather, what is distinctive of the practice of philosophical argumentation is the aim with which arguments, whatever their merits may turn out to be, are deployed—namely, to have the nature of their persuasive power dialectically illuminated by virtue of nuanced contrast. By this I do not mean merely that we put arguments forth to see how convincing they are, but, as I said, in what manner they are or fail to be convincing with regard to the subject matter; we are testing not just our thoughts, our beliefs, but the tools of our thinking, and the only way to do that is comparatively. The illumination that results from argumentation is not of an incidental quality of what we express, as the power of some consideration to sway a particular person might be taken to be an incidental property of that argument. Rather, such dialectical illumination is an expansion, a production of the meaning of what comes to expression; philosophical discourse does not map out a preexisting conceptual structure, but employs the tensions present in our concepts to create new possibilities for us to appropriate and consider. This point is an expression of the historicized conception of meaning that is at the core of naturalistic pragmatism.

It must be clear that I am not, absurdly, suggesting a picture of philosophical thought that depicts it as alogical. After all, inferential intuition is what generates the tensions we exploit, and are driven by, as we seek to make discursive room for new perspectives. Even a philosopher who swallows a contradiction is thereby paying a price for a preferred inference pattern. But the sense in which logical structure, or inferential intuition, plays a critical role as an engine for philosophical thought is not a sense which will ground a methodological distinction. To strive to think logically is not to follow a methodological norm; it is just to try to think. The virtue of philosophical argumentation lies in the constructive exploitation of tensions that exist by virtue of inferential intuition. Genuinely methodological norms, norms that meet both the substance condition and the autonomy condition, cannot tell us how, in general, to achieve this, and so cannot provide the core of an account of what philosophy is.

What we are left with here is a conception of philosophical rationality that is a moral stance rather than a methodological notion; it reflects the fact that neither the significance nor indeed even the content of what we say is settled as long as people continue to talk in response. It is the virtue of taking with full seriousness the Hegelian idea that the meaning of what you, or I, or anyone, says is never fully present until that very moment when it ceases entirely to matter as a discursive act. It is a conception which builds in an appeal to experience, not as an epistemic court of appeal, but as the practice of living in which any theoretical proposal or descriptive strategy comes to its actual content and in terms of which it must be evaluated. It demands of us a willingness to put our thoughts in the hands of others, and to be willing to stand, in some measure, refuted, at least to the point of having the limitation of the force of one's considerations highlighted by one who remains, on consideration, unconvinced. To face resistance of this sort and to grapple with is a way to understand more of one's own position, even where disagreement continues to prevail; this kind of dialogical exchange, however argumentative, is as fundamentally a discovery of what one thinks as it is a discovery of the truth or falsehoods of one's opinions. Philosophical rationality cannot be methodologized because it is fundamentally a moral response to the essential incompleteness of our discursive efforts, the dependence of all our thinking on what others will do or not do in response to the words we offer. Though its normative significance cannot be cashed in methodological terms, it is not without force, or discriminating power. It is what we draw on, for example, when we, taking our cue from Plato, criticize what Plato thought he saw in the Sophists: the tendency to treat argument as technique, a means, amongst others, for securing assent to a claim.

By invoking Plato at this point, I intend to return to the question that has been the theme of this chapter: if we agree with Rorty that philosophy has neither Subject Form nor Subject Matter, are we left with nothing but hit lists of texts and sociological reports? Putting the point with reference to Plato: is Plato's significance with respect to the question of the nature of philosophy simply that he kicked off the sequence we now refer to as the history of Western philosophy? If we are tempted, as Rorty is tempted, to answer in the affirmative, we are in danger of jeopardizing the idea of philosophy as a tradition—as, in Rorty's terms, a conversation. Rorty himself articulates a role for philosophical reflection, but in the context of his antiessentialism, which in its extreme form becomes what I called a bland pluralism, this recommendation is in danger of losing its power as a redescription or interpretation of philosophy as a tradition. The idea of a tradition is a normative one; to properly characterize it is to offer clues as to what we should do with the books we read; it is to provide a tool for self-understanding. We learn something about what we ourselves are doing as philosophers when we come to understand how stylistically and rhetorically very different intellectual endeavors are also exercises of philosophical reflection—not by decree, or by sociological or organizational happenstance, but by virtue of what they attempt to achieve.

A characterization of a tradition must express, however vaguely, some kind of unity of goal, of purpose, towards which current practitioners, even reformist or revolutionary practitioners, must comport themselves. To belong to a tradition, to be a part of a tradition, is to see oneself as having, under some description, goals or purposes in common with those who make up that tradition. To be sure, a living, changing tradition will constantly be reconceiving itself; it is a dynamic, evolving, blurry-bordered thing. However, the dynamic which drives such change, the crucible within which the pressure to redescribe can mount to the point of precipitation, is constituted precisely by the effort to see others as somehow, and in some sense, engaged in the same endeavor as oneself. The point, then, in formulating answers to the question of the nature of philosophy is not to obtain a formula defining the activities constituting the tradition. Rather, the point is to find a way to engage with particular others, to converse with some others about a subject, while placing at issue, or at least not taking for granted, exactly what that subject is— the point, that is to say, is to participate in a tradition by constantly making and remaking the tradition. And that is just how a tradition lives.

We can put the same point in terms of Rorty's notion of conversation. Indeed, what makes an exchange a part of a conversation, and not simply a sequence of remarks, is just the teleological, or metateleological, unity presupposed in the idea of a living tradition. We need not imagine that this requires a substantial sameness of views, capturable in terms of some minimum body of necessary commitments, substantive or methodological. Rather, we are talking about a kind of metateleological unity: a common commitment to find a sameness in what one is doing. That is the shared effort which relates the remarks of one interlocutor to those of another, however much they disagree. If that attempt is lacking, there is no conversation. Of course, the exchange may nevertheless serve a variety of more or less important ends. But the exchange is not a philosophical dialogue; it is not structured by the attempt to achieve the sort of illumination that argumentation provides, which is to say that the parties are forgoing an opportunity not only to learn from one another about some subject matter, but also—and thereby—to deepen their understandings of their own efforts to come to grips with the subject.

Rorty's dismissal of the question of the nature of philosophy therefore seems to be at odds with the very conversation to which he remains committed—it hobbles his own understanding of what philosophy could be. However, there is a certain danger here of smugly exaggerating the significance of this appearance, and so losing from sight the critical point that expresses itself in Rorty's dismissive attitude toward this question. For it would be consonant with Rorty's own intention to "move everything over into cultural politics," and indeed with the picture of philosophy I am here reading into Rorty, to reconceive what is framed as a vacuously pluralistic answer to a conceptual question rather as a kind of warning, as a rhetorical device intended to remind us of the moral nakedness of our decisions to include and exclude voices from the conversation. Accounts of the essence of a subject, what it is, certainly are often made to conceal this nakedness, and to limit, aprioristically, our opportunities for dialogical understanding. Entrenching a definition of what we do may serve as a substitute for the hard work of attempting dialogue, which is to say, for placing one's own self-conception as a philosopher and one's preconception of another at real risk. Of course, we cannot talk to everybody. The point, rather, of a vacuously pluralistic definition of philosophy is to remind us that every time we do, as we undoubtedly must, rely on a fixed conception of our subject to preclude from serious consideration some text or author, we are giving in to expediency, relying on ad hoc specifications of what we do by aprioristically circumscribing the "we."

Read this way, the positive intent behind Rorty's scepticism toward a normative account of philosophy is to assert the primacy of dialogical engagement, of actual interpretive effort, over essence-wielding. It is to deny that the act of exclusion by definition is groundable in anything but expedience. It is to remind us that the pretence of grounding such exclusion in purported insight into the nature of the discipline is always questionable, because, in the end, there is no shortcut to the justification of such exclusion; terms of justification other than expedience require the sort of careful consideration of the text or view in question that can be obtained only through the attempt to enter into genuine dialogue with it.

Of course, the point I here attribute to Rorty is not that we should feel committed to enter into dialogue with all comers. Rather, the point is that we should not try to make our refusal to do so into a nobler thing than it is by construing it as resting upon an insight into the nature of philosophy.

Conclusion

I have tried to show that we can heed this warning while preserving the idea of philosophical argumentation as defined with reference to a normatively significant ideal of rationality, and thereby also preserve our understanding of ourselves as participants in a genuine conversation, a tradition. The warning against essentialism and aprioristic demarcation is heeded because the ideal itself is constructed around an affirmation of the temporality of the content of the conversation, the essential incompleteness of all contributions. But we no longer find ourselves driven to a bland pluralism. Thus, when Rorty depicts philosophical argumentation as redescription which aims to reform and expand the discursive space we operate in, we can take this proposal to be a genuine interpretation, a redescription of philosophy, a recipe for reading the great masters of the past and guiding future thought. The dialogical conception of philosophical argumentation allows us to see past the misleading contrast between rational argument and creative, vocabulary-innovative reflection. In this way, we can conceive philosophical argumentation as manifesting, and responding to, the contingency and temporality Rorty finds in all thinking, but as no less worthwhile, and no less demanding, for all that.

The point in reconceiving Rorty's historicism as I have done here can be brought out with reference to Plato's significance for the question of the nature of philosophy. In the terms that I recommend, the normative bearing of Plato's thought on the adequacy of any characterization of our tradition is acknowledged in a way that Rorty's approach will not easily permit. Plato's self-conscious questioning of the nature of good thinking provides us with the seeds for the very idea of theory. This is an idea we are still struggling to work out, which means that Plato's thought remains dynamically incomplete, continuing to shape and be shaped by our responses. This is just what it means to be in dialogue with Plato, but this is also why it is misleading to construe Plato's significance for philosophy in causal-chronological or sociohistorical terms. Plato's thought is not simply a causal or even a genealogical antecedent to what philosophy now happens to have become. Rather, by its very incompleteness it remains an active force in the shaping of the options that we discursively conceive. That is why, although no questions are philosophical by their intrinsic nature and no methods capture the virtue of philosophical argumentation, it remains right to say of Plato, as so many have said, that the conversation of the West remains his conversation—at least it is his as much as ours, or Rorty's. No descriptive strategy or technique, no method, no decision to change topics, subject, or style can make what we say less dependent on the living indeterminacy of the contributions of those who keep making it possible for us to say it.

Notes

This essay was originally published in Portuguese as "Rorty e os Instrumentos da Filosofia." In Paulo Roberto Margutti Pinto et al. (eds.), *Filosofia Analítica, Pragmatismo e Ciência*. Editora UFMG: Belo Horizonte, Minas Gerais, 1998. Reprinted with permission from the publisher.

1. Dennett's self-ironic deflationism employs the "Rorty-Factor"; "take whatever Rorty says about anyone's views and multiply it by .742" (Dennett 1982, 349).

2. Unlike the demonizers I discuss, my deflationist is a composite. This reflects the fact that deflationists tend not to write much about Rorty, usually offering their view of Rorty

in footnotes and other asides, or in oral responses to queries; while there are many deflationists about, the position is underrepresented in the literature. One who has commented
quite extensively on Rorty, and who shares many of the traits of my composite, is Dennett. But his case is complicated. Though Dennett until fairly recently has shied away
from the topic, his metaphilosophical position is very close to Rorty's. Dennett on qualia
(1988; 1991), could serve as a textbook illustration of Rorty's (1995b) characterization of
productive philosophical activity. Until *Consciousness Explained*, however, Dennett's strategy has been whenever possible to back away from explicit metaphilosophical argument,
partly on the presumption, I surmise, that such discussion would distract from the issues
Dennett is principally interested in debating. Another reason is that Dennett doubts—for
reasons Rorty would probably be sympathetic toward—that polemic at that level of abstraction and generality is likely to amount to anything but a definition of postures. However, recent writing (Dennett 1991; 1994) clearly shows that Dennett recognizes the great
extent to which metaphilosophical issues are at stake in the persistent disagreements between himself and critics like Fodor, Block, Searle, and Rey, and even Rosenthal and the
Churchlands. Of late Dennett has become increasingly willing to articulate these differences, and take a self-consciously pragmatic metaphilosophical stand. But see Dennett
(1994) for reservations: "I see," Dennett there claims, "both general and specific problems
with the radical positions Rorty thinks I should hold" (233).

3. Haack, a demonizer I discuss briefly below, "would go so far as to say that a discipline
in which problems had ceased to evolve would be dead" (Haack 1994, 129).

4. Including Rorty. Referring to Putnam, he says: "We seem, both to me and to philosophers who find both our views absurd, to be in much the same line of business. But Putnam sees us as doing something quite different and I do not know why" (Rorty 1993, 459).

5. In an endnote, Putnam informs us that the position he here criticizes "is the way
Rorty presented his view at a conference on Truth in Paris (May 3, 1990)" (Putnam 1995,
81). However, while Putnam is right that Rorty wants to say that "we are connected to
the world 'causally but not semantically'" (Putnam 1995, 74), I doubt that Rorty would
accept as his the thought that we "cannot so much as refer" to the world. Rorty's point is
of course not that we are, alas, unable to refer to the world, but that we should think of
our use of words as events in the world to be described in terms of their causal relations
to each other and to other kinds of events. The imputation of idealism is just off point.
And the "scientism" label seems equally unmotivated, since Rorty sees no philosophical
point in reduction; as descriptions of causal relations, intentional-language explanations
are no less capable of being literally true than are explanations couched in terms of the
projectible predicates of our basic natural science, even though there is no prospect of reducing the former to the latter. It is ironic that Putnam in *Pragmatism* (1995) uses Rorty,
of all people, as a principal foil for the strategy Putnam extracts from Wittgenstein: "In
sum, there is an enormous difference between Kantian tone, which Rorty retains by saying that we can't describe reality as it is in itself, and the Wittgensteinian tone which is
to try to make his reader not want to say either 'we can describe reality as it is in itself' or
'we can't describe reality as it is in itself'" (Putnam 1995, 40).

6. Incontestably, a key element in Rorty's thinking is Darwinian naturalism—a decision to take evolutionary biology as providing a baseline stricture on any vocabulary

within which we pursue pretensions to situate ourselves in the world. "To be a naturalist, in this sense," says Rorty,

> is to be the kind of antiessentialist who, like Dewey, sees no breaks in the hierarchy of increasingly complex adjustments to novel stimulation—the hierarchy which has amoeba adjusting themselves to changed water temperature at the bottom, bees dancing and chess players check-mating in the middle, and people fomenting scientific, artistic, and political revolutions at the top. (1991, 109)

To take this view, as I understand it, is not to view the vocabulary of evolutionary biology as of a unique or privileged order; it is to recommend a secularized picture of language-users which encourages us to see any vocabulary, including the vocabularies of natural science, including the vocabulary of evolutionary biology, as evolving tools of evolving creatures for coping with the world. Typically, vocabularies that run afoul of the stricture thus imposed are metavocabularies—philosophers' tools. In particular, Rorty has wanted to demonstrate, metavocabularies pitched with an eye to demarcation and legitimation of various aspects of linguistically saturated human practice are able to sustain these ambitions only insofar as their designers are able to cover up the contingency of their aims as well as of their criteria of success. Darwinian secularism requires that we evaluate vocabularies as we evaluate tools—with respect to their purposes. Moreover, such evaluation requires a degree of specificity; it will not do to say, as some might be tempted to say, that we might evaluate vocabularies with respect to their ability to uncover the truth. That would be like claiming to evaluate tools for their ability to help us get what we want—not for their ability to help us realize this or that particular goal, or kind of goal, but just what we want, in full generality. Is the hammer or the stapler better—in general? Here, I think, we come to the critical difference between Rorty's pragmatic naturalism and the deflationist's naturalism. For the pragmatist, any vocabulary, also that of evolutionary explanation, is a tool for a purpose, and therefore subject to teleological assessment. For Rorty, as for Nietzsche, such assessment must in the end appeal to experience, to actual human living. Rorty's theoretical project in philosophy, facilitating the spread of evolutionary naturalism, is grounded in a conviction of this sort: were we to develop a fully secularized vocabulary of self-description built around an affirmation of contingency, we would be less compelled than we presently are by ideologies of intolerance, ideologies which cause us—by purporting to give us reasons—to restrict the scope of solidarity. Theory is assessed, ultimately, with reference to hunches about the effects of various ways of talking on human practice. For the deflationist, by contrast, science simply tells us how things are—metatheoretical considerations of the sort that a Rortyan pragmatist will ultimately appeal to seem strictly instrumental, irrelevant to an assessment of the epistemic value of our theorizing.

7. Haack pointed out to me that it might be fair to mention that the critique of Rorty comes as a chapter in a book, and is preceded by detailed development of the position from which the criticism is launched. She is right. But it is also true that nowhere in the preceding chapters does Haack entertain the kind of metamethodological challenge to the presuppositions of her project that I here take Rorty to be raising.

8. McDowell, like Rorty, assumes "that philosophical concerns about the possibility of knowledge express at root the same anxiety as philosophical concerns about how content is possible, an anxiety about the felt distance between mind and world. Davidson and Rorty usually focus on concerns of the former sort, whereas I focus on concerns of the latter sort; I take it that the underlying thought is the same, that we ought to exorcize the feeling of distance rather than trying [sic] to bridge the felt gap" (McDowell 1994, 146–47).

9. Rorty's use of Davidson is the clearest example. See Rorty's account (1986a) of Davidson's (1986) antisceptical use of interpretivism. While Davidson thinks he is offering an argument against scepticism, Rorty suggests Davidson is really "telling the sceptic to get lost."

10. It seems fair to say that this claim drives his deconstructive diagnoses of a wide range of philosophical projects and controversies, as well as of the pretensions of social theory. It also crucially informs Rorty's articulation of the virtues of liberal politics. Rorty is explicit that what supports and gives shape to his affirmation of the ethnocentric condition is "an anti-representationalist view of inquiry." For Rorty, there is a direct link between the negative antirepresentationalist thesis (or theses), and the recommendation that we "view warrant as a sociological matter, to be ascertained by observing the reception of S's statements by her peers" (1993, 449).

Bibliography

Davidson, D. (1986) "A Coherence Theory of Truth and Knowledge," in Lepore (1986).
Dennett, D. (1982) "Comments on Rorty," *Synthese* 53.
——— . (1988) "Quining Qualia." In A. Marcel and E. Bisiach (eds.), *Consciousness in Contemporary Science*. Oxford: Oxford University Press.
——— . (1991) *Consciousness Explained*. New York: Little, Brown.
——— . (1993) "Comments," in Bo Dahlbom (ed.), *Dennett and His Critics*. Oxford: Blackwell.
Haack, S. (1994) "Vulgar Pragmatism: An Unedifying Concept." In Herman Saatkamp (ed.), *Rorty and Pragmatism*. Nashville, Tenn.: Vanderbilt University Press.
Lepore, E. (ed.) (1986) *Truth and Interpretation*. Oxford: Blackwell.
McDowell, J. (1994) *Mind and World*. Cambridge, Mass.: Harvard University Press.
Putnam, H. (1990) *Realism with a Human Face*. Cambridge, Mass.: Harvard University Press.
——— . (1995) *Pragmatism: An Open Question*. Oxford, Blackwell.
Rorty, R. (1976) "Keeping Philosophy Pure," reprinted in 1982b.
——— . "Philosophy as a Kind of Writing: An Essay on Derrida," reprinted in 1982b.
——— . (1989) *Philosophy and the Mirror of Nature*. Princeton, N.J.: Princeton University Press.
——— . (1981) "Nineteenth-Century Idealism and Twentieth-Century Textualism," reprinted in 1982b.
——— . (1982a) "Philosophy in America Today," reprinted in 1982b.

————. (1982b) *Consequences of Pragmatism*. Minneapolis: University of Minnesota Press.

————. (1985) "Solidarity or Objectivity," reprinted in 1991.

————. (1986a) "Pragmatism, Davidson, and Truth." In Lepore, reprinted in 1991.

————. (1986b) "Beyond Realism and Anti-realism." In Ludwig Nagl and Richard Heinrich (eds.), *Wo Steht die Analytische Philosophie Heute?* Vienna: R. Oldenbourg Verlag.

————. (1987) "Science as Solidarity," reprinted in 1991.

————. (1988a) "Is Natural Science a Natural Kind?" reprinted in 1991.

————. (1988b) "Representation, Social Practice, and Truth," reprinted in 1991.

————. (1988c) "Inquiry as Recontextualization: An Anti-dualist Account of Interpretation," reprinted in 1991.

————. (1989) *Contingency, Irony, and Solidarity*. Cambridge: Cambridge University Press.

————. (1991) *Objectivity, Relativism, and Truth*. Cambridge: Cambridge University Press.

————. (1993) "Putnam and the Relativist Menace," *Journal of Philosophy* 90, no. 9.

————. (1995a) Philosophy and the Future." In Herman Saatkamp (ed.), *Rorty and Pragmatism*. Nashville, Tenn.: Vanderbilt University Press.

————. (1995b) "Is Truth a Goal of Inquiry? Donald Davidson vs. Crispin Wright," *The Philosophical Quarterly* 45: 281–300.

CHAPTER TWO

Rorty, Metaphysics, and the Education of Human Potential

Jim Garrison

Rorty deems Dewey's efforts to evolve a "naturalistic metaphysics" a "contra-diction in terms" (1925–1981, 81). He proclaims:

> [N]o man can serve both Locke and Hegel. Nobody can claim to offer an "empiri-cal account" of something called "the inclusive integrity of 'experience'" nor take this integrated unity as the starting point for philosophic thought, if he also agrees with Hegel that the starting point of philosophic thought is bound to be the dialec-tical situation in which one finds oneself caught in one's own historical period. (81)

Dewey, we are told, turns to "Lockean modes of thought, under the aegis of Darwin" (81). The connection between the empiricism of Locke and the biology of Darwin, though, is unclear. Rorty shows that Locke confuses the causal account of how one comes to have a belief with the justification of the belief. In spite of the fact that Dewey's radical empiricism is as far from that of Locke as it is for an empiricism to get, Dewey's biologically oriented psy-chology is somehow supposed to commit the same mistake. It does not, as any reader of his 1938 *Logic* knows; the formation of linguistic meanings and logical judgment involves a long process of symbolic and physical operations on existence. Although logic has a biological matrix, it also has a cultural matrix. Rorty thinks it is a mistake to "cross the line between physiology and sociology" (81). Dewey thought both were part of the existential matrix of inquiry, a part of the context of thought, and part of every dialectical situa-tion. That is because when existential problems arise, they involve a context that includes our body as well as our culture.

Rorty makes the wrong distinction and then constructs a dualism out of it. Dewey makes a more discerning distinction and refuses to allow it to harden into a dualism by carefully distinguishing *existence* from *essence*. Existence simply is; logical essence emerges when existence takes on the form or structures the cultural arts of science and morality give it. Existence is the topic of metaphysics (not experience) and essence the topic of logic. Existential causal antecedents do not determine logical essence for Dewey. To think it does leads to what Dewey (1925/1981) calls "the philosophic fallacy," by which he means "the conversion of eventual functions into antecedent existence" (34). For example, causation for Dewey is a logical concept, not ontological. It is a consequence of inquiry and not an antecedent condition. Ignoring the intuitive, precognitive qualitative situation, including the operations of selective interests, forming the background of cognition as Rorty does is an example of what Dewey later (1931/1985) would call "the neglect of context." The philosophic fallacy involves failing to understand that we cannot have the linguistic or logical cognitive product without the entire artistic process. Rorty commits the philosophic fallacy because he confuses existence with essence. No one creates ex nihilo, and any good sculptor must know her materials. I'm afraid Rorty flirts with linguistic idealism.

Rorty (1982a) regrets that Dewey thought a Hegelian "criticism of culture had to take the form of a redescription of 'nature' or 'experience' or both" (85). I suspect he subscribes to an unacknowledged "culture" versus "nature" dualism just as he advocates a dualism between the private and the public. Education is the site of cultural reproduction and on Rorty's account, presumably, does not involve descriptions of nature, the body, or experience. Rorty thinks Dewey would have arrived at this happy conclusion if only he "felt able to forget the Aristotelian and Kantian models [of metaphysics] and been Hegelian all the way" (85). He seems to think Dewey has a "metaphysics of experience" since Rorty uses that phrase repeatedly; small wonder he reads Dewey as if he were an Aristotelian or a Kantian. In fact, Dewey directly repudiates Kant's metaphysics of experience in favor of a metaphysics of existence. He also completely reconstructs Aristotle so Dewey can provide an account for change. While Aristotle thinks metaphysics "First Philosophy," Dewey thinks it last philosophy; one should turn toward metaphysics only after the arts of cultural inquiry have done their work. To think otherwise is to commit the philosophic fallacy of ignoring the cultural context of all knowing, including metaphysical knowing.

Regarding metaphysics, Rorty writes that he cannot understand "why we *need* a discipline at that level of generality, nor how the results of such 'discoveries' can be anything but trivial" (77). In this chapter, I will show why education needs such a discipline, why it is not trivial, and why Rorty himself owes allegiance not only to metaphysics, but also to one very much like that of Dewey. Specifically, I will show that if we accept Dewey deconstruction of the metaphysics of presence and his reconstruction of Aristotle's theory of potentiality, we will have to rethink completely the ideas of human development and education. Dewey could not possibly have held the kind of metaphysics Rorty attributes to him. If Rorty does not like the metaphysics Dewey actually holds, at the very least he will need to give us an entirely different set of arguments.

Deconstructing the Metaphysics of Presence: Heidegger, Derrida, and Dewey[1]

The metaphysics of presence has dominated thinking in the West since the pre-Socratic philosophers. The most influential challenge to the metaphysics of presence is Martin Heidegger's (1927/1962) *Being and Time*. Jacques Derrida frequently refers to "the metaphysics of presence," and carries out a sustained assault that surpasses that of Heidegger. Dewey did the same over a decade before Heidegger, and before publishing *Democracy and Education* in 1916, though no one noticed. If we do not comprehend Dewey's comprehensive rejection of the metaphysics of presence, we fail to recognize the radical character of his thought and the hidden reason so many reject his educational philosophy.

Traditional metaphysics places ultimate ontology (identity, essence, categories, etc.) somewhere beyond time, contingency, and change, then uses these supernal entities "rationally" to order all existence. Heidegger resolves that the "treatment of the question of the meaning of Being must enable us to show that *the central problematic of all ontology is rooted in the phenomena of time, if rightly seen and rightly explained,* and we must show how this is the case" (40).[2] Dewey is not interested in the meaning of so abstract a noun as Being, though for him "temporal quality" is a trait of all existences.

Heidegger observes that in Western ontology, "Entities are grasped in their Being as 'presence'; this means that they are understood with regard to a definite mode of time—the 'Present'" (47). This is the metaphysics of presence; the doctrine that somehow we may come into the presence, the center, of eternal, immutable essence. Jacques Derrida (1978) concludes a consideration of centeredness and the metaphysics of presence with this comment:

> [T]he entire history of the concept of structure . . . must be thought of as a series of
> substitutions of center for center. . . . The history of metaphysics . . . is the history

of these metaphors and metonymies. Its matrix . . . is the determination of Being as presence in all senses of this word. It could be shown that all names related to fundamentals, to principles, or to the center have always designated an invariable presence—*eidos, arche, telos, energeia, ousia* (essence, existence, substance, subject) . . . transcendentality, consciousness, God, man, and so forth. (279–80)

Here Derrida provides us with most of the aspects of the metaphysics of presence I wish to consider. He also provides us with a hint as to why contemplating the rejection of that metaphysics is so disturbing.

So, what composes the metaphysics of presence? The primary concept is that of essence, or what the ancient Greeks called *eidos*. Something's *eidos* designates its unique form, characteristic property, or basic nature that makes the entity what it is. *Eidos* is the center of the metaphysics of presence, the ultimate explanatory principle of action; toward it, everything else converges. In what follows, I develop the metaphysics of presence from the perspective of Aristotle's *Metaphysica*. I do so because Aristotle's theory of development, which assumes the metaphysics of presence, dominates most modern theories of education. Such theories assume ultimate centers of action such as I. Q., Rationality, God's design, or perhaps selfish genes control human development. The assumption that there is "essential knowledge" everyone must learn drives curriculum and the recurring call for "educational standards." There is a hidden terror in rejecting the metaphysics of presence. If there are no fixed and final essences, then there are no such essences of Truth, Rationality, or Man. In fact, that is Dewey's existentially disturbing thesis.

The next four aspects all center on the concept of *eidos* and derive their meaning from their function in actualizing something's essence. The first is *energeia*, the correlative concept of which is *dynamis*. *Dynamis* refers to something's latent potential or power for change; it is something's capacity to become its essence. *Energeia* refers to the actual, activity, or act, as opposed to potential. Aristotle understood *energeia* functionally as what something "by nature" is suited to do or be. *Energeia* functions to actualize a latent potential (*dynamis*) to achieve its full actualization. Achieving full actualization means that something achieves its essence. *Energeia* conjoins with *entelecheia* to yield the perfect self-actualization of the entity. *Entelecheia* refers to a state of perfection; it is complete self-actualization. Again, the *eidos* is the state of completion toward which the development tends. *Energeia* and *entelecheia* are very nearly synonymous. *Telos* refers to completion, end, or purpose; it also connects with *entelecheia*. The fully actualized essence functions to actualize perfectly the latent potential of an entity to achieve the perfect completion of its telos. For instance, a normal, properly functioning acorn will necessarily develop into a giant oak. Fixed and final *energeia*, *telos*, and *entelecheia* dominate the vast majority of educational theories.

Ousia refers to ultimate entity, subject, or substance. For Aristotle, the ultimate subject or substance is the *eidos* because something's essence makes it what it is. Another important concept for the metaphysics of presence is that of the *arche*, which refers to ultimate origins, foundations, or absolute first principles. Again, for Aristotle, something's essence is the ultimate origin of action and the foundation or first principle in the explanation of development.

Dewey either completely rejects or dramatically reconstructs every fundamental concept associated with the metaphysics of presence. His reconstruction has major consequences for the analysis of human education and development. He rejects the metaphysics of presence in favor of naturalism so prosaic it is difficult to notice Dewey affects a decentering "Copernican revolution."[3]

> Neither self nor world . . . nor nature (in the sense of something isolated and finished in its isolation) is the centre, any more than either earth or sun is the absolute centre of a single universal and necessary frame of reference. There is a moving whole of interacting parts; a centre emerges wherever there is effort to change them in a particular direction . . . . Mind is no longer a spectator. . . . The mind is within the world as a part of the latter's own ongoing process. (232)

For Dewey, human nature is a part of nature and the mind and the self a participant in the flux of events, not a spectator. There is no absolute, eternal, and immutable center of existence, no absolute frame of reference, and no fixed context of action. There are only interactions among individual events.

Dewey carefully distinguishes existence from essence. It is a distinction especially useful for theorists of education and development because it allows us to distinguish antecedent existential events (the metaphysically given) from linguistically constructed meanings, or logically constructed essences. Here is how Dewey (1925/1981) describes the relation between existence and essence:

> Essence . . . is but a pronounced instance of [linguistic] meaning; to be partial, and to assign a meaning to a thing as *the* meaning is but to evince human subjection to bias . . . . Essence is never existence, and yet it is the essence, the distilled import of existence: the significant thing about it, its intellectual voucher. (144)

Dewey is a constuctivist about knowledge. The assignment of any one essence to an individual human being, or group of such beings, is always the

contingent product of cultural inquiry. Dewey is as Hegelian as one can become without falling into the hole of Hegel's philosophical idealism, as Rorty
does.[4]

So, what connects existence to essence? Dewey answers:

> [T]here is a natural bridge that joins the gap between existence and essence;
> namely communication, language, discourse. Failure to acknowledge the presence
> and operation of natural interaction in the form of communication creates the gulf
> between existence and essence, and that gulf is factitious and gratuitous. (133)

Essences emerge in the course of inquiry, the constructive process of forming logical judgments. Similarly, an inquiry into human development involves a *constructive* process of forming judgments about the meaning and
essence of human being.

Existence resembles iron ore in the earth. Linguistic meanings resemble
pig iron produced by the practical art of smelting. Logical essences, the product of inquiry, resemble steel, the refined essence of iron ore. Dewey transfers
most of the concepts found in the metaphysics of presence to the *lógos* active
as language or logic.[5] We cannot create ex nihilo and what we are *given* con-
strains what we may *make* of existence. One can mix talk of antecedent natural conditions and the cultural formation of logical judgment as readily as
one may mix talk of iron ore in the earth with steel for socially constructed
skyscrapers. All meanings and essences, including the essence of human being, are the contingent products of constructive processes themselves subject
to human need, interest, and purpose.

Dewey's destruction of Western metaphysics amounts to little more than
doing for philosophy what Darwin did for biology. A species is the ultimate
ontological subject of evolutionary theory. The word "species" is also the
Latin for the Greek word *eidos*. Dewey did for all essences what Darwin did
for species. In "The Influence of Darwinism on Philosophy," Dewey
(1909/1977) concludes that for classical and modern philosophy, "The conception of εἶδος, species, a fixed form and final cause, was the central principle of knowledge as well as of nature. Upon it rested the logic of science"
(6). After Darwin, Dewey thought we must rethink the logic of science.
Dewey recognizes the determination of *telos* by *eidos* when he states that "the
classic notion of species carried with it the idea of purpose" (8). Tradition-
ally, most assume the *telos* of inquiry is knowledge of eternal, immutable
essence, including the essence of Truth itself. The development of knowledge, in other words, assumes the same metaphysics of presence as biological
and cultural development.

Estimates are that 99 percent of all species that have ever existed are now extinct.[6] Dewey's neo-Darwinian insight is to realize what holds for biological forms or essences also holds for linguistic meanings and logical forms as well. Dewey (1925/1981) insists that "even the solid earth mountains, the emblems of constancy, appear and disappear like the clouds. . . . A thing may endure *secula seculorum* and yet not be everlasting; it will crumble before the gnawing tooth of time, as it exceeds a certain measure. Every existence is an event" (63). For Dewey, individual events have no *antecedent* fixed meanings or essences; instead, meaning and essence emerge as a *consequence* of linguistic and logical interaction between human beings and the rest of nature.

Events are not substances (*ousia*), so they do not have simple locations in time or place. Dewey insists that "events, being events and not rigid and lumpy substances, are ongoing and hence as such unfinished, incomplete, indeterminate" (126–27). We are especially interested in the events involved in human biological and social development. When Dewey finishes reconstructing *eidos*, it is an entirely temporal and contingent concept that no longer resides in the metaphysical domain.

Dewey's strategy involves draining the swamp of Western metaphysics into the basin of the *lógos*, that is, language or logic, until it is fit for human habitation. The following passage drains off a great deal: "Philosophy forswears inquiry after absolute origins and absolute finalities in order to explore specific values and the specific conditions that generate them" (1910/1977, 10). All theories of education should do the same.

Reconstructing the Subject Matter of Metaphysical Inquiry: Evolutionary Change, Diversity, and Interaction

In his "The Subject-Matter of Metaphysical Inquiry," Dewey (1915/1979) begins to consider the prospects for metaphysics once all of the constituents associated with the metaphysics of presence have undergone reconstruction, or have been discarded. Dewey turns the reconstructed constituents over to language or logic:

> I am not concerned to develop a metaphysics; but simply to indicate one way of conceiving the problem of metaphysical inquiry as distinct from that of the special sciences, a way which settles upon the more ultimate traits of the world as defining its subject-matter, but which frees these traits from confusion with ultimate origins [*arche*] and ultimate ends [*telos*]—that is, from questions of creation and eschatology [*entelecheia*]. (13)

Dewey maintains it possible to say something about existence at large beyond the specific cultural arts, including the arts of science and logic. He draws a careful distinction between the subject matter of the sciences, or their logic, and the subject matter of metaphysics. Further, there is no subject matter that deals with the eternal and immutable because no such things, forms, or *eidos* exist, hence it is impossible to secure their presence.

Dewey thinks we should understand questions regarding *arche, energeia, telos, entelecheia, ousia,* etc., in terms of their *functioning* in the *lógos,* either language or logic, while relinquishing their metaphysical connotations entirely. Dewey notes:

Hence it may be said that a question about ultimate origin [*arche*] or ultimate causation [*entelecheia, energeia,* or *eidos*] is either a meaningless question, or else the words are used in a relative sense to designate the point in the past at which a particular inquiry breaks off. (5)

We may simply eliminate those metaphysical concepts that we cannot substitute for "origin" or "causation" in this passage. What about the metaphysics Dewey does consider. He writes:

I wish to suggest that while one may accept as a preliminary demarcation of metaphysics from science the more "ultimate traits" with which the former deals, it is not necessary to identify these ultimate traits with empirically original traits—that, in fact, there are good reasons why we should not do so. We may also mark off the metaphysical subject-matter by reference to certain irreducible traits found in any and every subject of scientific inquiry. (4)

Dewey wants to consider a metaphysics capable of uniting diverse forms of inquiry in a contingent and evolutionary Darwinian universe.

The question is, are there any "irreducible traits" of existence sure to turn up in all domains of inquiry? Dewey thinks the answer is yes:

In all such investigations . . . we find at least such traits as the following: Specifically diverse existences, interaction, change . . . . As such they may be made the object of a kind of inquiry differing from that which deals with the genesis of a particular group of existences, a kind of inquiry to which the name metaphysical may be given. (6)

These simple ideas, diverse existence, interaction (later transaction), and change, do not seem a very promising beginning to a revolutionary new way of thinking about metaphysics, but in an unfinished and unfinishable Darwinian Universe, they are.

Aristotle's Theory of Potential

Aristotle discusses the potential and the actual in Book IX of his *Metaphysics*. He recognizes that it is impossible to explain change without potentiality (see chapter 3). Neither can we explain change solely by potential; nothing's potential becomes actualized without the intervention of something already actual. For Aristotle, existence is a mixture of the actual and the potential. The actual is the ultimate, eternal, and immutable form *eidos* that something is functioning to become, while potential is matter, latent capacity, or *dynamis*, the passive power to achieve the change. The essence of "man," for instance, is active reason that manifests the presence of divine reason in human souls.

The ratio of the mixture of the actual and potential determines the entities' place on the hierarchy of Being. At the bottom is pure potential or pure materiality, completely uninformed by any *eidos*. Latent potentiality is entirely passive and incapable of movement for without any actuality it has no agency. At the top is the Divine essence that is perfectly actualized and devoid of any materiality; the Divine is "the prime mover," the ultimate agent of all change that moves everything else, but is unmoved itself. The *eidos* is the *telos* and perfect *entelechy* for everything's development. On this theory, "normal" acorns become giant oaks because that is their latent potential.

Dewey (1920/1982) realizes that development and change in the ancient and medieval world-picture was fixed, predetermined, and repetitive. Such change is hyperrationalized:

> Only changes that lead to some defined or fixed outcome of form are of any account and can have any account—any *logos* or reason—made of them. The growth of plants and animals illustrates the highest kind of change that is possible in the sublunary or mundane sphere. They go from one definite fixed form to another . . . . Development holds merely of the course of changes which takes place within a particular member of the species. It is only a name for the predetermined movement from the acorn to the oak tree. (112)

Again, acorns "naturally" become oak trees because that is what they already are in their latent essence.

Dewey recognizes Aristotle's metaphysics describes a hierarchy of Being from the lowest pure potentially to the highest completely actualized entity, the God of St. Thomas Aquinas. It also forms a hierarchy of value. The complete and perfect Being, the Divine, or eternal prime mover is infinitely valuable, while the uninformed matter, if there is such, at the bottom is entirely devoid of value. Dewey also notices it is an epistemological hierarchy. Dewey

(1925/1981) makes the following observation about ancient thought that applies to Plato as much as Aristotle:

> There were higher and lower forms of knowledge; but all stages of knowledge were alike realization of some level of Being, so that appearance in contrast with reality meant only a lower degree of Being, being imperfect or not fully actualized. (111)

The notion that there are degrees of reality still haunts modern philosophy as the distinction between appearance and reality.

Rorty (1982a) refers to Dewey's student, Sydney Hook, who writes:

> Traditional metaphysics has always been a violent and logically impossible attempt to impose some parochial scheme of values upon the cosmos in order to justify or undermine a set of existing social institutions by a pretended deduction from the nature of reality. (74)

Dewey is as concerned to ameliorate metaphysical violence as Emmanuel Levinas, Jacques Derrida, or Rorty.

Dewey's Reconstruction of Aristotle's Theory of Potentiality: Time and Individuality

Although Dewey rejects almost the entirety of Western metaphysics, he does want to preserve a place for a radically reconstructed theory of the actual (*energeia*) and the potential (*dynamis*). The best way to begin understanding the metaphysics Dewey does consider is to see it as a reconstruction of Aristotle's metaphysics of the actual and the potential. Dewey notes that we never appeal to the term potential "except where there is change or a process of becoming" (1915/1979, 11). In a contingent, ever-evolving Darwinian universe this simple statement makes sense.

Change, development, and evolution championed by Aristotle and his medieval admirers involve entities guided toward their predetermined, fully actualized (*energeia*), and eternal immutable *eidos* by their intrinsic substance (*ousia*), imminent *telos*, and *entelecheia*. Consider Dewey's (1920/1982) remarks on the classical concept of development:

> Development, evolution, never means, as in modern science, origin of new forms, a mutation from an old species, but only the monotonous traversing of a previously plotted cycle of change. So potentiality never means, as in modern life, the possibility of novelty, of invention, of radical deviation, but only that principle in virtue of which the acorn becomes the oak .... Potentiality instead of implying the emergence of anything novel means merely the facility with which a particular thing re-

peats the recurrent process of its kind, and thus becomes a specific case of the eternal forms in and through which all things are constituted. (112–13)

Dewey recognizes that potentiality is required to account for change, but rejects latent potentiality, fixed essence, or fixed *telos*. Instead, he wants to preserve a place for creative emergence through interaction among diverse individuals.

Dewey (1940/1991) begins his amazing essay, "Time and Individuality," with some reflections on the human existential needs satisfied by classical and modern metaphysics:

> It was not then for metaphysical reasons that classic philosophy maintained that change, and consequently time, are marks of inferior reality, holding that true and ultimate reality is immutable and eternal . . . . The grounds for the belief are couched in the technical language of philosophy, but the cause for the grounds is the heart's desire for surcease from change, struggle, and uncertainty. The eternal and immutable is the consummation of mortal man's quest for certainty. (98–99)

In a dangerous, ever-changing world, we desire something eternal, immutable, and indubitable to quell metaphysical anxiety. The quest for certainty can only complete itself in some supernal realm beyond space, time, chance, and change. Even today, the quest of many scientists and philosophers is for eternal, fixed causal laws that deny change to the "really real." Dewey affirms: "Fixed laws which govern change and fixed ends toward which changes tend are both the products of a backward look, one that ignores the forward movement of life" (100). Following out the logic of these theories, Dewey (1940/1991) thought they all "hold to a closed universe in which there is no room for novelty and adventure" (101). They "sacrifice individuality and all the values, moral and aesthetic which hang upon individuality . . . the individual is simply a part determined by the whole of which he is a part" (101). Totalizing theories, like totalitarian societies, sacrifice creativity to a false sense of security and diverse individuality to the system. We may say the same for totalizing theories of education. In a Darwinian universe, this is not only unaesthetic and immoral; it is dumb.

Change, evolution, and time are the consequences of interactions among diverse existences. The existence of a plurality of *unique* individuals, i.e., diverse existence, is, therefore, a crucial concept in Dewey's theory of change. Dewey's most common example of individuality is human individuality:

> Take the account of the life of any person, whether the account is a biography or an autobiography. The story begins with birth, a temporal incident; it extends to include the temporal existence of parents and ancestry. It does not end with death,

for it takes in the influence upon subsequent events of the words and deeds of the one whose life is told. Everything recorded is an historical event; it is something temporal . . . . [It] is an extensive event. (102)

The particular individual whose interactions and changes (evolutionary development) Dewey selects is Abraham Lincoln. There is a sense in which an existential participant in the drama of existence has an intuitive pretheoretical and preontological understanding of existence. Hence, examining what is closest to hand, human individuality, its interactions with other existences, and the resulting changes, should provide clues to the general characteristics of individuality, interaction, and change. Human being in its "average understanding" of everydayness as a user of tools, and the tool of tools (language and the self for Dewey) provides an existential clue to the nature of all existence.

Any individual is a unique product of prior physical, biological, and cultural interactions. Dewey derives his entire educational theory from this basic insight. As a product of biological interactions (e.g., mating), they inherit genes that individuate them as a unique one-time-only individual in the history of cosmos. Even if two biological beings could share exactly the same biological inheritance, they cannot occupy the same identical durational-extensional expanse, so their differential experiences soon render them unique. Experience for Dewey (1934/1987) is just our interactions with other physical, biological, and cultural individuals: "Experience occurs continuously, because the interaction of the live creature and environing conditions is involved in the very process of living" (42). Cultural interactions are crucial to the emergence of a truly unique mind and self.

"Genuine time," Dewey (1940/1991) writes, "if it exists as anything else except the measure of motion in space, is all one with the existence of individuals as individuals" (112). For example, Lincoln "did not just exist in a time which externally surround him, but time was the heart of his existence" (102). This statement is true because each individual becomes what they experience, their interactions with diverse environing conditions. Dewey states the obvious conclusion bluntly: "Temporal seriality is the very essence, then, of the human individual . . . . Lincoln as an individual *is* a history" (102). Individuals of all kinds are not *in* time; their interactions with other individuals *are* time. This insight has the power to revolutionize our thinking about time, evolution, and development, including theories of human development. There are many barriers to thinking of time this way; the myth of flux is perhaps the greatest obstacle. Let us begin to struggle with it here.

We often think of time as a flowing Heraclitean stream. D. C. Williams (1951) called this conception of time "the myth of passage." Motion in space is motion with respect to time (e.g., rate of motion equals feet per second). The motion of time, though, cannot be motion in time with respect to time (e.g., rate of motion, or flux, equals seconds per what?). Time, we might suppose, must move with respect to something; call it hypertime. The motion of hypertime would then be with respect to hyper-hypertime, and so on ad infinitum. The myth of passage breaks down. Time does not flow; rather events are constantly interacting, constantly changing. Time is not a flowing substance (*ousia*); it is a *function* of interacting, or more precisely, transacting, events, or those durationally-extensionally contracted events we call "objects." Dewey dismisses another false notion of time that claims it is like an empty space filled by events. Time is no more that than it is some "thing," some substance. Dewey (1934/1987) concludes: "Time as empty does not exist; time as an entity does not exist. What exists are things acting and changing" (214). Time is an interaction among diverse events, including those objects, ontology, etc., that eventuate in human experience as the products of linguistic and logical processes.

If we can get over the notion that time is some sort of homogenous flowing substance then we are a long way toward appreciating the connections among diverse individuals, interaction, change, evolution, and development. Dewey believes that if we ever fully recognize these relations, then we will acknowledge that time involves change and change involves transformation. He thinks two major educational implications arise from such a transformational understanding of time and individuality. Dewey (1915/1979) writes:

First and negatively, the idea . . . is excluded that development is process of unfolding what was previously implicit or latent. Positively it is implied that potentiality is a category of existence, for development cannot occur unless an individual has powers or capacity that are not actualized at a given time. (109)

We have seen how Dewey revives the metaphysical notion of potential while rejecting the notion of "latent" potential. There is something here, though, that we overlooked earlier. Potentiality, for Dewey, is not passive; rather, it is the *active* power of some actual individual to change, evolve, and develop. Every actual individual has potential and may change and develop but only through interaction with *other* equally unique actual individuals. Once we abandon self-action, it becomes clear that we need others different from ourselves to grow and prosper. Just as diversity is the key to biological survival and growth, so too is diversity the key to cultural survival and growth. The neo-Darwinian knows the racist is simply wrong.

Because of the uniqueness of actual individuals, we cannot specify the potential of a novel *interaction* until *after* the event:

> When the idea that development is due to some indwelling end [*telos*] which tends to control the series of changes passed through is abandoned, potentialities [*dynamis*] must be thought of in terms of consequences of interactions with other things. Hence potentialities cannot be known until after the interactions have occurred. There are at a given time unactualized potentialities in an individual because and in as far as there are in existence other things with which it has not as yet interacted. (109)

Potentiality is an *active* category of existence that only discloses itself when individuals engage in transaction; it is a *consequence* of these transactions, not an antecedent latent condition. For decades, Dewey used an interactional vocabulary to express transactional ideas. The passage above is one such instance, yet on the very next page he states, "There is no such thing as interaction that is merely a one-way movement" (110). When two events "interact" the actualized in the one event actualizes the potential in the second and, transactionally, the actualized in the second event actualizes the potential in the first. Every good teacher knows this truth well. In the remainder of this chapter, though, I retain the term interaction.

Remember our old friend the acorn. We usually assume "normal" acorns become oak trees (their *eidos*), a fine instance of believing in a self-acting *entelechy* (immanent *telos*). In fact, acorns may just as easily become stored for food in winter; such an interaction is perfectly normal; potentiality is as fully actualized in this interaction as in the acorn becoming an oak tree. To become an oak tree the acorn must engage in many interactions that include soil, nutrients, sunshine, atmosphere, and water (while avoiding interactions with such events as squirrels). What the developmental potential of a given acorn is, we can never know for sure until *after* the interaction. Instead of antecedently existing latent potentials, we only have changes that emerge after diverse existences interact. Dewey (1915/1979) writes, "Potentiality thus signifies a certain limitation of present powers, due to the limited number of conditions with which they are in interaction plus the fact of the manifestation of new powers under different conditions" (11). Potentiality thus implies not merely diversity, but a progressively increasing *emergent* diversification of a specific thing in a particular direction as a *consequence* of interaction.

Emergent diversification, the realization of potential, is unpredictable. We do not know what will happen until after the transaction. Dewey (1940/1991) insists:

> Individuality conceived as a temporal development involves uncertainty, indeterminacy, or contingency. Individuality is the source of whatever is unpredictable in the world. The indeterminate is not change in the sense of violation of law . . . . When a change occurs, *after* it has occurred it belongs to the observable world. (111)

Only after an interaction, we can perhaps establish lawlike relations for repeating patterns. The same holds for the artistic construction of linguistic meaning and logical essence.

The Artistic Operations of Creative Inquiry: Toward a Science of Education

The key to survival and growth, including educational development, lies in controlling the sequence and kind of interactions an individual participates in. That is the supreme task of the species *Homo sapiens* in a contingent ever-evolving universe. Dewey reminds us:

> The striving to make stability of meaning prevail over the instability of events is the main task of intelligent human effort. But when the function is dropped from the province of art and treated as a property of given things, whether cosmological or logical, effort is rendered useless. (49)

Traditional metaphysics drops the function by placing the stability of meaning and essence in a supernal realm beyond time and chance. Let us focus on the art of inquiry, especially scientific inquiry.

The interactions (operations) involved in inquiry artfully actualize the potentials of existence; it *creates* essences from existence. We avoid confusion if we separate existential potential from logical essence, the product of the process of inquiry. In a debate with Ernest Nagel over the sphere of application of the logical law of excluded middle, Dewey (1929a/1984) accuses Nagel of failing to make this fundamental distinction. How Dewey concludes his first response to Nagel is especially useful for our purposes:

> I do deny that existence, apart from reflection [inquiry], conditions reflection as an existence, nor that the latter has a temporal continuity with prior existences. The union of stability and precariousness is, as I have tried to show elsewhere, a condition of the occurrence of thought, whose ulterior function is, accordingly, to give

to other existences a stability or determination they would not possess without it. My position may perhaps be made clearer by a distinction between the potential and the actual. To use a barbarous locution, I hold that existence apart from that of reflection is logici*ble*, but not logici*zed*. Similarly, certain stuffs in nature are ed-*ible* but not eat*en* until certain operations of organisms supervene. These operations produce distinctive additive consequences. Through them, qualities and relations previously potential become actualized. (208)

Most notably for the remainder of this chapter are the artistic "operations" required to actualize the potential of a given existential situation. Note, though, that Rorty would not allow us to mix the vocabulary of the edible with that of the eaten.

Dewey understood inquiry as fundamentally involving operations that de-termine consequences capable of transforming a given individual situation. Such operations involve interactions among existential individuals. In *Logic: The Theory of Inquiry*, Dewey (1938/1986) explains:

> Existence in general must be such as to be capable of taking on logical form, and existences in particular must be capable of taking on differential logical forms. But the operations which constitute controlled inquiry are necessary in order to give actuality to these capacities or potentialities. (387)

Systematic and repeatable methodological operations actualize the poten-tial of antecedent existence to yield essences and other logical forms by in-stituting systematically controlled interactions among diverse existences. In *The Quest for Certainty*, Dewey (1929a/1984) writes:

> With the surrender of unchangeable substances [*ousia*] having properties fixed in isolation and unaffected by interactions, must go the notion that certainty is at-tained by attachment to fixed objects with fixed characters [*eidos*] . . . . Henceforth the quest for certainty becomes the search for methods of control; that is, regula-tion of conditions of change with respect to their consequences. (103)

The regulation of change involves controlling interactions by systematic, repeatable operations that arrive at sought-for consequences. Dewey insists:

> It was logically inevitable that as science proceeded on its experimental path it would sooner or later become clear that all conceptions, all intellectual descrip-tions, must be formulated in terms of operations, actual or imaginatively possible. There are no conceivable ways in which the existence of ultimate unchangeable substances which interact without undergoing change in themselves can be reached by means of experimental operations. (95)

Dewey (1938/1986) asserts, "*The subject-matter of logic is determined operationally*" (22). Operations fall into two general types: "There are operations that are performed upon and with existential material—as in experimental observation" and there are symbolic operations (22). In the latter case "the symbols . . . stand for *possible* final existential operations" (22). In illustrating what he means, Dewey draws his examples "from the operations of industrial arts" (23).

If we can find the right operations to perform, we can actualize the possibilities of some problematic situation, thereby idealizing existence in some way, large or small. Dewey writes:

> The relation between objects as known and objects with respect to value is that between the actual and the possible. "The actual" consists of given conditions; "the possible" denotes ends or consequences not now existing but which the actual may through its use brings into existence. The possible in respect to any given actual situation is this an ideal for that situation, from the standpoint of operational definition—of thinking in terms of action—the ideal and the possible are equivalent ideas. (239)

Exercising the art of intelligent inquiry by carrying out sagacious operations allows us to transform the world, thereby actualizing ideal possibilities, ends-in-view, or, if you would, values. That is not all though. As Dewey (1940/1991) asserts:

> The artist in realizing his own individuality reveals potentialities hitherto unrealized. This revelation is the inspiration of other individuals to make the potentialities real, for it is not sheer revolt against things as they are which stirs human endeavor to its depths, but vision of what might be and is not. (114)

This result is possible because our ever-evolving human "nature" is a part of nature and, therefore, participates in its interactions. As Dewey saw it, "The intelligent activity of man is not something brought to bear upon nature from without; it is nature realizing its own potentialities" (170). Ultimately, pluralistic democracy is so desirable because it realizes human potential better than any other form of social relations currently known; something Heidegger failed to realize.

We can now understand why Dewey (1934/1987) would say that "science itself is but a central art auxiliary to the generation and utilization of other arts" (33). We may also understand what Dewey meant by a science of education. In "The Sources of a Science of Education" Dewey (1929b/1984) concludes, "In concrete operation, education is an art . . . . If there were an opposition between science and art, I should be compelled to side with those who assert that education is an art" (6). There is no opposition, though. Education is the art, informed by other arts (the sciences) that yield experimental knowledge of human interactions. Generations of educators have terribly misread Dewey's remarks on the role of science in education.

Conclusion

We have seen how Dewey dismantles the metaphysics of atemporal presence while recovering a reconstructed metaphysics of potentiality that rejects Aristotle's latent potential in favor of an account of change that relies on interaction among diverse individuals. Drawing on the development of human potential as a physical, biological, and social interaction as an example, Dewey develops a general account of emergent evolution that overcomes the myth of passage. Whether or not Peirce influences Dewey's reconstruction of metaphysics, Dewey's position on Firsts, Seconds, potentiality, and interaction resembles that of Peirce in some important ways. We have also seen how Dewey's reconstruction of the concept of potential provides insights into Dewey's generic traits of existence.

Without potentiality, it is impossible to account for change. One Dewey version, realization of potential and change, occurs when actual existential individuals interact. Drawing a careful distinction between existence and essence, Dewey recognizes that our existential task is to make the stability of meanings and essences prevail over the instability of existential events. The artistic operations of the *lógos*, of language and logic, whose artifacts are meanings, identities, essences, logical forms, and warranted assertions, achieve relative stability. When human beings actualize the antecedent potentialities of existence, including their own unique potential, they can complete the quest for meaning and value in the universe, although they cannot complete the quest for certainty. The philosophical fallacy occurs when we mistake the products of the *lógos* (language and logic) for antecedent reality. In their effort to complete the quest for certainty they hope will relieve them of the existential burdens of fear, anxiety, and fatigue, human beings cut themselves off from the miracle of creation. This effort is doubly tragic, for it also cuts them off from the only genuine source of their deliverance.

What are we to say to Rorty when he laments that Dewey composed a metaphysic? One thing we can say is that Dewey could not possibly have held a traditional version of Aristotelian, Lockean, Kantian, or Hegelian metaphysics. Another thing we can do is to point out that it is impossible to account for change without potentiality, or something synonymous with it from Dewey's list of generic traits. Rorty (1989) recognizes the inevitability of change; indeed, he dreams of the day we arrive at the point "where we treat *everything*—our language, our conscience, our community—as a product of time and chance" (22). In order to fulfill his dream, Rorty commits himself to the doctrine that *everything* is contingent. Of course Dewey (1925/1981) would agree with this manifestly metaphysical statement, only he would speak of the "ineradicable union in nature of the relatively stable and the relatively contingent" (56). For Dewey, "Barely to note and register that contingency is a trait of natural events has nothing to do with wisdom" (309). In his opinion "necessity implies the precarious and contingent. A world that was all necessity would not be a world of necessity; it would just be. For in its being, nothing would be necessary for anything else" (59). Among other things, his statement is a reminder that the potential cannot actualize itself without interacting with the actual (relatively stable). I suspect Rorty (1956) understands this metaphysical claim; after all, the title of his dissertation was "The Concept of Potential." Metaphysics always buries its undertakers, so we may appreciate the possibilities of Dewey's reconstructed metaphysics.

Notes

1. This section and the next owe a great deal to Garrison (1999).
2. Nowhere in this chapter have I added emphasis to cited material.
3. J. Dewey (1929a/1984, 229, 230, 232, 235, 238, 245).
4. See Rorty (1982b).
5. The analogy is not perfect because in it we name the iron ore before any interaction with it.
6. See Parker (1992).

Bibliography

Dewey, J. (1909/1977). The Influence of Darwinism on Philosophy. In Jo Ann Boydston (ed.), *John Dewey: The Middle Works, Volume 4* (3–14). Carbondale, Ill.: Southern Illinois University Press.

———. (1915/1979). The Subject-Matter of Metaphysical Inquiry. In Jo Ann Boydston (ed.), *John Dewey: The Middle Works, Volume 8* (3–13). Carbondale, Ill.: Southern Illinois University Press.

———. (1920/1982). Reconstruction in Philosophy. In Jo Ann Boydston (ed.), *John Dewey: The Middle Works, Volume 12*. Carbondale, Ill.: Southern Illinois University Press.

66 ～ Jim Garrison

———. (1925/1981). Experience and Nature. In Jo Ann Boydston (ed.), *John Dewey: The Later Works, Volume 1*. Carbondale, Ill.: Southern Illinois University Press.

———. (1929a/1984). The Quest for Certainty. In Jo Ann Boydston (ed.), *John Dewey: The Later Works, Volume 4*. Carbondale, Ill.: Southern Illinois University Press.

———. (1929b/1984). The Sources of a Science of Education. In Jo Ann Boydston (ed.), *John Dewey: The Later Works, Volume 5* (3–40). Carbondale, Ill.: Southern Illinois University Press.

———. (1931/1985). Context and Thought. In Jo Ann Boydston (ed.), *John Dewey: The Later Works, Volume 6* (3–21). Carbondale, Ill.: Southern Illinois University Press.

———. (1934/1987). Art as Experience. In Jo Ann Boydston (ed.), *John Dewey: The Later Works, Volume 10*. Carbondale, Ill.: Southern Illinois University Press.

———. (1938/1986). Logic: The Theory of Inquiry. In Jo Ann Boydston (ed.), *John Dewey: The Later Works, Volume 12*. Carbondale, Ill.: Southern Illinois University Press.

———. (1940/1991) Time and Individuality. In Jo Ann Boydston (ed.), *John Dewey: The Later Works, Volume 14* (98–114). Carbondale, Ill.: Southern Illinois University Press.

Garrison, J. (1999) John Dewey, Jacques Derrida, and the Metaphysics of Presence. *Transactions of the Charles S. Peirce Society* 35, no. 2, 346–72.

Heidegger, M. (1927/1962) *Being and Time*. John Macquarrie and Edward Robinson (trans.). New York: Harper & Row.

Parker, S. (ed.) (1992) *McGraw-Hill Encyclopedia of Science and Technology*, vol. 6 (7th ed., 570–72). New York: McGraw-Hill.

Rorty, R. (1956) The Concept of Potential. *Dissertation Abstracts Online*.

———. (1982a) Dewey's Metaphysics. In *Consequences of Pragmatism* (72–89). Minneapolis: University of Minnesota Press.

———. (1982b) The World Well Lost. In *Consequences of Pragmatism* (3–18). Minneapolis: University of Minnesota Press.

———. (1989). *Contingency, Irony, and Solidarity*. Cambridge: Cambridge University Press.

Williams, D. C. (1951) The Myth of Passage. *Journal of Philosophy* 48, 457–72.

CHAPTER THREE

❧

Truth, Trust, and Metaphor: Rorty's Davidsonian Philosophy of Education

Paulo Ghiraldelli Jr.

Rorty's philosophy of education is a discourse built on two elements: a criticism of the traditional notion of truth and an exaltation for a democratic society nurtured by trust between their citizens.

Briefly, Rorty's philosophy of education tells us the following (see Rorty 1999a; 1999b; see Ghiraldelli 1999): the social function of education is not the promotion of the truth, in a specific sense. In American society and other democratic societies, precollege education aims to *socialize* children and young people. Precollege education wants young people to hold the values and knowledge of society. On the other hand, higher education, or better, nonvocational education at college, aims to produce *individuals*—free and critical persons. For Rorty, this is right, because, as he says, education is not socialization *or* individualization. Education is socialization and individualization. But, he says, we needn't think that socialization promotes only people like John Wayne as model Americans for young people—people who say that American values lie in the war against aliens, inside or outside the United States. And it is not imperative that individualization should be carried out showing that America is exclusively a sexist, racist, and imperialist society, one in which mutual trust is dead. For Rorty, socialization could be conducted by a certain kind of teacher. For example, the teacher that reminded their students that the militants of the Civil Rights Movement were American men. Individualization could be conducted by teachers that showed that Great Books and the books from the Left were never incompatible readings—both sets of books show us that trust is a possible thing and

67

that *that* is the core of a democratic social life that gives us what we believe as true. Rorty believes that this is something that happened and happens in the United States, rather than only a *mere* dream.

Rorty's critics have attacked both sides of Rorty's philosophy of education. I choose, in this text, to talk about two critical positions. The first was a position developed directly against Rorty by Jürgen Habermas, in a debate in the Institute of Philosophy and Sociology of the Polish Academy of Sciences, in 1995. The second was developed by several thinkers of the radical Left in the United States and Europe. But, in this case, I take as representing such positions a general criticism from Deleuze against American pragmatism, published in French in 1993; this position is not directly against Rorty, but I choose to use it because it is larger, and it covers several other positions from the radical Left against Rorty.

The first criticism is in the field of epistemology. The second criticism is in the field of politics. In the first position, Habermas disagrees with Rorty's deflationary position about truth. In the second position, Deleuze disagrees with the pragmatist reliance on trust and thereby in the pragmatist hope that utopian American democracy will provide a better way of life in an uncertain future.

In both cases, Rorty's philosophy of education revolves around the nature of an aim. First: if Rorty cannot subscribe to the deflationary theory of truth, he would have to accept the strong notion of truth. In that case, he could not say, against the Right, that the social function of education is not to show the Truth, just because the Right assumes a strong notion of truth—education as a discourse that describes "Reality Like It Is." But Rorty sees this as a dogmatic position. Second: if Rorty cannot subscribe to the belief that trust is something that exists in American society, then education for individualization must be only a negative discourse—the discourse of the radical Left. So, if Habermas and Deleuze are right about all things, Rorty is wrong about his specific position.

In this chapter, I will deal with three things. First, I will talk about the Habermas-Rorty debate. After this, I will explain the political position of Rorty against the radical Left and thereby provide an answer to Deleuze. And finally, I will say something about philosophy of education and my general agreement with Rorty's perspective. As I read it, Rorty's perspective can be called a Davidsonian perspective.

Habermas versus Rorty

Rorty doesn't want the conversation about truth linked with epistemology or metaphysics. He believes that this kind of conversation is a thing of the past. Since his first books, Rorty sees truth to be an issue of semantics. We should ask, "How do we use the word 'true' or the word 'truth' in our declarations and sentences?" Instead we ask, "What is the truth?" Therefore, we should give up questions concerned with epistemology or metaphysics and we should continue moving on from the old pragmatists in the observation of our *experience* or, to put it better, our *linguistic behavior*.

Habermas has no doubts about this. He agrees with Rorty about what he has made known as "linguistic turn" and "pragmatic-linguistic turn"—the way that we did philosophy in the twentieth century and the way that we will continue doing it now, in the twenty-first century. But whereas Rorty thinks that a lot of philosophical problems could be *dissolved*, Habermas believes that there still are authentic problems that need attention—they should be *resolved*. Habermas wants to show that such a conclusion can be taken from a reading of Rorty's perspective about truth. For Habermas, the Rortyan analysis of linguistic behavior in the use of 'truth' or 'true' would lead us to conclusions, that contradict Rorty's position. I need to explore this before I explain the Rortyan way of talking about truth.

Following the idea that philosophical problems should be dissolved, Rorty thinks that as a result we would not have a "pragmatist theory of truth," in a constructive sense, but just a historical set about the uses of 'true'. As he says, "this dissolution would start from the claim that 'true' has no explanatory use, but merely the following uses: 'an endorsing use', 'a disquotational use' and 'a cautionary use'" (see Rorty 1991, 127–28). What do these terms mean? I will talk about each one, and I will show that the third use is the use on which Habermas depends for his objections to Rorty's deflationary position about truth.

First: 'endorsing use'. It happens when we say "true!" as "certain!", "I agree!", "go on!", "I think the same way, you must continue!" and so on.

Second: 'disquotational use'. For example: you can use the following sentence: Now the doctors tell me "ulceration is caused by the bacteria W." This declaration is not your declaration, but the doctors' declaration and therefore you use quotes. But, at a certain moment, you believe in this declaration, and then you give up the quotes—you *disquote*: it is true that ulceration is caused by the bacteria W. Your disquotational operation asked the word "true?" You answered true and then you used the declaration without quotes. In a more general way, the disquotational use appears to say metalinguistic things of the form "S" is true if and only if _____.

Third: 'cautionary use'. It happens when we want say things such as "Your declaration that John is an honest man is well justified, but perhaps not true." In this case, such a sentence is a warning—it is not rare that we, humans, are wrong about a lot of things that we believed to be correct.

So, for Rorty, whatever the meanings of "truth" or "true" they are put in our phrases in a way which does not involve a metaphysical question such as "what is the truth?" or, in the epistemological field, the question "What is true knowledge?" "Truth" and "true" are words that have their "language games"—contexts where they acquire meanings. These "language games" need not make the word "truth" equivalent to "Reality As It Is." In all these "language games" the "truth" or the "true" work rather as a semantic expedient than as a metaphysical element.

Habermas would not agree with this last paragraph (see Habermas 1996). For him, the 'cautionary use', shows that there is a common performance linguistic need, in itself, of a *strong* distinction between "well justified" and "true"—a substantive and explanatory distinction. The common person, Habermas says, knows that "well justified" is just "well justified" as "true" is "true." If the person didn't distinguish, in a strong way, between "well justified" and "true", the use 'cautionary use' wouldn't be a cautionary use. It is not a warning. It is a warning, Habermas says, because there is an ideal field, linked to language, where we understand "well justified" as "well justified" and "true" as "well justified in all place and all time." This ideal field is an area that belongs to epistemology: a hierarchy of words strongly distinguished from each other. For Habermas then, remarks about the pragmatic use of declarations and sentences, in the case of "truth" or "true", do not show a deflationary use but, rather, a reinflationary use.

Habermas thinks, then, that we must not give up our worry about the truth but, instead, show in a clear way which society is more like the ideal society in which ideal linguistic communication happens.

Rorty doesn't think that Habermas is completely wrong. He thinks that Habermas is undertaking a useless operation—Habermas is putting more philosophy than is necessary in the business. The building of a ideal field for language can be made, Rorty says, but when we, looking at a declaration or phrase, or sentence, etc., want to know if it is true or not true, we ask for justifications and more and better justifications, nothing more. And we know that a new and better justification than we could even imagine might appear—and then we would have the *truth*. So, for Rorty, "well justified for all place and time" is *just* a case of "justified for all place and time in *this place and in this time*"—true, of course, but *here* and *now*.

Rorty says

My attempt amounts to thinking of the contrast between the merely justified and the true not as the contrast between the actual and the ideal, but simply as the contrast between justification to us as we are here and now and justification to a superior version of ourselves, the version we hope our descendants will exemplify.

Consider what I call the "cautionary use of truth", the use of 'true' in the phrase "unjustifiable to all of you but maybe true anyway" . . . I think of the contrast which is drawn in such phrases as a contrast between this age of the world and a possible future, better, age of the world—not "the end of inquiry" or "the ideal cognitive situation", but just a better age than ours. . . .

So I think of the cautionary use of 'true', the use it swings free of present practices of justification, as the voice of prophecy. This voice says, some day the world will be changed, and then this proposition may turn out to be true. The romantic hope for another world which is yet to come is at the heart of the anti-Platonist's quest for spiritual perfection. (Rorty 1996b, 50)

The field of ideal communication suggested by Habermas would be more an ad hoc theory than a discovery in epistemology. But, Rorty says, among ad hoc theories, he prefers the pragmatist deflationary theory because it does not deny that it is a *merely* ad hoc theory. An ad hoc theory is not a Theory, just a theory—for example, a semantical list about truth such as Rorty's list above. A list in which the truth does not claim to be "Reality As It Is" because maybe "reality", the future, could be completely different and better.

Though Habermas works in the field of the linguistic turn, he *still* seeks a philosophical foundation for communication, and thereby, for democracy. Rorty, conversely, believes that democracy—as contingent experience—is sufficient for itself, even because there is no other way. So, in the Habermasian project, the philosophy of education would still have a foundational task. But in the Rortyan project the philosophy of education is free—it can spend energy on other things, such as, for example, imagining new stories for the increase of freedom. Perhaps, with luck, such stories will support democracy and social justice.

Deleuze versus Rorty

The parties of the Left in the United States and other countries do not agree with Rorty about the possibility of a new task for the philosophy of education. Generally, the argument from old and dogmatic positions has been learned from hard-line Marxism or traditional philosophical thought. I see a major part of the criticism from the Left as being without value. Many people from the Left do not understand Rorty just as Bertrand Russell and Max Horkheimer did not understand William James or John Dewey. In the past, Russell and Horkheimer made several criticisms of pragmatism. Linking pragmatism to mere blind behavior, they delineated Dewey and James as promoters of violence and alienation. This kind of criticism was not capable of understanding that "instrumental reason" (Horkheimer) was different from the "pragmatical rationality" defended by Dewey and James. Deleuze's criticism of American pragmatism doesn't replay old or wrong positions. It is an elegant criticism.

Like Rorty, Deleuze sees American society as founded in politics, that is, built on the social compromise between citizens. He sees pragmatism as the expression of a society made only by brothers and sisters, without parents. Such a society needs mutual trust—solidarity. Like Rorty, Deleuze understands that in such a society, if we want to say what is true or what is false and what is right and what is wrong, we have only one way: the answers acquired by consensus through free meetings. In such a society the appeal to superior entities has no value.

Since before independence, Deleuze says, the American people thought about the State in a new form that was compatible with one's vocation. The American people did not want a State like the European State. They thought not about tradition, heritage, and family, but about the federation of men and goods, a community of anarchist individuals, with inspiration coming from Jefferson, Thoreau, and Melville (see Deleuze 1997a, 98). Several of Rorty's texts, like those of Deleuze, remind us that the American vocation is the only American destiny. The American people were destined to a historical democratic experience because it had denied the past—England, parents, and superiors. This society did not have other things on its hands, except for mutual conversation and, thereby, democracy. For Deleuze, the United States is an archipelago and a place of hope, and therefore, the American people must seek trust between the several islands of the archipelago in order to achieve the nation. In this place, the community gets the truth through trust. So, pragmatism, for Deleuze, will always be a struggle on two fronts. Pragmatism will be against the particularities that put the men in mutual opposition causing the distrust to grow, and pragmatism will be against The Universal, The Whole, the fusion of souls by "great love" or "charity" (see Deleuze 1997a, 100–101).

Pragmatism, for Rorty and Deleuze, means that truth is fruit of the trust, and objectivity is intersubjectivity—solidarity. But, if for Rorty this is alive, for Deleuze it is dead. America, Deleuze says, thought itself to be making revolution with the energy from universal immigration, just as Russia thought it was making the other revolution with the energy from the universal creation of the proletarian. But in Deleuze's judgment, the eventualities were not good. The society of friendship is the American dream, the dream of Whitman, but a dream was betrayed even before the Soviet project started. Both revolutions—the pragmatical and the dialectical—failed. The first failed and its proof was the Civil War. The second failed too and its proof was the end of "soviets." For Deleuze, all this is delineated in the mutation of the word "trust": it meant friendship between citizens but now it means the link between corporations *against* citizens (see Deleuze 1997b, 72).

What would Rorty answer to Deleuze? I have found good arguments against Deleuze in Rorty's *Achieving Our Country* where he compares Dewey and Whitman. As Rorty describes Whitman and Dewey, there appears a version of American history in which the events are better justified than in Deleuze's version.

Rorty believes that there is little difference in doctrine between Dewey and Whitman, but there is an obvious difference in emphasis: "the difference between talking mostly about love and talking mostly about citizenship." And Rorty continues:

> Whitman's image of democracy was of lovers embracing. Dewey's was of a town meeting. Dewey dwelt on the need to create what the Israeli philosopher Avishai Margalit has called a *decent* society, defined as one in which *institutions* do not humiliate. Whitman's hopes were centered on the creation of what Margalit calls, by contrast, a *civilized* society, defined as one in which *individuals* do not humiliate each other—in which tolerance for other people's fantasies and choices is instinctive and habitual. Dewey's principal target was institutionalized selfishness, whereas Whitman's was the socially acceptable sadism which is a consequence of sexual repression, and of the inability to love.
>
> Dewey disliked and distrusted Franklin D. Roosevelt, but many of his ideas came into their own in the New Deal. Whitman's hopes, on the other hand, began to be realized only in the youth culture of the 1960s. Whitman would have been delighted by rock-and-roll, drugs, and the kind of casual, friendly copulation which is insouciant about the homosexual-heterosexual distinction . . . Dewey might have approved of the rock-and-roll in a guarded and deliberate way, but Whitman would have thrown himself into it wholeheartedly. (Rorty 1997, 25–26)

Rorty's reply to Deleuze would be simple: events in American history show that the American democratic dream was not destroyed in the time of the Civil War, but was made a reality just after the Civil War, and later in the building of the American Welfare State in the twentieth century. So, when Rorty cites the happenings that he would like to constitute the content of the socialization process in education, he talks about things of our era rather than of the Civil War era—but he shows that the Civil War era was also a moment of struggle involving the American dream. And he talks about the realization of a Deweyan dream:

> For Dewey, this socialization consisted in acquiring an image of themselves as heirs to tradition of increasing liberty and rising hope. Updating Dewey a bit, we can

think of him as wanting the children to come to think of themselves as proud and loyal citizens of a country that, slowly and painfully, threw off a foreign yoke, freed its slaves, enfranchised its women, restrained its robber barons and licensed its trade unions, liberalized its religious practices, broadened its religious and moral tolerance, and built colleges in which 50 per cent of its population could enroll—a country that numbered Jefferson, Thoreau, Susan B. Anthony, Eugene Debs, Woodrow Wilson, Walter Reuther, Franklin Delano Roosevelt, Rosa Parks and James Baldwin among its citizens. Dewey wanted the inculcation of this narrative of freedom and hope to be the core of the socializing process. (Rorty 1999a, 121–22)

Thereby, against Deleuze, Rorty could easily bring the chronological history in which social gain in American democracy is not juxtaposed with the social prejudices of the Stalin era in Russia. To see the dialectical or pragmatic revolutions as great failings is to see the end of history, but history doesn't have an end.

Rorty's Strategy

As against Habermas, Rorty's argument would be much the same as against Deleuzian criticisms. He has a characteristic tactic: the radical historicism argument. He tries to stop Habermas and would try to stop Deleuze using the number one enemy of Philosophy: contingency. To Habermas he says that one can appear and put on the table a drawing never seen before. To the French philosopher he would say that Deleuze's drawing has one error: it wants to finish exactly at the point when all is just starting.

If we accept the play of Habermas and Deleuze we need to understand what Rorty calls the notion of language as a puzzle. In the idea of language as a puzzle there is a possibility of the new, but it is a "new" that has been expected. People know that it would come, and yet that it had never arrived. We can have a puzzle without a piece, but we know that puzzle without a piece—that piece. A piece that is in any place—real, ideal, virtual, imaginary, logical, transcendental, transcendent, divine, and so on. One day it will arrive. The notion of history in this case must be a weak notion: the new is just the old with a new dress. The new is just unpublished. But the new is not the new, because at least its mode is given in the puzzle. The owl flies in the afternoon, but it is a neurotic owl that never can fly out of its borders. Philosophy is a neurotic activity. Philosophy of education is boring. In Habermas's terms, philosophy of education would seek fundamentals for educational theory. In the field of Deleuze it would be nonsense because philosophy of education by definition is a search for new ways for education, but it cannot be a true search if history is finished.

Now, I want to put my position. I want to return to the philosophy of education.

I love Rorty's alternative because I don't love death. Nietzsche taught us that Philosophy since the Greeks sought death. Socrates, Nietzsche said, sought death and he was happy when it arrived. Philosophy, then, was marked: instead of life and contingency, philosophy wanted the World of Ideas (Plato) or a Transcendental Field (Kant) or a Universal Linguistic Field (Habermas) or the End of History (Deleuze). That places and elements and situation are the warranty of the replay. The vocabulary is a puzzle. The philosopher knows that the problem is to find the piece and to finish the game.

Education, thereby, does not amount to anything more than waiting for the moment of replay: in Adorno, education is a critical autoreflection in that man gives up his cruelty, his Nazi tendency, and shows a human pure core—a *human and good* nucleus. In Plato, education is the moment in which man remembers the True, the place of Ideas, his intellectual soul. So, education in traditional philosophy is a calm, silent world, the moment in which man escapes from the confusion and perturbation of history and contingency. Rorty, in a debate with Carol Nicholson, refuses this calm. He says that the biped without feathers can be a piece in an infinite construction made by our language games. And this can happen during the moment of the socialization of children, because children can learn to admire the heroes who strove for freedom. There is no human nature, but there are cultures—almost all—in which heroes who sought liberty existed. Education, then, is not a process of drawing out the human core, but is an open endless play. It is linked to our capacity to talk about ourselves and others and the world differently, making evident the behavior of other bipeds without feathers—behaviors which are similar to heroes.

So, I see education in Adorno and Plato as a limited, weak process. It cannot transform behavior. But I see education in Rorty as a strong process: our conversation can turn the biped without feathers into something else—fantastic, different—because history is endless and the biped doesn't have a human nucleus.

But there are in Rorty two ways to transform the biped without feathers and with luck put it in a better democratic situation. First, we can talk about sentimental stories. In a pragmatic way, such stories bring different people to look at themselves and then they will want to trace a common heritage with others that they don't regard "humans." However, such stories serve just to hold onto rights already known. Democracy is protected, but it holds on to its limits. Democracy is transformed if we invent *new rights*. So, we have the second point. With luck, democracy is enlarged if our conversation is broken with a metaphor. The conversation with the metaphor can bring rights never dreamed of. But here, we must understand "the metaphor" in agreement with Donald Davidson read by Rorty.

Philosophy of Education and the Theory of Metaphor

Now, we do not remain in the epistemological field, as Habermas would have us do. We don't stay in the area of Political Philosophy, as in the debate with Deleuze. We are in the proper area of philosophy of education past the linguistic and pragmatic turn: the field of Rorty-Davidson. The theory of metaphor is the central point in that philosophy of education.

Our traditional understanding of the metaphor is that it is a message that hides a true content. It is like the superficial cream on a cake. It makes the cake very beautiful. We eat the cream but it is merely decoration of the cake. So, on this understanding, the metaphor is saying something in a different way—it is a version of a literal sentence or declaration. Language, then, is a set of words and sentences and a semantical complex that is established a priori. Everything in language is metaphor or literal expression, but metaphor is simply a case of literal expression. Thereby, metaphor and literal expression are two faces of the same coin.

The problem with that conception is the following: metaphor doesn't generate paraphrase. Davidson argues:

> What I deny is that metaphor does its work by having a special meaning, a specific cognitive content. . . . If this is right, what we attempt in "paraphrasing" a metaphor cannot be to give its meaning, for that lies on the surface; rather we attempt to evoke what the metaphor brings to our attention. . . . When we try to say what a metaphor "means", we soon realize there is no end to what we want to mention. (Davidson 1996, 424–25)

Rorty reads Davidson and draws from him a theory about the transformation of language, helping to establish his own historicism. I argue that the transformation of language is a strategy in philosophy of education, or better still, a new philosophy of education. In an interesting passage of *Contingency, Irony, and Solidarity*, Rorty writes on metaphor in Davidson:

> To have a meaning is to have a place in a language game. Metaphors, by definition, do not. Davidson denies, in his words, "a thesis that associated with a metaphor is a cognitive content that its author wishes to convey and that the interpreter must grasp if he is to get the message." In his view, tossing a metaphor into a conversa-

tion is like suddenly breaking off the conversation long enough to make a face, or pulling a photograph out your pocket and displaying it, or pointing at a feature of the surroundings, or slapping your interlocutor's face, or kissing him. Tossing a metaphor into a text is like using italics, or illustrations, or odd punctuation or formats.

All these are ways of producing effects on your interlocutor or your reader, but not ways of conveying a message. To none of these is it appropriate to respond with "What exactly are you trying to say?" If one had wanted to say something—if one had wanted to utter a sentence with a meaning—one would presumably have done so. But instead one thought that one's aim could be better carried out by other means. That one uses familiar words in unfamiliar ways—rather than slaps, kisses, pictures, gestures, or grimaces—does not show that what one said must have a meaning. An attempt to state that meaning would be an attempt to find some familiar (that is, literal) use of words—some sentence which already had a place in the language game—and, to claim that one might just as well have had *that*. But the unparaphraseability of metaphor is just the unsuitability of any such familiar sentence of one's purpose.

Uttering a sentence without a fixed place in a language game is . . . to utter something which is neither true nor false—something which is not . . . a "truth-value candidate." This because it is a sentence which one cannot confirm or disconfirm, argue for or against. One can only savor it or spit it out. But this is not to say that it may not, in time, *become* a truth-value candidate. If it is savored rather that spat out, the sentence may be repeated, caught up, bandied out. Then it will gradually require a habitual use, a familiar place in the language game. It will thereby have ceased to be a metaphor—or, if you like, it will become what most sentences of our language are, a dead metaphor. It will be just one more, literally true or literally false, sentence of the language. (Rorty 1996a, 18)

I didn't hesitate to insert this long passage because it is Rorty's central dissertation about metaphor and the borrowing of the traditional distinction between literal sense and metaphor. It is with metaphor, that is, with the breaking off of the communication process that there is the impact necessary to create the new in language. So, I doubt that Galileo knew—as we know—what he was saying when he said to the Catholic priest "The Hearth moves." I doubt that the Black Movement knew what the phrase "Black is beautiful!" was when they tossed this into the debate with conservatives. Just like today, I doubt that one may explain the meaning of "Gay is good!" If one were to try, the result would be disaster, a spectacle of bad taste explaining nothing. But "Gay is good!" in several countries has created an impact, causing people to discuss the possibility of new democratic rights and the possibility of marriage between people of the same sex.

If we have to talk about "the Hearth moves" nowadays we talk about science. If we have to tell children about the "Black is beautiful!" we can talk about conservative scare tactics. But nowadays, if we have to explain "Gay is good!" we cannot do it. In the future, perhaps, we can tell a happy story about the discussions from conservatives when they exclaimed "gay is good!" and the young people understood a different *meaning* of "gay is good"!

So, the Rortyan professor is one that is alert to metaphors and alternative vocabularies in society. In these language places—in alternative vocabularies—new rights can appear. Then, if we are intelligent teachers and we are lucky, we can use metaphor in a democratic direction.

Now, if we go along with Habermas, our attention will be focused on the cake, and the metaphors will not be the motor of change. And if we go along with Deleuze, metaphor would be a good thing, but history would come to an end, and then metaphor could not help to develop new rights—nothing would be radically new! I think that the philosophy of education in such a context would be a boring task whether or not it had something useful to do.

Bibliography

Davidson, D. (1996) What Metaphors Mean. In A. Martinich, ed. *The Philosophy of Language*. New York: Oxford Press.

Deleuze, G. (1997a) Bartleby, ou a fórmula. Peter Pál Pelbart, trans. In *Critica e clínica*. São Paulo: Editora 34.

———. (1997b) Whitman. Peter Pál Pelbart, trans. In *Critica e clínica*. São Paulo; Editora 34.

Ghiraldelli, P., Jr. (1999). *Richard Rorty—A filosofia do Novo Mundo em busca de novos mundos*. Petrópolis: Editora Vozes.

Habermas, J. (1996). Coping with Contingencies—The Return of Historicism. In J. Niznik and J. Sanders (eds.). *Debating the State of Philosophy*. London: Praeger.

Rorty, R. (1991). *Objectivity, Relativism, and Truth*. Cambridge: Cambridge University Press.

———. (1996a). *Contingency, Irony, and Solidarity*. Cambridge: Cambridge University Press.

———. (1996b). On Moral Obligation, Truth, and Common Sense. In J. Niznik and J. Sanders (eds.). *Debating the State of Philosophy*. London: Praeger.

———. (1999a). Education as Socialization and as Individualization. In *Philosophy and Social Hope*. London: Penguin Books.

———. (1999b). *Para realizar a América—o pensamento da esquerda nos Estados Unidos no século XX*. Introduction of Paulo Ghiraldelli Jr. Traction of Paulo Ghiraldelli Jr., Alberto Tosi Rodrigues and Leoni Henning and Antonio Marcus Pereira. Rio de Janeiro: DPA Editora.

CHAPTER FOUR

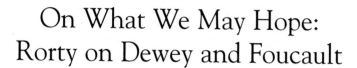

On What We May Hope:
Rorty on Dewey and Foucault

James D. Marshall

Introduction

Richard Rorty (1982) argued that there is little essential philosophical difference between John Dewey and Michel Foucault. He sees what differences
that do exist as not being over theoretical issues but "over what we may
hope" (Rorty 1982, 204). Whilst he attempts to make their differences more
obvious (Rorty 1991), nevertheless he still retains the Deweyan and American notion of hope or optimism as the reason for following that tradition
rather than the closely aligned post-Nietzschean European tradition.[1] First,
whilst I do find some positive message of hope in Foucault—he is certainly
not nihilistic—it is not a Deweyan progressive and optimistic message of
hope. Second, Rorty, in running together the traditions of post-Darwinian
American philosophy and post-Nietzschean European philosophy so that the
latter has an important role to play (Rorty 1999, xix–xxii), appears to downplay less hopeful, if not pessimistic, messages, that are to be found in the European tradition (and in Foucault). This perhaps can be best exhibited by
Rorty's approach to history, whereby he, and the post-Darwinian American
philosophical tradition, attempt to build more upon uplifting stories, vener-
ating the past and ignoring such things as the genocide of indigenous Indians
and the Afro-American slave economy. On the other hand the Nietzschean
inspired philosophers of suspicion offer a critique of the past and uplifting
stories from a critical and genealogical history of the 'truths' of the present
(Peters 2001). Such differences mark a much more fundamental dissocia-
tion between the optimistic progressive view of Rorty and post-Darwinian

American philosophy, and Foucault and post-Nietzschean European philosophy, than Rorty fully acknowledges. Thus it is not clear, as he claims, that the post-Nietzschean thinkers can be caught as playing a role, important but minor, or subservient to Dewey et al., in the 'grand' pragmatism, or liberal bourgeois tradition, of Rorty.

Foucault's writing has an optimistic side even though it is submersed in a Nietzschean European tradition of a critique of history. But it is certainly not part of a post-Darwinian (and Hegelian) progressive view of human existence, which seems to underlie Rorty's account of Dewey's message of hope. Rorty's message is directed perhaps at what sort of *society* we should have: we must start from where we are, privilege our own group (Rorty 1991, 29) and go forward, aiming at an egalitarian society. For Foucault where we are at the present is a problem, one which, in the case of the self, must be overturned. For Rorty this seems to be a form of defiant and lonely individualism if not, as in Nietzsche's case, a form of "resentful idiosyncratic idealisations of silence, solitude and violence" (Rorty 1991, 33). In essence Dewey's concern is first with society and then with the individual, whereas Foucault's emphasis philosophically is on a philosophy of the self.

Rorty's (1982) early argument is to the effect that if "we get rid of traditional notions of 'objectivity' and 'scientific method' we shall be able to see the social sciences as continuous with literature" (1982, 203). Rorty claims that when the notion of knowledge as representation goes then there is no longer any requirement for knowledge to be split into discrete 'bits', as the normal notions of 'logical' demarcation, between different 'forms' of knowledge, also go. These logical lines of demarcation go and the lines between novels and the human sciences become blurred lines, drawn only pragmatically by existing current concerns, be they 'theoretical' or practical. By 1991 he is expressing this slightly differently (Rorty 1991, 15):

> Most of my critics on the left are fairly well disposed toward the antirepresenta-
> tionalism I advocate, for this view is Nietzsches's and Foucault's as much as
> Dewey's or Davidson's. But they think of themselves as standing outside of the so-
> ciopolitical culture of liberalism with which Dewey identified, a culture with
> which I continue to identify . . . I, however, find it hard to see them as outsiders
> to this culture; they look to me like people playing a role—an important role—
> within it. I do not see them as having developed an alternative culture, nor even
> as having envisaged one.

The major difference then seems to be that whereas the "Deweyan liberal left and the Marxist radical left of my youth both tried to work out Utopian visions. . . . the Foucauldean left (has failed) to offer such visions and encouragement" (Rorty 1991, 16). This comment directed at the philosophers of suspicion obviously applies to Foucault himself.

In speaking of a tradition, a group of 'so-called relativists' and 'anti-Platonists', drawn from post-Nietzschean European philosophy and post-Darwinian American philosophy (i.e., pragmatism), he includes both Foucault and Dewey in that tradition (Rorty 1999, xix), adding: "[T]he most important thing that links the great names of each tradition to one another . . . is suspicion of the same set of Greek distinctions which make it possible, natural, and almost inevitable to ask, 'Found or made?', 'Absolute or relative?', 'Real or apparent?'"

But another way of exhibiting the differences between the traditions, says Rorty, is to say that "the Europeans have typically put forward a distinctive new, post-Nietzschean 'method' for philosophers to employ," whereas "the Americans have not been much given to such proclamations" (1999, xx). But this requires Rorty to immediately downplay the importance of Dewey's notion of scientific method: "he never was able to explain what this method was." Thereby Rorty, in this source, is able to argue for the superiority of post-Darwinian American philosophy over post-Nietzschean European philosophy in solving philosophical problems. 'We' pragmatists can climb the (Wittgensteinean) ladder, if we wish, but throw it away because "we have different problems to solve than those which perplexed our ancestors" (1999, xxi). I will argue in section 2 that in Foucault's case Rorty is not correct about a distinctive 'method' and then, in downplaying Dewey's account of method, he 'constructs' a difference that is not there, but one which he goes on to take sides with.

Rorty continues to suggest that the differences between these two traditions are over what we may hope, "to achieve agreement among human beings about what to do, to bring about consensus on the ends to be achieved and the means to be used to achieve those ends . . . [as] . . . all areas of culture are parts of the same endeavour to make life better" (1999, xxv). The accord between the two strands of this tradition is not as straightforward as Rorty suggests, nor are the similarities and differences between Dewey and Foucault (Marshall 1995). There are, he says, two ways to go, and he adopts the side of the tradition that follows from Dewey, James, and Peirce. But Dewey, the alleged optimist, may hope but may not be able to deliver in certain areas, and Foucault, the alleged pessimist, hopes, but cannot deliver in certain other areas. But the areas for both are quite different. And this is what is obscured by Rorty's general thesis on hope and pessimism.

It is not my intention to repeat earlier arguments against Rorty here in full, though I will summarize them in the first section. I wish to explore further the alleged differences between Dewey and Foucault on the notion of methodology. This I do in the next section, arguing that Rorty must downplay Dewey's notion of scientific method so that it is reducible "to the virtues of curiosity, open-mindedness and conversability." On the other hand, he must elevate Foucault to the status of methodologist, as propounding philosophical theories or methodologies—archaeology and/or genealogy (Rorty 1999, xxi). In my view neither the downplaying of Dewey's account of the method of inquiry, nor the 'upgrading' of Foucault to methodologist is justified. (Derrida seems to be excluded by Rorty from the category of methodologist.) In which case Rorty must provide more specific arguments that this is a general tendency of post-Nietzschean European philosophy. My conclusion is that Rorty is mistaken if his argument for the superiority of post-Darwinian American philosophy depends in part upon an alleged difference between Dewey and Foucault on philosophical methodology.

Arguments against the Accord of the Two Paths

My earlier arguments against Rorty's accord between Foucault and Dewey (Marshall 1995) were grouped under the following headings: the social sciences; methodology; rationality; the individual and community; and, the subject. In this section I will summarize those arguments only, with the exception of the section on methodology, which will be the concern of section 2.

The Social Sciences
At first sight there are differences on the nature of the social sciences between Dewey and Foucault, as Dewey emphasized the moral importance of the social sciences (Rorty 1982, 203), their role in the Enlightenment message of improving the human condition through the advance of knowledge and, thereby, the opening up of new views of community (1982, 204). On the other hand, Foucault emphasized the ways in which the social sciences "have served as instruments of 'the disciplinary society'" in what Rorty describes as "the best account of this dark side of the social sciences" (1982, 204).

Elsewhere he says that for Foucault "the social scientists have often been, and are always likely to be, coopted by the bad guys" (1982, 207). But Rorty quickly assures us that this should not be interpreted as a methodological difference however, not as a "Galilean-vs-hermeneutic" or an "explanation-vs-understanding" or as the politicized obverse of emancipation and domination but, rather, "over what we may hope". What Rorty glosses over here is that Dewey and Foucault have fundamentally different views of the social sciences, and their relationship to the natural sciences and to ordinary discourse. They are not just "saying the same thing but putting a different spin upon it" (1982, 205).

First Dewey is adamant that there is continuity between ordinary everyday problem solving and, say, the problem solving of the theoretical physicist (Dewey 1938a; chapters 4 and 24). What gives continuity here is Dewey's version of problem solving through inquiry, which he also calls scientific method. According to Dewey scientific method pervades all of our thought and action. The theory of inquiry is fully treated in *Logic: The Theory of Inquiry* and there is little doubt that he saw himself as advancing a totalizing theory about all kinds of inquiry and belief formation (see section 2).

Foucault does not see such continuity. First his work is almost essentially in the area which the French call the human sciences (and which is wider than the Anglo-Saxon social sciences—e.g., it includes psychoanalytic theory). Whilst he recognizes that truth in the exact sciences is not divorced from power, the exact sciences have resolved issues in the 'moves in power games' which do not make them as problematic and dangerous as the social sciences, through the institutionalization of science in the universities, for example. In answer to an explicit question as to whether his analyses of the relations between knowledge and power concern the exact sciences as well as the human sciences, Foucault responded (Foucault 1984b, 106): "Oh no, not at all! I would not make such a claim for myself. And, anyway, you know, I'm an empiricist: I don't try to advance things without seeing whether they are applicable." Rorty then glosses over substantial differences between Dewey and Foucault respectively on continuity and discontinuity between the natural sciences, social sciences, and common sense.

Rationality

According to Rorty, both Dewey and Foucault agree on abandoning traditional views of rationality: "they agree that rationality is what history and society make it" (1982, 204). But that is not the end of the matter for they have a different view of the 'unfolding' of rationality through time and of the Enlightenment message that rationality (scientific method as exemplified by the theory of inquiry) will improve the lot of mankind.

In his many discussions of problem solving and scientific method Dewey seems committed to rationality being sited in sociohistorical circumstances. In addition, however, he clearly had a view that both rationality and humankind were improving, in parallel, through rational problem solving. Dewey would see the changes in punishment as exhibited by Foucault's account in *Discipline and Punish* of the execution of Damiens and the treatment of the young offenders in Faucher's 'reformatory' as indicative of both an improvement in rationality and of human beings. In general he would have supported the humanitarian notions of improvement of human beings through the more humane treatment of offenders. But Foucault exposes those notions as refinements of technocratic rationality, techniques of governance and as early versions of bio-power, as punishment becomes *disciplinary* (in Foucault's sense).

Dewey believed that modern technology exemplifies problem solving at its best (Dewey 1916; chapter 23). He believes that whilst education should not be narrowly vocational and that the study of technology is critically important for the young for advanced technology exemplifies advanced rationality. In his view of scientific method, as science advances and progresses holistically we have a historical and teleological unfolding of reason.

But Foucault gives us no teleological unfolding of reason. Indeed he argues quite convincingly that what appears as irrational to us in the twentieth century in the practice of torture is quite rational given certain assumptions of the time about guilt (here Charles Taylor says that he finds Foucault quite convincing [Taylor 1986, 71]). There is no Enlightenment future for mankind then, according to Foucault, because reason is embedded in sociohistorical conditions and there is no rational unfolding of history in any developmental or improving sense. Neither reason then nor history offers us liberation or, indeed, a return to the abyss (if his earlier writings up to *Discipline and Punish* are pessimistic, his later writings are much more optimistic).

Foucault, in his earlier writings, had launched a total attack upon Western reason (see Boyne 1990). That was done in *Folie et Déraison*, originally published in 1961, but that attack was excluded from the English translation in 1965 of a very much abridged 1964 French edition. Foucault launched an attack upon the form that modern reason had taken post-Descartes because he wished to escape from a form of reason that had come to constitute madness, its treatment, and the modern world. Here he was probably heavily influenced by Bataille, which he acknowledged, especially his views concerning the death of history and the *unreasonableness of reason* (Descombes 1980, 14), and hence the need to explore the 'irrationality' of madness to find rationality. There is talk by Foucault of a search for a 'higher' form of reason in the 1961 source, but this search was abandoned.

The Individual and the Community
There is a dualism implied in this subtitle—one of many dualisms rejected by Dewey—but if there is a distinction in *language* identified by the symbols 'individual' and 'community', for Dewey there was no distinction in *reality*. Dewey's version of individualism is very much that of a socially formed indi-

vidual, in which the beliefs, thoughts, habits, and interests are formed through social interaction within the scientific and/or democratic community. Dewey makes this very clear in the opening chapters of *Democracy and Education* (Dewey 1916, 2f.):

> Each individual, each unit who is the carrier of the life experience of his group, in time passes away. Yet the life of the group goes on. . . . Society exists through a process of transmission quite as much as biological life. This transmission occurs by means of communication of habits of doing, thinking, and feeling from the older to the younger. Without this communication of ideals, hopes, expectations, standards, opinions from those members of society who are passing out of the group life to those who are coming into it, social life could not survive . . . [education] is a work of necessity.

He continues (1916, 5): "Not only is social life identical with communication, but all communication (and hence all genuine social life) is educative." Because of the complexity of the modern world the school occupied a crucial position in the necessary education of the young (1916, 20): "It is the business of the school environment to eliminate, as far as possible, the unworthy features of the existing environment from influences upon mental habitudes. . . . Selection aims not only at simplifying but at weeding out what is undesirable. . . . it strives to reinforce the power of this best."

At certain points the community controls the individual in Dewey's thought. For example, if we consider Dewey's views on problem solving and meaning within the scientific community, it is clear that meaning can be imposed. In their problem solving learners are to follow scientific method— the method of inquiry—which involves shared decision making on matters such as meaning and 'truth'. Clearly when meaning and truth depend upon a democratic decision there is considerable pressure upon the individual dissenter, or creative hypothesizer, to conform to the group's decisions on these matters.

Similarly in matters of social control Dewey sees that conformity to the rules of the democratic decisions of society is necessary. In the classroom this means that, like a game in which people participate willingly in accordance with the rules (Dewey 1938b, chapter 4), children will participate in their learning activities because social rules govern the 'game' of learning and of life. To participate in life is to communicate, according to the rules of communication, and not to wish to live is not on the agenda for Dewey. Every living being struggles to survive, to continue and to renew its life form. For this to occur and not to lapse into barbarism social life must continue and grow (Dewey 1916, chapter 1).

Dewey is not arguing for a closed system of meanings, habits, and social rules. But he does mean that changes in what we know, and in how we behave, must be subject to appraisal in accordance with the theory of inquiry and agreement as to such changes by the 'scientific' community. He is opposed to original ideas being suppressed by a majority vote based upon custom but, instead, applauds the critical approach taken by scientific method which has liberated us from mere custom (Dewey 1916, 296). But intellectual individualism cannot provide the connections with others to unite an individual with his fellows. Instead humans must act in a common and public world and critical consciousness can only overcome tradition and custom where individuals are identified with democratic and scientific communities.

There seems little or no place in Dewey, then, for the isolate, for the scientist who claims that 1,001 other scientists are wrong, and for those who recognize the other and argue for difference. Indeed Dewey is almost unashamedly an acculturist, as his educational proposals were certainly couched within the problems of late nineteenth and early twentieth-century United States of America, which was faced with large influxes of immigrants, with widely different languages and cultures, and from diverse parts of Europe. Here we can understand his criteria for the assessment of a democratic community in terms of shared interests as being the breaking down of ethnic and cultural diversity leading to a multicultural and homogenous society, as opposed to a multicultural and diverse society. The problems which this leads to are the loss of language and culture of the minority groups in the assimilations and the loss of personal identity and esteem that can accompany such assimilation into a dominant culture.

Foucault, like Dewey, does not believe in any such thing as an 'innate' human nature. In attacking the Cartesian individual as an isolated center of consciousness, he was also attacking epistemological individualism. But on the relation between individual and society he begins to part company with Dewey. Whereas for Dewey there is a social and moral aspect to individualism such that necessarily the individual cannot be hived off from society, for Foucault any understanding of modern society requires not only such possibilities but in terms of security of state, governmentality in the modern state must ensure that individuals are both respected as individuals and treated as such, free from interference from others in any form (Gordon 1991). At times, and in his own behavior, Foucault seemed almost to hold a neoliberal form of individualism (he is certainly not a neoliberal in any Hayaekean form). But individualism was necessary, Foucault argued, for the *security* of the modern state. This requires different forms of interaction between the individual and others from both Dewey and his earlier writings (e.g., Foucault 1979). If

Foucault agrees with Dewey then in denying any form of epistemological individualism and agrees upon the development of consciousness, needs, interests, and habits through social interaction, he stops short at seeing the necessary social, moral, and political aspects to individualism that Dewey saw as necessary.

First in his account of power relations Foucault talks about micropower and how power relations work from the bottom up (though he does try in his later work to accommodate this analysis with macro- and state power). The point about power relations, particularly in his later work, is that the individual must be conceived as a free agent in order for power relations to exist, for power to be exerted over her or him (Foucault 1983). Dewey's claim is that society only exists through communication. But, insofar as power relations are closely associated with communication at the micro-level then, theoretically, as power relations can always be resisted, then the Deweyan basis of the necessary relation between individual and society is called in question. Morally and politically it is better in Foucault to resist oppression, to resist objectifying classifications, and to resist subjection. It seems that morally and socially Foucault is saying that it may be better for the individual to maintain a distance from society. Certainly there is no necessary relationship between individual and society on the moral, social, or political parameters.

At the epistemological level there is at first some agreement. Consciousness becomes shaped in various ways through discourse—here they agree. But they disagree here on the role of the human sciences, especially as they have merged with everyday language and everyday understandings. Rather their emergence on the stage as discourses—the human sciences—has been very much an odd affair, one which is probably reversible, but one which has come to dominate the modern world so that we are governable. As Rorty notes, Foucault points to the dark side of the social sciences in shaping up individuals and society. But this is not all that he is talking about for he has a much more positive point about freedom. This may only be obtained by resisting rules of the game, though not in merely reversing them. Hence freedom, according to Foucault, is not necessarily to be obtained as in Dewey by participating or operating within democratically designed social constraints.

Foucault found certain social relations as not merely overpowering and intimidating but restrictive of freedom. As he said of himself early in his professional life (Foucault 1982b, 5): "Anyway I have suffered and I still suffer from a lot of things in French social and political life. That was the reason why I left France in 1955." Foucault said that each of his works were part of his own biography (Foucault 1981, 339; 1982a, 11). He claimed to be directing questions to those who worked in institutions which exercised power over individuals. Certainly, he regarded his own education in the lycées as 'unerotic' (Foucault 1974) and as involving a forced feeding, if not manipulative period of his life. He found living with others at the École Normale Supérieure extremely difficult and sought isolation and privacy as soon as he could (Eribon 1991, chapter 3). But at this time he was not coping well with his homosexuality and his mental health was a matter of some concern. Then there comes the period at Hôpital St. Anne which is to lead to certain insights in *Folie et Déraison* (Foucault 1982b, 5). Contrary to Dewey, the assertion of the other, the rejection of Western reason (e.g., in *Folie et Déraison*), the rejection of other students, and the flight to Sweden in 1955 can be seen, together, as a general rejection of the necessity of the social and of the need for communication. There were other ways to know and understand, and to be free. Indeed Foucault noted his early rejection of the obligation to communicate (Foucault 1982b, 4), and argued positively for a need for silence and of not talking about oneself, exposing one's inner thoughts and thereby placing oneself under the power of others (e.g., Foucault 1980).

Dewey and Foucault then can be seen as differing considerably upon the notion of the relationship between the individual and society. If Dewey sees this relation as both necessary and positive for the ultimate happiness of human beings, Foucault is much less optimistic. It is not that the human sciences have done nothing good for human beings, but that they are dangerous, and we do not have the autonomy promised in the Enlightenment message (Marshall 1996). If Foucault is optimistic, it is in a Nietzschean sense of going *beyond* good and evil.

The Subject or Self

On the subject, the individual, or the person, much of what Dewey has to say has already been covered above. But to add to the sketch above it must be noted that Dewey protested against the mind/body dualism, the identification of personal identity with consciousness and, thereby, the sharp demarcation of individual minds from one another and from the world (see e.g., Dewey 1916; chapter 22). Also he must have devoted a million words to cast doubt on the nature of human nature as being a given or as fixed (Hollis 1972, 56). For Dewey man was to be conceived as an organism, a fusion of mind and body and, essentially, as a creature of habits on the one side of the coin and a set of beliefs on the other side of the coin, where habits and beliefs are but obverse 'pictures' of one another (1938b). But for Dewey it was a self always in a mode of becoming (the Hegelian influence) because the mind is not passive but active, and knowledge and habits are the outcome of active problem solving on the part of the organism in response to indeterminate situations.

For Dewey then the subject is a creature of habits and beliefs. But these beliefs and habits have not been acquired willy-nilly but evolve, or become, in response to indeterminate situations, the use of the theory of inquiry, and the reconstruction of experience in problem solving. But the hypotheses advanced, or the habits adopted, have to be evaluated against a holistic worldview or set of habits (1938a). In other words there is a presupposition of continuity of the creature either through a set of habits or proclivities to respond to situations, or in the holistic set of beliefs held by the creature. There is certainly no notion of slipping from one identity to another, and then back again. The creature may change but only against a continuous and rational background concerned with both the *continuity* and *preservation* of the creature. Thus, the subject or self is always an *individuated* subject or self.

Much of what Dewey has to say about the subject, about the theory of inquiry, and about the relationship between the individual and society, is predicated upon the fundamental notion of survival. Living beings struggle to survive according to Dewey (see e.g., Dewey 1916, chapter 1), and they are defined, accordingly, as follows (1916, 2): "a living being is one that subjugates and controls for its own continued activity the energies that would otherwise use it up. Life is a self continuing process through action upon the environment."

Foucault, like Dewey, has no truck with human nature. For both of them, if what is meant is that there is some common essence that one brings into the world, there is no such thing. They both seem to see human beings as capable of considerable change, if not infinite malleability. Each see the subject as capable of acting upon the world, and resisting dangererous situations, but neither provides rational criteria either for the felt situation of danger, or for knowing when to resist power. Both reject any Cartesian ego. But there the similarities on the subject begin to run into the sands.

If the subject can change for Dewey it does not seem to be more than qualitative change, whereas for Foucault there can be quantitative change. Underlying Dewey's notion of qualitative change there is continuity and an enduring and individuated subject of change (the creature with a set of habits [beliefs] X which amends them to X+1 or to set Y). This is not the case in Foucault.

For Foucault subjects arise through processes closely associated with discursive practices. His earlier position was that human beings are turned into subjects in two main ways. First, there were the discourses on Man concerned with the speaking subject, the laboring subject, and the living economic subject.

Second, there were the dividing practices which classify and objectify humans in various ways, e.g., as sane or insane, and the discourses which construct the self, particularly through the notion of sexuality. Here his general question can be seen as: "how are human beings made into subjects?" The later answer is that subjects are both constituted and constituting, i.e., that subjects can constitute themselves in various ways.

But Foucault admits a stronger position that not only are subjects changing through these processes of constitution, but that the subject may switch to and fro at will, from one subject to another. Thus he talked of the importance of education in permitting "the individual to change at will" (1980, 329).

His concerns were with how discursive practices positioned, objectified, and dominated individuals. Different discursive practices could constitute the subject in quantitatively different ways. However, such objectifications could always be resisted, and by care of the self subjects could not only resist but constitute themselves differently. Hence there are potentially many subjects in Foucault's account of how human beings are turned into subjects.

This position is most clearly stated in one of his last interviews (Foucault 1984a). From 1979 Michel Foucault began to pursue questions of the self vigorously, particularly in his important article 'What is Enlightenment?' (Foucault 1984c). His question was: "who are we in the present, what is this fragile moment from which we can't detach our identity and which will carry that identity away with itself?" In Nietzschean fashion he was to answer this question by turning to experience, as opposed to starting from a committed and perhaps theoretical philosophical position, and ask questions about *how* we constitute the self. As he said (1984a, 290):

> What I rejected was the idea of starting out with a theory of the subject. . . . What I wanted to try to show was how the subject constituted itself, in one specific form or another . . . it is not a substance. It is a form, and this form is not always identical to itself . . . in each case one plays, one establishes a different relation to oneself.

Foucault does not hold the mystical view of the "I" that is to be found in Schopenhauer and, in part, in Wittgenstein (1961; 1971). As in Nietzsche the self is part of the organic (and inorganic) world. It is neither something that is given nor is it something which is open to biological, sociological, etc., description. For Foucault the Man which is dead, and cannot serve as a posit of "human" theory, is not just *the* Man of the human sciences, with all of the humanistic baggage that Man there carries. It is also the subject post-Kant to which these attributes are accorded, which is not the self of Schopenhauer, Nietzsche, Wittgenstein, and Foucault.

On the self Foucault essentially holds a Nietzschean position (Nietzsche 1983, 127): "Be yourself. You are none of the things you now do, think, desire." (According to Miller [1993, 69] this was Schopenhauer's influence upon Nietzsche, and Nietzsche's upon Foucault.) "One's way of no longer remaining the same is, by definition, the most singular part of what I am" (quoted in Rabinow 1997, xix). But for both Nietzsche and Foucault: "Our body is but a social structure" (Nietzsche 1966, 19), and the self is contingent, and hanging because of shifting social and cultural forces (Nietzsche 1968). Nietzsche thought that we had come to hate the body and its Dionysian untamed frenzies because of Christianity and, deeply immersed in social and cultural traditions, it had become difficult "to become what one is." To transcend the self that appears as a given, Nietzsche begins in *Thus Spake Zarathustra* (Nietzsche 1976) with the discovery of the Dionysian frenzy of life by communing again with the world: for the later Foucault it is to care for the self. For both Nietzsche and Foucault: "Nobody can build you the bridge over which you must cross the river of life, nobody but you alone" (Nietzsche 1983, 129).

Foucault's own position on the self is stated quite clearly (Foucault 1984a). For Foucault, as for Schopenhauer and Wittgenstein, the self is not an individuated object or substance. Instead it is said to be a *form*, something conceptual, which our conceptualizing of ourselves at any particular time may take up, in a complex interplay of intellect, character, and action. The form is like a category, or a logical placeholder, which may be filled in various ways. Thus you may not have the same relationship to yourself when you constitute yourself as a coach of a sporting team and as a father speaking to a daughter or son at dinner. We cannot assert an identity relationship such as "a = b" between these two forms, because these two forms may not be identical, he argues. Another way to understand Foucault is to realize that his concern is with how the intellect, character, and action can be reconciled in living in the context of practical affairs in the present. The singularity of the present in its games of truth and practices of power may either require a certain form of the self, or present the opportunity to constitute one's self actively in a form of transfiguration of other forms of the self. But these practices are not something entirely invented, as we are influenced by models: in Foucault's case by Kant on the historical singularity of reason and Baudelaire on the stylization of the self, though not in an artistic or narcissistic sense (Rabinow 1997, xxxii). But other models are available, and are proposed and suggested (sometimes imposed) by the culture, society, and social group (Foucault 1984a, 293). We are also influenced by mentors. But all of these models must be subjected to historical and philosophical examination. There are a number of pedagogical issues here (see Marshall 2000).

Methodology

John Dewey

As mentioned above, Rorty claims that if Dewey had a particular methodology, then he was not able to explain it. But Dewey has a particular methodology, and he went to great lengths to explain it, especially in what he saw as his major work, *Logic: The theory of Inquiry* (Dewey 1938a). It is perhaps unfortunate that philosophers of education mistakenly adopted (an alleged version of) Dewey's theory of enquiry which, in fact, has been positivistically inclined, and that generally they have misunderstood his version of induction. In my view it was not so much that education was left with an out-of-date version of scientific method (Newton 1975), but that the version adopted was inadequate and impossible to defend (Marshall 1984).

Some philosophers (e.g., Brodbeck 1961) have identified Dewey's theory of inquiry as an early version of the hypothetico-deductive account of scientific method to be found later, especially in the work of Karl Popper (e.g., Popper 1959), and widely in education through the work of Denis (D. C.) Phillips. However, Dewey's views on enquiry or scientific method should not be seen either as an early or as an ill-formed version of hypothetico-deductive method. This is because Dewey did not draw a distinction between what has been called, on the one hand, a logic of discovery and, on the other hand, a logic of justification (Reichenbach 1951; Popper 1959; Medawar 1969), and because he held to a version of discovery which he called '*induction*', though this was not induction in any Baconian or Millean sense.

Dewey said that what characterized scientific thinking was the *activity* of reflective thinking. Thus he refused to concern himself solely with the abstract content of scientific thought and with its logical reconstructions. He saw the latter as important but limited. Instead he identified both logic and scientific method with the activity of inquiry. Even though he was criticized for introducing psychological elements into logic (e.g., Russell 1946) he was dealing essentially with a logical structure and not with a temporal structure. Thus in the *Logic* (1938a, 105f.) he defines enquiry as follows: "Inquiry is the controlled or directed transformation of an indeterminate situation into one which is so determinate in its constituent distinctions and relations as to convert the elements of the original situation into a complete whole." The activity of inquiry converts a confused or indeterminate situation, a result of an unsatisfactory interaction of an organism with its environment, into a satisfactory and ordered situation by imposing new meaning upon that situation. Knowledge, encapsulated into a hypothetical form—if A, and if B, then C—is the outcome or end of inquiry (Dewey 1938a, 6).

Inquiry originates in an indeterminate situation when the organism is not sure of what to do because the outcomes of possible courses of action are unclear. Inquiry resolves that psychological indeterminate state and the results are knowledge and a new habit (in his special sense of the term 'habit'). Dewey identifies various 'stages' in the process of inquiry from felt difficulty to definition of the problem, to the advancement of a hypothesis and its testing, and finally to the formulation of knowledge (in his sense of the term 'knowledge'). Inquiry is divided into two aspects—induction or the sum of the empirical aspects of inquiry, and deduction, which is the rational aspect of inquiry. Clearly this account is incompatible with those accounts which, since Reichenbach and Popper, distinguish sharply between a 'logic' of discovery and a logic of justification.

However, whilst Dewey considers activities under the notion of a logic of discovery, he said that nothing meaningful can be said about any process or *method* for discovering hypotheses (e.g., 1938a, 109). He did nevertheless talk about stages of inquiry, though these were not to be understood in any fixed, categorial, or temporal sense (1938a, 115). Second, he referred to induction but not in any Millean or Baconian sense. Indeed, he was quite scathing about induction in Mill's sense. Instead induction was (1938a, 407) "the complex of experimental operations by which antecedently existing conditions are so modified that data are obtained which indicate and test proposed modes of solution." The use of the term 'induction', with its accompanying historical baggage, was perhaps then unfortunate.

In these brief comments I have tried to indicate that Dewey's theory of enquiry was explicable. Rorty says that Dewey has failed to explain this method. Yet he has argued (Rorty 1991, 21–45) that "all that remains of Peirce's, Dewey's and Popper's praise of science is praise of certain moral values—those of an open society—rather than any specific epistemic strategy" (Rorty 1999, 36). Presumably to argue in such a manner requires *understanding* what Dewey attempted to say about his method, i.e., that it was sufficiently explained. Perhaps the position is better put by Jim Tiles. According to Tiles (1988, 107), Dewey was

> recommending a change of subject. Dewey does not share the concerns of, and hence does not appear to have anything to say to, those who are working in philosophical logic. But a sign that Dewey is not off somewhere else, looking into a different subject altogether, is the way Dewey's account of intellectual advance or 'inquiry' differs radically from that offered by someone whose concerns are much closer to those of contemporary philosophical logicians.

At least some philosophers then can make sense of Dewey's theory of inquiry.

Michel Foucault

The theory of inquiry is fully treated by Dewy in *Logic: The Theory of Inquiry* and there is little doubt that he saw himself as advancing a totalizing theory about all kinds of inquiry and belief formation. Foucault does not see such continuity, and he was opposed to theory and totalizing theories. First his work is almost essentially in the area which the French call the human sciences (and which is wider than the Anglo-Saxon social sciences—e.g., it includes psychoanalytic theory). Whilst he recognizes that truth in the exact sciences is not divorced from power, he believed that the exact sciences had resolved issues in the 'moves in power games', through the institutionalization of science in the universities, for example. Such 'resolution' did not make them as problematic and dangerous as the social sciences.

Foucault was strongly influenced in his approach to the sciences by Gaston Bachelard and Georges Canguilhem. But Foucault was too much of a rebel (or perhaps transgressor), even in his school days, to merely accept ideas because they were those of his teachers, or to become a disciple of them, or of others. Therefore, ideas are not simply adopted, as he also *adapts* them and uses them for his own purposes. Foucault talks of "the beautiful, very formal sciences like mathematics and theoretical physics" (Foucault 1969, 53). As we saw above, he denied that his analyses of knowledge and power applied to the natural sciences (Foucault 1984a, 106). Apart from Foucault's rejection of grand totalizing theories, his point is that, unlike the human sciences, he had not studied the actual work of practicing scientists and hence anything which he might say would be mere speculation. Here he is influenced by Bachelard who had totally rejected any general a priori application of philosophical theory(ies) to the sciences. According to Bachelard the application of philosophical theories to science was but groundless speculation about what there is, and what, and how, we can know about what there is. Instead, for Bachelard, the nature of the world and how we know about the world is to be understood through the study of the successful actual applications of reason in the world. Philosophy then is a form of reflection upon the sciences, but is not part of science itself. Thus, Gary Gutting claims (1989, 52), Foucault's position on science is essentially Bachelardian.

Many of his views on the philosophy of science are 'adopted' by Foucault—especially ruptures, continuities, epistemological breaks, and epistemological profiles. But these are adapted. Ruptures, for example, are not absolute in Foucault's work. He is not a philosopher who bases his work on any absolute notion of a rupture (see his objections to such claims in Foucault 1984a, 100). But arguably ruptures are important in *The Order of Things*. Foucault argues that these discontinuities are problems which must be resolved, for there may be (always?) underlying continuities—e.g., the continuity of the exercise of power in *Discipline and Punish* between two apparently different and dissociated forms of punishment. Continuities then may be obscured, or hidden, or experienced as *effects* (e.g., power). Nor did he see the break between Ricardo and Marx in the sense that Althusser had—i.e., as an *epistemological* break (Foucault 1967, 14). Ruptures or discontinuities are important, then, not because they represent a 'real' break, but because they are problems which must be resolved (Foucault 1967, 14). Nevertheless there are epistemological breaks between ordinary everyday descriptions and putative scientific descriptions (contrary to Dewey). These are clearly exhibited by the competing discourses in *I Pierre Rivière, Having Slaughtered My Mother, My Sister and My Brother* . . . where there are the competing and juxtaposed stories of the priest, the policeman, the magistrate, and the psychiatrists, as well as Pierre Rivière's own lucid statement (Foucault 1982a).

He does not seem, however, to have been so enthusiastic about Bachelard's notions of certainty about the present and progress (admittedly qualified by Bachelard) in the human sciences. Yet for Foucault truth did matter, but it was a qualified truth (qualified by archaeology and genealogy). Thus (Foucault 1984a, 295): "All those who say that for me truth doesn't exist are simple minded." But his point against truth is that what we take for truth in the present is not the outcome of some developing rationality or progress but, instead, is the outcome of sociohistorical contingencies.

Canguilhem, an historian of science rather than a philosopher of science, took as his major sources biology and medicine, causing a change of course in French History of Science. But his concern was with concepts, and the primacy of concepts over theories in the history of science. This position also clearly influenced Foucault, for his analyses of notions such as madness, illness, and punishment, for example, reflect the primacy of the concept over theory. In *Discipline and Punish* there is a clear and unequivocal rejection of penal and legal theory, and of the general enlightenment improvement thesis about the more humane forms of punishment. Instead, historically, Foucault looks at who gets punished and *how* they are punished; it is the actual practices of punishment that determine the concept of punishment. Indeed, his notion of disciplinary punishment is established, empirically, in this way. According to Gutting (1989, 54) something like Canguilhem's history of concepts is also discernible in *Folie et Déraison, Birth of the Clinic,* and *The Order of Things.*

In his account of the history of concepts Canguilhem points to the futility of any search for precursors—or Nietzschean origin. Canguilhem objects to such searches because of the danger that science originates in some 'golden

age'. That would be the end of any history of science as Canguilhem understood it. Whilst Foucault is perhaps more Nietzschean here, he rejects also
any notion of a golden age in the history of the concept 'Man', the concept
that permeates his work on the human sciences. If anything 'Man' has a lowly
origin, and 'his' horizons are becoming circumscribed through critique.

Foucault did not seem to fit into any discernible discipline or academic category. Was he philosopher, historian, social theorist, or . . . ? He entitled his
own position at Le Collège de France as 'Professor of the History of Thought'
(but this was not history of *ideas*). At times he was categorized as a structuralist, archaeologist, and genealogist. But he strenuously denied that he was ever
a structuralist, that he was advancing a *theory* of archaeology or genealogy, and
that his books provided a method for others to follow. Indeed, his own genealogical studies differ both between themselves and from Nietzsche. His
books then, he said, were to be used as bombs! Foucault then was antitheory
and antimethod. Nor was he interested in establishing a legacy of Foucauldean scholars—though that seems to have happened (see e.g., O'Farrell
1997).

Conclusion

What the arguments above establish, in my view, is that there are quite major
differences between Dewey and Foucault. If these are taken as representatives,
or exemplars, of post-Darwinian American philosophy and post-Nietzschean
European philosophy, then there seem to me to be wider differences between
these two traditions than Rorty acknowledges.

Whilst Rorty, in his later work, is more careful to identify and talk of differences between these two philosophers, his general pragmatic position requires him to de-emphasize what Dewy said on scientific method. Then, in
these sources, to choose Dewey over Foucault (and post-Darwinian American philosophy over post-Nietzschean European philosophy) he alleges that
Foucault is a methodologist. This is at best to emphasize the earlier Foucault
and, at the same time, to ignore what Foucault said concerning himself as
theorist and methodologist. But, further, Dewey left intact much of what
Rorty stigmatizes as Philosophy. He presented Philosophy as instrumental to
the conduct of 'philosophy' and, certainly, in his *Logic* he considered himself
to be doing Philosophy (Tiles 1988, 2–4). In Foucault's case, his Ph.D. ex-
aminers noted explicitly that the emphasis of his work was Philosophical,
and he headed the Department of Philosophy at Vincennes in 1968.

Rorty also retains the vision of hope in the choice of the path of post-
Darwinian American philosophy over that of post-Nietzschean philosophy

(the message of hope in Rorty 1982). His aim is to improve society. However, Kojève (1954, 252) wrote that there is no essential difference between the philosopher and the tyrant. If Kojève is wrong that all philosophers fall into that category, he may be correct that some philosophers do, insofar as they attempt to impose a universal worldview upon others. Foucault is right in my view to be suspicious of the totalizing effects of such worldviews. He therefore stands aside from Dewey (and Rorty) in offering a philosophy of the self and a way for individuals to care for the self, and not a universal philosophy of the progress of society and humankind. There is no world path to salvation in his philosophical position.

Note

1. Some of the arguments produced in section 1 were originally contained in my (1994/5) On What We May Hope: Rorty on Dewey and Foucault, *Studies in Philosophy and Education*, 13(4), 307–23; reprinted in J. Garrison, ed. (1995), *The New Scholarship on Dewey*, Dordrecht: Kluwer, 139–55.

Bibliography

Boyne, R. (1990) *Foucault and Derrida: The other side of reason*. London: Unwin.

Brodbeck, M. (1961) The Philosophy of John Dewey, *Indian Journal of Philosophy* 3, 69–101.

Descombes, V. (1980) *Modern French Philosophy*, trans. L. Scott-Fox and J. M. Harding. Cambridge: Cambridge University Press.

Dewey, J. (1916) *Democracy and Education*. New York: MacMillan.

——— . (1938a) *Logic: The Theory of Inquiry*. New York: Holt, Rhinehart, Winston.

——— . (1938b) *Experience and Education*. New York: Phi Kappa Delta.

Eribon, D. (1991) *Michel Foucault*, trans. Betsy Wing. Cambridge, Mass.: Harvard University Press.

Foucault, M. (1967) The Discourse of History, reprinted in (1989) *Foucault Live: Interviews 1966–1984*. New York: Semiotexte.

——— . (1969) Michel Foucault Explique Son Dernier Livre, *Le Magazine Litéraire* 28: 23–25.

——— . (1974) Michel Foucault: An Interview, *Impulse*, 50–55.

——— . (1979) *Discipline and Punish: The Birth of the Prison*. New York: Vintage.

——— . (1980) *The History of Sexuality*, Vol. 1. New York: Vintage.

——— . (1981) L'Intellectual et les Pouvoirs, *La Revue Nouvelle* 80(10), October 1984, 328–331.

——— . (1982a) *I Piere Rivière, having slaughtered my mother, my sister, my brother* . . . Lincoln: University of Nebraska Press. Originally published in 1973.

98   ~ James D. Marshall

———. (1982b) Michel Foucault: An Interview, *Ethos* 1(2), 1983, 4–9. Republished in Lawrence Kritzman, 1988, 3–16, as The Minimalist Self.

———. (1983) Afterword, in Hubert Dreyfus and Paul Rabinow (1983), *Michel Foucault: Beyond Structuralism and Hermeneutics*. Brighton, Sussex: Harvester Press, 208–66.

———. (1984a) The Ethics of the Concern for Self as a Practice of Freedom. In Paul Rabinow (ed.) (1997), *Michel Foucault: Ethics, Subjectivity, Truth*. New York: New Press, 281–301.

———. (1984b) On Power. An interview begun in 1978 with fragments appearing in *L'Express* in July 1984, shortly after his death. Republished in Kritzman, 1988, 96–109.

———. (1984c) What Is Enlightenment? In Paul Rabinow (ed.) 1984, *The Foucault Reader*. New York: Pantheon, 32–50.

Gordon, C. (1991) Governmental Rationality: An Introduction. In G. Burchell, C. Gordon, and Miller, eds., *The Foucault Effect: Studies in Governmentality*, Chicago: University of Chicago Press.

Gutting, G. (1989) *Michel Foucault's Archaeology of Knowledge*. Cambridge: Cambridge University Press.

Hollis, M. (1972) 'The Self in Action', in (ed.) R. S. Peters, *John Dewey Reconsidered*. London: Routledge and Kegan Paul, 56–75.

Kojève, A. (1954) *Tyrannie et Sagesse*. Paris: Gallimard.

Kritzman, L. D., ed. (1988) *Michel Foucault: Politics, Philosophy, Culture*. London: Routledge.

Marshall, J. D. (1984) John Dewey and Educational Research, *Journal of Research and Development in Education* 17(3), 66–77.

———. (1994/95) On What We May Hope: Rorty on Dewey and Foucault, *Studies in Philosophy and Education* 13(4), 307–23; reprinted in J. Garrison (ed.) (1995), *The New Scholarship on Dewey*. Dordrecht: Kluwer, 139–155.

———. (1996) *Michel Foucault: Personal autonomy as an aim of education*. Dordrecht: Kluwer Academic Press.

———. (2000) Michel Foucault: The pedagogy of caring for a self. In *Proceedings of the Philosophy of Education Society of Great Britain Annual Conference*, New College, Oxford, April.

Medawar, P. (1969) *Induction and Intuition in Scientific Thought*. London: Methuen.

Miller, J. (1993) *The Passion of Michel Foucault*. New York: Simon & Schuster.

Newton, R. F. (1975) Inquiry: Science and pedgagogy in conflict, *Teachers College Record* 77(1) 107–21.

Nietzsche, F. (1966) *Beyond Good and Evil*. Trans. W. Kaufmann. New York: Viking Press.

———. (1968). *On the Genealogy of Morals*. Trans. W. Kaufmann and R. J. Hollingdale. New York: Vintage Books.

———. (1976) *Thus Spake Zarathustra*, in Walter Kaufmann, 1976. Trans. and ed. *The Portable Nietzsche*. Harmondsworth: Penguin, 103–429.

———. (1983). *Untimely Meditations*, trans. R. J. Hollingdale. Cambridge: Cambridge University Press.

O'Farrell, Clare (1997) *Foucault: The legacy*. Brisbane: Queensland University Press.

Peters, M. (2001) "Achieving America: Postmodernism and Rorty's Critique of the Cultural Left," this volume.

Popper, K. (1959) *The Logic of Scientific Discovery*. London: Hutchinson.

Poster, M. (1984) *Foucault, Marxism, History*. New York: Polity Press.

Rabinow, P. (1997) (ed.) *Michel Foucault: Ethics, Subjectivity, Truth*. New York: New Press.

Reichenbach, H. (1951) *The Rise of Scientific Philosophy*. Los Angeles: University of California Press.

Rorty, R. (1982) Method, Social Science, and Social Hope, in *Consequences of Pragmatism (Essays: 1972–1980)*. Brighton: Harvester Press, 191–210.

——. (1991) *Objectivity, Relativism, and Truth*. Cambridge: Cambridge University Press.

——. (1999) *Philosophy and Social Hope*. Harmondsworth: Penguin.

Russell, B. (1946) *A History of Western Philosophy*. London: George Allen & Unwin.

Taylor, C. (1986) Foucault on Freedom and Truth, in D. C. Hoy (ed.), *Foucault: A critical reader*. Oxford: Blackwell, 69–102.

Tiles, J. E. (1988) *Dewey*. London: Routledge.

Wittgenstein, L. (1961). *Notebooks, 1914–1916*. Oxford: Blackwell.

——. (1971). *Tractatus-Logico-Philosophicus*. Oxford: Blackwell.

CHAPTER FIVE

Richard Rorty
and Postmodern Theory

Steven Best and Douglas Kellner

In theorizing the postmodern, one inevitably encounters the postmodern assault on theory, such as Lyotard's and Foucault's attack on modern theory for
its alleged totalizing and essentializing character. The argument is ironic, of
course, since it falsely homogenizes a heterogeneous "modern tradition" and
since postmodern theorists like Foucault and Baudrillard are often as totalizing as any modern thinker (Kellner 1989; Best 1995). But where Lyotard
seeks justification of theory within localized language games, arguing that no
universal criteria are possible to ground objective truths or universal values,
Foucault steadfastly resists any efforts, local or otherwise, to validate normative concepts and theoretical perspectives. For Foucault, justification en-
snares one in metaphysical illusions like "truth" and the only concern of the
philosopher-critic is to dismantle old ways of thinking, to attack existing traditions and institutions, and to open up new horizons of experience for
greater individual freedom. What matters, then, is results, and if actions
bring greater freedom, the theoretical perspectives informing them are "justified." From this perspective, theoretical discourse is seen not so much as
"correct" or "true," but as "efficacious," as producing positive effects.

Continuing along this path, postmodernists have attacked theory per se as
at best irrelevant to practice and at worst a barrier to it. Rorty assails both
metatheory—reflection on the status of theory itself which often is concerned with epistemological and normative justification of claims and values—and theory, which he critiques in three related ways that emerge
through his own articulation of the "end of philosophy" thesis. Rigorously

trained in analytic philosophy, Rorty became turncoat and abandoned the professional dogma that philosophy was "queen of the sciences" or the universal arbiter of values whose task was to provide foundations for truth and value claims. Philosophy has no special knowledge or truth claims because it, like any other cultural phenomenon, is a thoroughly linguistic phenomenon. For Rorty, language is a poetic construction that creates worlds, not a mirror that reflects "reality," and there are no presuppositionless or neutral truths that evade the contingencies of historically shaped selfhood. Consequently, there is no noncircular, Archimedean point for grounding theory. Language can only provide us with a "description" of the world that is thoroughly historical and contingent in nature.

Thus, the first plank in Rorty's assault on theory is an attack on the idea that theory can provide objective foundations for knowledge and ethics. Alleged universal truths are merely local, time-bound perspectives and masks for a "Real" that cannot be known. The second plank immediately follows: if there are no universal or objective truths, no neutral language to arbitrate competing claims, then "theory" has no power to adjudicate among competing languages or descriptions, a task which inevitably transforms theory into metatheory once the conditions of argumentation themselves become sufficiently problematic.

Hence, Rorty denies that the theorist can properly criticize, argue, evaluate, or even "deconstruct," since there is no fulcrum from which to push one claim as "right," "correct," or "better" than another. The theorist is replaced by the ironist, one who is aware of the ineliminable contingency of selfhood and discourse. Accepting the new limitations, the ironist can only "redescribe" the older theories in new languages and offer new descriptions for ourselves and others. We adopt values and ideologies on emotive rather than rational grounds. Every vocabulary is incommensurable with another and there is no "final vocabulary" with which one can arbitrate normative and epistemological claims. Thus, for Rorty:

> The method is to redescribe lots and lots of things in new ways, until you have created a pattern of linguistic behavior which will tempt the rising generation to adopt it. . . . This sort of philosophy does not work piece by piece, analyzing concept after concept, or testing thesis after thesis. Rather it works holistically and pragmatically. It says things like 'try thinking of it this way'—or more specifically, 'try to ignore the apparently futile traditional questions by substituting the following new and possibly interesting questions'. It does not pretend to have a better candidate for doing the same old things which we did when we spoke in the old way. . . . Conforming to my own precepts, I am not going to offer arguments against the vocabulary I want to replace. Instead, I am going to try to make the vocabulary I favor

look more attractive by showing how it may be used to describe a variety of topics. (1989, 9)

One would think this would commit Rorty to relativism, but he denies the term on the grounds that it belongs to a discredited foundationalist framework, as the term "blasphemy" makes no sense within an atheistic logic. Whether or not we can say Rorty is a relativist in the sense of someone who cannot demonstrate one viewpoint is more true than another, he is not a "relativist" in the sense of someone who thinks all claims are equally good or viable. Clearly, Rorty is pushing for some descriptions—those that celebrate contingency, irony, solidarity, and liberal values—over others, but he claims that one cannot "argue" for the new description. On this level, the attack on theory means simply that it is useless to provide arguments for one's positions; the only thing one can do is to offer new descriptions and hope others will find them appealing and more useful for (liberal) society. Dethroning philosophy, Rorty claims that literature is a far more powerful mode of interpreting the world and offering the descriptions needed for self-creation and social progress. Fiction takes the place of theory. Of course, Rorty cannot help but argue for his positions, and is himself still writing philosophy not fiction.

From this step follows the third plank in Rorty's attack on theory. The "theorist" should abandon all attempts to radically criticize social institutions. First, as we have seen, "critique" has no force for Rorty and, ultimately, one description is as good as any other. But "theory" on this level also means for Rorty the attempt, classically inscribed in Plato's *Republic*, to merge public and private concerns, to unite the private quest for perfection with social justice. Here, Rorty is guided by the assumption that tradition and convention are far more powerful forces than reason in the social construction of life, in holding the "social glue" together.

Rorty holds that philosophical views on topics such as the nature of the self or the meaning of the good life are as irrelevant to politics as are arguments about the existence of God. He wants to revive liberal values without feeling the need to defend them on a philosophical level: "What is needed is a sort of intellectual analogue of civic virtue—tolerance, irony, and a willingness to let spheres of culture flourish without worrying too much about their 'common ground,' their unification, the 'intrinsic ideals' they suggest, or what picture of man they 'presuppose'" (1989, 168). Since philosophy can provide no shared or viable foundation for a political concept of justice, it should be abandoned, replaced with historical narratives and poetic descriptions. Ultimately, Rorty's goal is to redescribe modern culture and the vocabulary of Enlightenment rationalism in strongly historicist and pragmatist terms.

Taking a giant leap to the right of Foucault, Rorty claims not only that philosophy provides no foundation for politics, but that it plays no political role whatsoever. Despite his assault on foundationalism, Foucault was a tireless militant and "engaged intellectual" who used theory as a weapon for political struggle. For Rorty, however, philosophy has no public or political role. Reviving the classic liberal distinction between the public and private, Rorty claims philosophy should be reserved for private life, where it can be ironic at best, while leaving political and moral traditions to govern public life. Even Derrida, master of subversion and irony, insisted that deconstruction entails political commitments and at least made public and political gestures, however vague or problematic.

We agree with Rorty's initial premise that consciousness, language, and subjectivity are historical and contingent in nature, that our relation to the world is mediated many times over, but we reject most of his conclusions. First, although we too are against foundationalism, we hold that it is possible for theory to construct *nonarbitrary* grounds to assess competing factual and value claims. These grounds are not metaphysical or ahistorical; they are found in the criteria of logic and argumentation which are *reasonable to hold*, and in shared social values that are the assumptions of a liberal democracy which Rorty himself affirms. Rejecting the implication of Rorty's position, we do not find it *arbitrary* to say racism is wrong, or that critiques of racism or sexism are merely good "descriptions" with which we hope others would agree. Rather, we find the arguments for racism, for example, far weaker than the arguments against racism and counter to liberal values that enlightened citizens hold— or should hold. The assumptions of these antiracist arguments are of course themselves historical; they stem from the modern liberal tradition that proclaims the rights of all human beings to a life of freedom and dignity. Rorty would rightly see this as a "tradition," but it is one that was constituted with a strong rational component and has compelling force for those who wish—and clearly not all do—to play the "language game" of democratic argumentation.

Similarly, while we do not know what the nature of the universe ultimately is, we find that astronomy provides a better "description" than astrology, that evolutionary theory is more compelling that creationism. Our court of appeal is reason, facts, verified bodies of knowledge, and our experience of the world itself, which is not infinitely malleable to any and all descriptions, such as the one which says the earth is flat. Symptomatic of this problem, Rorty adopts a problematic consensus theory of truth which holds that "truth" emerges from free discussion; it is "whatever wins in a free and open encounter" (1989, 67). This ignores the fact that even the "freest" inquiry can still produce falsehood and that might continues to often make right.

Needless to say, the defense of such claims will require the tools of theory—science or philosophy—rather than fiction. Abandoning these tools, the ironist is disburdened of the need to defend one's claims and tries to evade argumentative responsibilities in ways we don't tolerate in our undergraduate students.[1] For Rorty, "Interesting philosophy is rarely an examination of the pros and cons of a thesis" (1989, 9). Admittedly, argumentation is difficult and not always sexy, especially to the mind of an impatient aestheticist who seeks beauty, novelty, and speed over rigor, fairness, and coherence. Rorty is only one step away from Baudrillard, the self-proclaimed "intellectual terrorist" who prefers simply to blow up ideas with unsubstantiated claims and outrageous exaggerations rather than attending to matters of evaluating truth or falsehood, or patient empirical demonstration of his claims.

Moreover, without some kind of metatheory, Rorty cannot plausibly claim that liberalism is good or convincingly show which practices are to be favored over others. If politics is strictly an aesthetic affair, what standards do we use to judge success from failure, good from bad politics? With Lyotard, Rorty seeks to proliferate ever new descriptions of the self and the world. This has the value of overcoming stale assumptions and entrenched dogmas, but it represents a fetishism of novelty over concern for truth and justice. On this scheme, there can be no gradual progress toward greater insight and knowledge; there is only succeeding and random points of discontinuity that scatter inquiry and knowledge in fragmented directions. Put in Rorty's own terms, our claim is that foundationalism, rationalism, and progressivist narratives of Western theory can be "redescribed" in better ways that make them more effective tools for historical analysis and social critique.

From our denial that theory is powerless to seek grounds of justification for claims, or to effectively challenge, counter, refute, or argue for specific positions, we hold that a crucial role of theory is to step beyond the circumscribed boundaries of individuality to assess the ways in which the social world shapes subjectivity. For Rorty, by contrast, the personal is no longer political. The question, of course, is not whether or not one should be theoretical, since all critical, philosophical, or political orientations are theoretical at least in their embedded assumptions that guide thought and action. No one hoping to speak intelligibly about the world can hope to avoid theory; one can either simply assume the validity of one's theory, or become reflexive about the sources of one's theoretical position, their compatibility, their validity, and their effects. The potential weakness and triviality of a nontheoretical approach is evident, for example, in the antitheoretical biases of much cultural studies that mindlessly celebrate media culture as interesting, fun, or meaningful, while ignoring its economic and ideological functions.

Theory is necessary to the extent that the world is not completely and immediately transparent to consciousness. Since this is never the case, especially in our own hypercapitalist culture where the shadows flickering on the walls of our caves stem principally from television sets, the corporate-dominated ideology machines that speak the language of deception and manipulation. As we show in our book *The Postmodern Adventure* (Best and Kellner 2001), which contains studies of Thomas Pynchon, Michael Herr, Mary Shelley, H. G. Wells, Philip K. Dick, and other imaginative writers, Rorty is right that fiction can powerfully illuminate the conditions of our lives, often in more concrete and illuminating ways than theory. Ultimately, we need to grant power to both theory and fiction, and understand their different perspectives and roles. For just as novels like Upton Sinclair's *The Jungle* had dramatic social impact, so too has the discourse of the Enlightenment, which provided the philosophical inspiration for the American and French Revolutions, as well as numerous succeeding revolts in history.

Postmodern attacks on theory are part and parcel of contemporary misology—the hatred of reason—that also manifests itself in the mysticism pervading some versions of deep ecology and ecofeminism, in antihumanist attacks from "biocentric" viewpoints that often see human beings as nothing more that a scourge on nature, in the layperson's rejection of philosophy for common sense, in the pragmatist celebration of the technological and practical, in the postmodern embrace of desire and spontaneity over reflection, and in the mindless "spiritualism" pervading our culture (see Boggs 2000, 166ff.). The positive value of pragmatic critiques of theory is to remind one to maintain a close relationship between theory and practice, to avoid excessively abstract analyses and becoming mired in a metatheory that becomes obsessed with the justification of theory over its application —a problem that frequently plagues Habermas's work (see Best 1995). The pragmatic critique helps keep theory from becoming an esoteric, specialized discourse manipulated and understood only by a cadre of academic experts. No doubt we are not alone in our dissatisfaction with the highly esoteric discourse that comes not only from modernists like Habermas, but also—and more so—from poststructuralist and postmodern champions of the ineffable and unreadable, or the terminally obscure and pompous.

Operating in the tradition of critical theory, we believe that the role of theory is to provide weapons for social critique and change, to illuminate the sources of human unhappiness, and to contribute to the goal of human emancipation. Against Rorty's very unpostmodern dichotomization of the public and private (itself a centerpiece of bourgeois ideology), we believe that the citizens of the "private realm" (itself a social and historical creation) have strong obligations to participate actively in the public realm through rational criticism and debate. With Rorty, we do not believe the theorist must seek to construct a perfect bridge between the public and the private, for the range of action and choice on the part of the individual always exceeds the minimal requirements of order in a free society. Rather, the role of the theorist is to help analyze what the conditions of freedom and human well-being should be, to ask whether or not they are being fulfilled, and to expose the forces of domination and oppression.

We see public intellectuals as specialists in critical thinking who can employ their skills to counter the abuses of the public realm in order to help reconstitute society and polity more democratically and to ensure that the private realm and its liberties and pleasures are not effaced through the ever-growing penetration of mass media, state administration, electronic surveillance, and the capitalist marketplace. Indeed, new media and computer technologies have created novel public spheres and thus unique opportunities for public intellectuals to exercise their skills of critique and argumentation (Kellner 1997).

In addition, we believe that theory can provide *social maps* and *historical narratives* which supply spatial and temporal contextualizations of the present age. Social maps study society holistically, moving from any point or mode of human experience into an ever-expanding macroscopic picture that may extend from the individual self to its network of everyday social relations, to its more encompassioning regional environment, to its national setting, and finally to the international arena of global capitalism. Within this holistic framework, social maps shift from one social level to another, articulating complex connections between economics, politics, the state, media culture, everyday life, and various ideologies and practices.

Historical narratives, similarly, contextualize the present by identifying both how the past has constituted the present and how the present opens up to alternative futures. As argued in the historicist tradition that began in the nineteenth century—in the work of Hegel, Dilthey, Marx, Weber, and others—all values, worldviews, traditions, social institutions, and individuals themselves must be understood historically as they change and evolve through time. As in the form of Foucault's genealogies or various popular histories, historical narratives chart the temporal trajectories of significant experiences and events, of political movements, or the forces constituting subjectivities. Against the postmodern tendency to randomize history as a disconnected series of events, we believe historical narratives should grasp both historical continuities and discontinuities, while analyzing how continuities embody developmental dynamics, such as moral and technical evolution, that have emancipatory possibilities and should be further developed in the future.

Together, social maps and historical narratives study the points of intersection between individuals and their cultures, between power and knowledge. To the fullest degree possible, they seek to lift the veils of ideology and expose the given as contingent and the present as historically constituted, while providing visions of alternative futures. Maps and narratives, then, are meant to overcome quietism and fatalism, to sharpen political vision, and to encourage translation of theory into practice in order to advance both personal freedom and social justice. Social maps and historical narratives should not be confused with the territories and times they analyze; they are approximations of a densely constituted human world that require theory and imagination. Nor should they ever be seen as final or complete, since they must be constantly rethought and revised in light of new information and changing situations. Finally, as we are suggesting, these maps can deploy the resources of either "theory" or "fiction," since both provide illuminations of social experience from different vantage points, each of which is useful and illuminating, and necessarily supplement each other.

The social maps called classical social theories are to some extent torn and tattered, in fragments, and in some cases outdated and obsolete. But we need to construct new ones from the sketches and fragments of the past to make sense of our current historical condition dominated by media culture, information explosion, new technologies, and a global restructuring of capitalism. Maps and theories provide orientation, overviews, and show how parts relate to each other and to a larger whole. If something new appears on the horizon, a good map will chart it, including sketches of some future configurations. And while some old maps and authorities are discredited and obsolete, some traditional theories continue to provide guideposts for current thought and action, as we have attempted to demonstrate in our various books that marshall both modern and postmodern theories to map and narrativize our present moment (see Best and Kellner 1997 and 2001).

Yet we also need new sketches of society and culture, and part of the postmodern adventure is sailing forth into new domains without complete maps, or with maps that are fragmentary and torn. Journeys into the postmodern thus thrust us into new worlds, making us explorers of uncharted, or poorly charted, domains. Our mappings can thus only be provisional, reports back from our explorations that require further investigation, testing, and revision. Yet the brave new worlds of postmodern culture and society are of sufficient interest, importance, and novelty to justify taking chances, leaving the familiar behind, and trying out new ideas and approaches.

Finally, we need new politics to deal with the problems of capitalist globalization and the failure of conventional politics. We fear that just as Rorty's assault on theory blocks attempts to map and critique the new social constellations of the present moment, so too does his attack on radical politics and defense of a reformist liberalism and pragmatism vitiate attempts to deal with the new global forces of technocapitalism. Demonstrations against the World Trade Organization meetings in Seattle in December 1999 and the subsequent antiglobalization movement (see Best and Kellner 2001) suggest that the radical spirit is still alive. Indeed, we believe that it is new social movements and the forces of radical opposition which provide the most promising avenues of radical democratic social transformation in the present moment.

Note

1. For further delineation of our own political perspectives of the present moment, see Best and Kellner 1997, 1998, 1999, and 2001.

Bibliography

Best, Steven. (1995) *The Politics of Historical Vision: Marx, Foucault, and Habermas*. New York: Guilford Press.

Best, Steven, and Douglas Kellner. (1997) *The Postmodern Turn*. New York and London: Guilford Press and Routledge.

Best, Steven, and Douglas Kellner. (1998) "Postmodern Politics and the Battle for the Future," *New Political Science* 20, no. 3: 283–99.

———. (1999) "Kevin Kelly's Complexity Theory: The Politics and Ideology of Self-Organizing Systems," *Organization and Environment* 12, no. 2: 141–62.

———. (2001) *The Postmodern Adventure*. New York and London: Guilford Press and Routledge.

Boggs, Carl. (2000) *The End of Politics*. New York: Guilford Press.

Kellner, Douglas. (1989) *Critical Theory, Marxism, and Modernity*. Cambridge, U.K., and Baltimore, Md.: Polity Press and Johns Hopkins University Press.

———. (1997) "Intellectuals, the Public Sphere, and New Technologies," *Research in Philosophy and Technology* 16: 15–32.

Rorty, Richard. (1989) *Contingency, Irony, and Solidarity*. Cambridge: Cambridge University Press.

CHAPTER SIX

~

The Political Liberalism of Richard Rorty

Alberto Tosi Rodrigues

Marx, above all for the political consequences of his thought, is the most important modern reference when one thinks about the establishment of correlations between social philosophy and political practice. As it is known, it is the Marxian theory of history that acts as a basis for the theory of proletarian revolution and serves as a source of intellectual and moral legitimation of communist utopia.

On the other hand, Rorty's antitheoreticism, such as it is expressed in his texts on political intervention, could not avoid the criticism against Marxism for this logical precedence of the theory in political action. Because Rorty sees in this type of invocation of "theory" the intellectual action for which the philosopher places himself in a position of having access to the essence of the real. He criticizes the theoreticism, therefore, in its metaphysical facet, that presupposes, *grosso modo*, that "true" is synonymous with "corresponding to the real" and that the Real (and therefore the truth) isn't accessible except for the mediation of the theory (and, also therefore, of philosophy).

Taking this subject as a starting point, this chapter presents, in the first place, the terms by which Rorty describes the contrast between Marxism and his own conception of political change. Soon after, it discusses some aspects of the thought of Castoriadis and Dewey in dialogue with Rorty. In conclusion, the chapter proposes a contrast between Rorty's anti-Marxism and the democratic effectiveness of the "really existent liberalism."

Marx's Essentialism and Rorty's Antilogocentrism

In a logocentric point of view, once the real is placed under the control of theory, this becomes the foundation and the key of political practice, in that only through it is it possible to detect the ultimate nature of the present social process, foresee the unfolding of political conflict, and to know, after all, to what fate one is directed for. Thus proceeds Marx, on Rorty's view.

In Rorty's procedure, such as he himself describes it, it doesn't make sense to believe that the political institutions of a given social order or that the moral cement responsible for the adhesion of the *demos* should presuppose a theory that bases and justifies them. It is not, for example, democratic theory that acts as a base for democracy, and therefore democratic theory is not the road for the amplification and of the deepening of liberal democracy. This road, for Rorty, is directly accessible for social-political actors, to their interactive practice. And, above all, it is not limited to the "necessary" relations of determination. It is basically contingent. Liberal democracy doesn't need, therefore, a philosophical justification.

> Those who share Dewey's pragmatism [writes Rorty] will say that although it may need philosophical articulation, it [democracy] does not need philosophical backup. On this view, the philosopher of liberal democracy may wish to develop a theory of the human self that comports with the institutions by reference to more fundamental premises, but the reverse: He or she is putting politics first and tailoring a philosophy to suit. (Rorty 1991, 178)

On this point of view, when Rorty looks at Marxism he sees a theory of the human self and of history, built in an ad hoc way with the intention of providing a base for political utopia. For him, Marx confuses two objects of distinct natures—social and political movement and philosophical movement—building among them a relationship of arbitrary determination. Two objects, in fact, not just different, but asymmetric in importance. Rorty argues that there is a relative insignificance of philosophical movements in comparison to social and political movements. For him, mixing socialism with dialectic materialism is mixing "something big" and that involves hopes for millions of people, as socialism, with "something relatively small and restricted," something that is no more than a set of philosophical responses to philosophical questions, as dialectic materialism.

For Rorty's pragmatism, the misleading nature of logocentric theory is derived itself from rationalism. He points out that the mystification of the daily life hasn't terminated with the denouncement of theological mystification completed by an illuminating reason. On the contrary, when substituting Reason for God, this Enlightenment made possible a new kind of mystification-rationalism, that began the process of construction of natural, social, or historical laws which should substitute for divine law. As a man holding to the scientificist tradition derived from Enlightenment, Marx would be pervaded by this inclination. As an illustration, it is enough to remind ourselves here of the passage in *Capital*, in which he affirms that the difference between the best bee and the worst architect is the capacity of the latter to build an object in his own mind, before turning it into reality, that is, the capacity to ratiocinate regarding what he does and what he will do. The break of the linkage that Rorty intends to effect between political practice and any attempt of basing it philosophically, of legitimating it theoretically, is for him an effort of continuity with the disenchantment of the world begun with the advent of modernity.

In summary, one may say that, in Rorty's mind, Marx's politics is derived from his philosophical attempt of demonstrating the *objective need* of transforming present social reality, something accessible in discovering the laws of history. Only after this discovery would it result in a moral community that is superior to the one possible under capitalism. On the other hand, Rorty's politics, in the way that he himself presents it, is pragmatic. It doesn't require a theoretical foundation, and it is an attempt to establish, communicatively, a better moral community under capitalism. He proposes a deepening of democracy and justice through institutional reinvention and social and political actors' redescriptions.

Let us unfold the opposition enunciated in the paragraph above, to make this point clearer. It is easy to find in Marx's and Engel's writings passages in which these authors present as necessary the work of *finding* the way for which human history works to produce its criticisims of capitalism. Marx believed to have found this mechanism in fact. Engels, in the speech that he uttered at Marx's funeral, highlighted two fundamental "discoveries" accomplished by the German thinker: the law of history and the law of surplus value.

> Just as Darwin discovered the law of development or organic nature, so Marx discovered the law of development of human history: the simple fact, hitherto concealed by an overgrowth of ideology, that mankind must first of all eat, drink, have shelter and clothing, before it can pursue politics, science, art, religion, etc.; that, therefore, the production of the immediate material means, and consequently the degree of economic development attained by a given people or during a given epoch, form the foundation upon which the state institutions, the legal conceptions, art, and even the ideas of religion, of the people concerned have evolved,

and in the light of which they must, therefore, be explained, instead of vice versa, as had hitherto been the case. But that is not all. Marx also discovered the special law governing the present-day capitalist mode of production, and bourgeois society that this mode of production has created. The discovery of surplus value suddenly threw light on a problem that both bourgeois economists and socialist critics had been groping in the dark trying to solve. (Engels 1974, 171–72)

The dialectic, for Marx, was not a method of investigation. Historical and dialectic materialism, as Marx had formulated it, was for him the discovery of the way in which the real operates or behaves. For him, history behaves, *objectively* (that is, independently of subjective wills) in a dialectical way. The dialectic is registered in the movement of the real, in the same way that the laws of physics describe natural phenomena. History is, *essentially*, dialectical.

This relentless law, summarized above in Engels' speech, is described, as we know, in *The German Ideology* (Feuerbach): it is through labor that man changes nature, submitting it to the satisfaction of his needs. With his genius, with the capacity to ratiocinate, which is missing in other animals, man is capable of increasing and improving the results of his labor. The establishment of property relations appears in sequence as a result of the process of the division of labor. The development of productive forces, which at first was amplified by the establishing of property relations, at a certain moment begins to come into contradiction with these same property relations. That is the dialectic from which moments of a social revolution and the subsequent structuring of a new order are opened. In this process, manual labor and intellectual reflection will never be separate, till the advent of capital.

The prevalence of a social class above the other ones, according to the capitalist relations of production, generated a *distortion* in the way by which men acquired consciousness of the relationship between the material world and the world of ideas. The property relations that are structured historically, pari passu to the development of the material productive forces, in the Marxian conception are the cause of the expropriation of a class by another one—a fact that becomes more generalized the more the social division of labor develops. Division of labor implies a separation among labor instruments or means, and labor itself. In consequence, the great transformations through which humanity has passed in its history were the transformations in the property relations, that is, from one *mode of production* to another: from the relations of ancient slavery to the realtions of servitude in the feudal world and, from these, as a last stage, to the modern wage system.

"Conceptions of the world" are, in this context, presentations that men provide regarding their lives, regarding the way social relationships *appear* in their daily experience. For Marx, such presentations imply, in the first instance, a *"false conscience,"* an *inverted conscience,* for they are based on *appearance* and they are not capable of capturing the *essence* of the relationships to which men are *really* submitted. Marx's supposition is that in capitalism the perception of the expropriation is blocked. Because of paid wages, labor, which is the result of each human being's work, is understood as something that doesn't belong to human beings. Labor, that has always been the means by which man relates to nature and to other men, is individually noticed as something that the worker has no control over. The worker is separated, by capitalism, from the autonomous control that he gets over his own labor and also over the fruit of that labor. Labor is then perceived by the worker as something outside of himself, something that belongs to someone else: here's the *alienation.* To the extent that workers share a conception of the world based only on its appearances, without being capable of understanding the real historical process, they are subjected to *ideology.* The slave of classic antiquity knew that his owner kept him under captivity and forced him to labor by means of physical violence, taking charge of his body, but the proletarian, this modern slave, thinks that it is fair that he is separated from the fruit of his own work because of the payment of wages. Marx's "discovery" is that, *objectively, any wage is unfair because the wage system is in essence unfair.* Subjectively, the supreme irony of capitalism is that those dominated think with the ruler's head, and that is the most visceral form of dominance. In capitalism, the workers sleep with the enemy, comfortably installed in his own mind, every day, without ever noticing it.

Marx believed he had discovered a scientific law of history and a scientific law of capitalist exploitation. This meant that there would be a moment in which the development of productive forces provided by capitalism would inevitably come into contradiction with capitalist forms of property and that, when that moment came, a time of social and political revolution would be opened, which would result in a new society, without exploiters or the exploited, without alienation and ideology, without social classes and the State—because the State for him is a manifestation of class relations, and it would cease to exist when classes no longer existed. In the new society—communist society—man would be reunited with himself; he would become an autonomous human being, self-centered and self-conscious, manual and intellectual worker at the same time. He would give to society, by his own will, all the effort and labor that he could, and would receive from it all that he needed, thanks to the material development provided by capitalism. Men and women would finally be complete and whole human beings. And, of course, they would be happy forever.

All this is essentialist, logocentric, and metaphysical silliness, Rorty tells us. The advent of a new society, or the moral progress of the current society, doesn't depend on the skill of seeing the reality "beyond" the illusions of superstition, prejudice, thoughtless habits, exploitation, or ideology. Essentialists distinguish between the "real" and the "apparent" and the philosopher will be able to unmask the first through the undoing of the mystification of the second. For Rorty, this distinction is not sustained, because there isn't anything that is intrinsic (to man, to nature, to history). The only "determining reason of the human behavior," as he says, is the existence of certain *shared practices*.

For Rorty's pragmatism, there isn't a way to unmask essences and, then, to project and to predict futures. Theorists or philosophers are not in a position of knowing what human beings *are*, for one cannot know which practices human beings can come to share with each other at any moment in the future. The establishment of a better moral community, therefore, is something possible just inside the possibilities that history updates every day. There isn't a way to appropriate the dialectical key which explains how history supposedly works (Rorty 1991b, 4).

In summary, specifically regarding Marx's "discoveries," Rorty expresses three basic criticisms:

1. The criticism of the Marxist conception of *justice*. According to it, Marx is making metaphysics when he sees injustice as intrinsic to the capitalist system, because injustice is contingent and it is not a part of the essence of any system.
2. The criticism of the Marxist conceptions of *alienation* and *ideology*. According to this criticism, Marx wouldn't be able to "reveal," with his theory of history, anything that is not *immediately* accessible to social and political actors, because "appearances" and "essences" don't exist.
3. The criticism of the Marxist conception of *politics*. According to this criticism, the Marxist theory of revolution should be evaluated on the point of view of its effectiveness and from this point of view it is useless, as was evidenced by the fall of the Berlin Wall.

Rorty expresses these criticisms especially in his comments on Rawls (Rorty 1991a) and on Derrida (Rorty 1999a).

Concerning the first point, when commenting on Rawls's theory of justice, Rorty suggests that we do not require a metaphysical and moral basis to justify our political conception of justice. The liberation of the human self through the invocation of reason is for him self-deceptive. It is an unnecessary attempt to do with philosophy what theology couldn't do. He finds in Rawls, therefore, the postulate that what seems to us fair or unfair should only have as a parameter the contingent and immediately accessible reality for men submitted in each situation.

> On the question of priority, as on the question of relativity of justice to historical situations, [. . .] [s]ince Rawls does not believe that for purposes of political theory, we need think of ourselves as having as essence that precedes and antedates history, he would not agree . . . that for these purposes, we need have an account of "the nature of the moral subject", which is "in some sense necessary, non-contingent and prior to any particular experience". Some of our ancestors may have required such an account, just as others of our ancestors required such an account of their relations to their putative Creator. But we—we heirs of the Enlightenment for whom justice has become the fist virtue—need neither. As citizens and as social theorists, we can be as indifferent to philosophical disagreements about the nature of the self as Jefferson was to theological differences about the nature of God. (Rorty 1991a, 181)

Therefore, if neither theology nor philosophy can provide foundation to politics, Marx's metaphysical discovery of the essence of the capitalist system and the consequent revealing of its supposed intrinsic injustice should serve as basis to understand the violent rupture with societal order. With greater reason if we remember that this intrinsic injustice that Marx speaks of would not be accessible to the proletariat except by means of Marxist theory. From this point of view, what is said is that if the proletariat follows Marxism, it will incorporate a superior parameter of justice. What Rorty admires in Rawls is just the opposite: *as justice becomes the main virtue of society, the need for philosophical legitimacy of political practices ceases to be necessary.* Such is the democratic society that figures in Rorty's utopia.

> [T]he philosophical tradition had accustomed us to the idea that anybody who is willing to listen to reason—to hear out all the arguments—can be brought around to the truth. This view, which . . . contrasted with the claim that our point of departure may be simply a historical event, is intertwined with the idea that the human self as a center (a divine spark, or a truth tracking faculty called "reason") and

that argumentation will, given time and patience, penetrate to this center. For Rawls's purposes, we do not need this picture. We are free to see the self as center-less, as a historical contingency all the way through. (Rorty 1991a, 188)

If the subject is centerless, contingent, therefore postmodern, then there is no more usefulness for the accusation, eminently modern, that Marx gives regarding the intrinsic injustice of the capitalist system. Because from it is de-rived the fact that the end of injustice is only possible with the complete de-feat of the capitalist order by means of a revolutionary process, as well as its substitution for a new institutional engineering and a new moral framework. A new man for a new society, institutionally and morally better, is what one can infer from the Marxian utopia. It is only possible if it is possible to demonstrate that there is a society, intrinsically fair (the communist one), registered as a "coming to be" in the heart of society, which is intrinsically unfair (the capitalist one).

> Justice, in other words, is what the metaphysics of presence keeps trying and fail-ing to identify with some set of institutions or principles. Such identification is im-possible, because every institution or principle will produce new, unexpected, in-justices of its own. Every imaginable utopia will need a social protest movement. Justice is a ghost that can never be laid. (Rorty 1999a, 213)

Regarding the second point—the criticism of the Marxist theory of alienation and ideology—the argument that Rorty's discourse expresses is that the "revelation" propitiated by the Marxist theory should be made relative for the loss of the innocence in the days that we live. As we know, Marx affirmed that the product of labor in all the previous production sys-tems was always a use value, but capitalism transformed it into a com-modity. Capitalism presents labor spent in the production of an object as an "objective" property of this object. For Marx, the "fetishism of the com-modity" reflects to men the social characteristics of their own labor as if they were physical characteristics of the products of the labor. For Rorty, it is as if the fact that the commodity is a social relationship, and the de-naturalization of the exploitation propitiated by this operation, only has some weight if it refers to capitalism and the existent labor class in the first half of the nineteenth century. Rorty seems to say that the demon-stration that a difference exists between use value and exchange value of the commodity, and that in capitalism the second prevails over the first, doesn't make sense any more nowadays and it doesn't reveal anything. In the text in which he comments on Derrida's book on Marx, Rorty ques-tions if we should still accept the Marxist theory of alienation and of ideology as revealing. Making use of irony, he refers indirectly to Marx's statements in item 4 of chapter 1 of *Capital*, and he affirms that the "unmaking" of the occultation of capitalist reality only makes sense today to the essentialist and logocentrist philosophers.

> There are, I suppose, some hick logocentrists who still think that some things or properties (the 'natural' and 'real' ones as opposed to the 'cultural' and 'artificial' ones) are what they are apart from any such relations. Such simple souls may still be impressed, or indignant, when the line between the natural and the social, the substantial and the relational, or the essential and the accidental, is blurred. But only such naïfs are still susceptible to the line of patter, which we antiessentialist philosophers have developed. ("Ha! Fooled you! You thought it was *real*, but now you see that it's only a *social construct!* You thought it was just a familiar object of sense-perception, but look! It has a supersensible, spectral, spiritual, backside!") . . . It's not really news that everything is what it is because of its difference from everything else. So it is hard to know who is going to be intrigued by the following deconstruction of Marx's distinction between use-value and commodity-value. (Rorty 1999a, 216–17)

Finally, in relation to the third point—the criticism of Marxist politics— what is once again questioned is the precedence of theory, or philosophy, on the vicissitudes of political practice. Why should we, Rorty wonders, continue to read and reread Marx, to whom the "philosophical revelation" of class exploitation was the key for the transformation of the world, if political practice that results from this philosophy was simply shown to be ineffective? Before that, Rorty confronts the Marxist theory of proletarian revolution in its own proposal of deepening liberal democracy.

The contemporary political phenomena that worry us—globalization, the increase of social apartheid, etc.—Rorty argues, don't need to be looked at from the point of view of a certain theoretical context. In that sense, Rorty is opposed to Derrida's idea that we should read and reread Marx as inspiration to face the contemporary problems.

> [T]he sort of thing we philosophers know, and the sort of changes we can help make in the way people think, may eventually do some social good, but only in the very long run, and in a very indirect way. There is no science of history, nor any big discovery (by Marx or anybody else) of the one right, proper, adequate context in which to place unemployment, mafias, merchants of death, globalized labour markets and the rest. Contexts provided by theories are tools for effecting change. The theories which provide new contexts are to be evaluated by their efficiency in effecting changes, not (as the logocentrists believed) by their adequacy to an object. Any tool is replaceable as soon as a handier, less clumsy, more easily portable tool

is invented. The sheer clumsiness of attempts to use "a problematic coming from the Marxist tradition" when dealing with contemporary problems is the most persuasive reason for doubting Derrida's claim that we must read and reread Marx. (Rorty 1999a, 220–21)

About his own utopia, on the other hand, Rorty says that liberal democracy can "walk alone," without philosophical presuppositions. For him, the goals of social theory are irrelevant for politics (cf. Rorty 1991a). The strategy is not "to unmask the real and then to change it." For Rorty, it is necessary to stop speaking about the need of "passing" from a distorted to a nondistorted perception of the reality, and begin to speak about the need of modifying our practices and of taking into account new descriptions of our practices (cf. Rorty 1991b).

Exactly because there isn't a "human essence" that makes every human being equal (everyone's God's children, or everyone possesses reason), a democratic society should base itself on *pluralism*, that is, on coexistence based on *difference*. Metaphysicians, says Rorty, asked themselves *"what we are?"* searching to know the intrinsic nature of human beings, and what differentiates us from other animals. If we wish, however, to create a better community or a more democratic one, we should, according to him, ask ourselves *"who are we?"* trying to forge more coherent moral identities. By doing so we are formulating a political question (Rorty 1996).

That change points to a different conception of the social subject, as well as to a new political strategy. Rorty proposes a "conversational strategy" for social and political change, for which a redescription of the social subjects is necessary. For such redescription to be possible it is necessary to change the terms by which social and political struggle is done by introducing a differentiated vocabulary in the heart of which it is possible to enlarge the argumentative potentialities of the oppressed. If Rorty discards a philosophy or a theory that justifies social practice, what he proposes, by contrast—a pragmatic argument—is that it should have usefulness and effectiveness, from the point of view of who practices it. In Rorty's pragmatist perspective it is not absolutely necessary to expose "theoretical" reasons. It is possible, simply, to expose

narratives, rational arguments and emotional motives in order to convince others of opting for our utopia, because it will give them advantages. We are able to provide many arguments and tell many stories that will help people to re-describe themselves and, thus, see themselves as advantageously inserted in the history of a democratizing society. It is this that will influence people to accept a "democratic utopia." (Ghiraldelli Jr. 1997, 15)

It is in this sense that Rorty criticizes "American multiculturalism" that intends to ennoble black culture and to stimulate in black people a pride that allows them to face prejudice. For Rorty, blacks need to see themself as members of the national community and to feel as important as whites in the construction of the nation (Rorty 1995). In the same sense, he claims that the memory of the American labor class must be rescued. The sons and grandsons of workers of the past must come to know their fights and privations, and therefore also feel participants of the construction of the nation (Rorty 1997). The individual, here, is always observed starting from social behavior and not through pure introspection. So, the subject, in Rorty's perspective, can be seen as a network of faiths and desires, as a crossroads of countless social interactions, which are the motivations of individual conduct.

This redescription of the subject, however, involves two movements. First, as we saw, it is the recounting of histories in which individuals are inserted that qualifies members of society as a moral community. The second movement is the change of vocabulary in which individual and collective lived experiences are expressed. Since the changes are given by conversational relationships, that is, by linguistic interaction, to change the way by which certain people and situations are ordinarily described—using words with differentiated sense or creating new ones—it can help to undress the social differences of current oppressive practices, such as race and sex prejudices, or relations of political oppression and economic exploitation.

In summary, these two movements—to recount one's own history (as individual or as collective) and redescribe yourself (also as individual or as collective), as well as through new vocabularies or through changing the sense of older ones—are mixed with the other and become crucial in the search for democratic utopia. Crucial because, in Rorty's perspective, they can enlarge the logical space (that is to say, enlarge the context in which the moral questions and its answers can appear) in the heart of which the conflict among oppressor and oppressed happens and, like this, gives to the oppressed new possibilities of overcoming oppression through the amplification of the terms by which each one perceives him- or herself and others as part of the same moral community.

That would be, for Rorty, much more effective than a proletarian revolution.

Castoriadis, Dewey, and Rorty's Anti-Marxism

As I suggested above, Rorty opposes an antiessentialist and antilogocentric argument to the Marxist conceptions of justice, alienation, and ideology. And to the Marxist conception of politics, he opposes the argument of the effectiveness (or, better, the political inefficacy) of Marxism.

Two influences are important for the constitution of these Rortyan arguments. Cornelius Castoriadis's influence can be seen in the criticism of the theoreticism of Marx's formulation concerning the proletarian revolution. Dewey's influence can be seen in the liberal-democratic criticism of the perverse effects of the market economy. Rorty reworks Dewey's criticisms as an antidote to the Marxist criticism of capitalism's effects of social exclusion.

Let us reexamine Castoriadis's and Dewey's arguments to provide us with a greater understanding of Rorty's position.

As Melkonian (1999, 119) points out, Rorty's criticisms owe a debt to Castoriadis's criticism of Marx. Leaving aside the complete argument (for this, see *The Imaginary Institution of the Society*), it is enough to remind ourselves of Castoriadis's forewords to his books *The Experience of the Labor Movement* (1985) and *Socialism or Barbarism* (1983).

In the first text, Castoriadis takes as his starting point the classic separation between the "trade unionist consciousness" and the "revolutionary consciousness." It presupposes arbitrary separations between the economy and politics, between the "immediate" and the "historical" and, therefore, among empirical political actors (the meat and bone proletarians) and a proletariat full of dreams—the receiver of an unprecedented revolutionary "mission" in human history. Castoriadis affirms, it is a contradiction in terms for Marxist theory: the proletariat that will build a new world is not capable of rioting against capitalist exploitation except in a moment of economic collapse, when it becomes possible for the revolutionary theoreticians to inject the class consciousness it requires.

In Castoriadis's vision, first presented in 1973, the precedence of theory, the logocentrism—that reduces to a metaphysical interpretation of social classes—is not a Leninist distortion, but really a characteristic of Marx's thought. It is not an "economicism," of the primacy of the economic over the political, Castoriadis says, but rather the primacy of the theoretical-speculative over the political-practical. In the context of the Marxist theory, the economic dimension is seen (deceptively) as scientifically theoreticizable and predictable.

Reminding us of a remarkably Hegelian passage in the young Marx, Castoriadis identifies the essentialist and logocentric matrix that pervades all the different traditions of political thought that received the name of Marxism. The exact terms are revealed by Castoriadis in the following quote.

> But, then, [he writes] who does know and theoretically possess "what is" the proletariat in an independent manner? Marx does in 1845—and, evidently, even better in 1867. *Where* is that "being" from the proletariat, that "will force it historically to

do" what must be done. It is in Marx's mind. What is the difference between all
those philosophers, who Marx criticizes mercilessly because they confound the history of the world with their own thought, and Marx himself? None. "What this or
that proletarian, or even the whole proletariat imagine", or, let us use the term, the
'immediate', or phenomenon or appearance, masks—here and everywhere else—
the being or the essence, appropriately inseparable from the necessity (presented as
'historical' imposition), and object of a knowledge based on necessary reasons.
With respect to that essence—as well as to the interpretation of the more or less
contingent appearances, as it is the case, for example, of 'representations' that the
proletarians elaborate concerning what they want, which are, at last instance, co-
ordinated and subordinated to it—, the theory and only the theory gives access; it
only allows to recognize whether, doing this or that, the proletariat acts based on
the domain of simple 'representations' or based on the imposition of its being.
When, then, is it possible to speak of autonomy or creativity of the proletariat?
Never; and, less than ever, at the moment of revolution, since, for him, that is precisely the moment of the absolute ontological necessity, in which history forces it
finally to manifest its being—a being that it ignores up to that time, but that others know for it. But, at least, is Marx autonomous when saying that? No, he is ser-
vant of Hegel, Aristotle and Plato: he sees (*theorei*) the being (*eidos*) of the proletariat, inspects its invoice, and discovers its occult potency (*dynamis*), which will
necessarily become a revolutionary act (*energeia*). (Castoriadis 1985, 14–15)

The vision that Marx has of history, in which everything is connected
with everything else and everything competes for the accomplishment of
everything, is, for Castoriadis, a clear sign of Marx's dependence on Hegelian
schemes. What turns Marx's position inconsistent is that he holds Hegel's position without discussion, in spite of the fact that in Hegel it is philosophically founded and that, at the same time, this foundation is denounced by
Marx himself as illusory or ideological. Although Marx inverts the terms,
substituting the Spirit for matter or for nature, the logic is strictly the same.
The rationalism that pervades Hegelian ontology, whose structure was, according to Castoriadis, integrally absorbed by Marx, doesn't take to its conclusion the other great theme of its thought: the idea that humanity's history
is the history of the struggle among classes. Marx works with an "objective"
definition of class, which is not dependent on the empirical activity of the
class itself. This activity is deducible from the objective definition.

Thus, class is defined by referring to relations of production, which are, in last instance, 'relations among people mediated by things'. The structure of the ontological relation essence/manifestation guarantees that knowledge of the essence allows
one to know its manifestations, since the essence produces, essentially, only its own
manifestations; and, inversely, the manifestations not determined in an essential

manner are, by definition, accidental. Stating that manifestations are determined by the essence means, evidently, that the phenomena obey laws; hence, as the same causes produce the same effects due to the principle of identity, we know—limited only by imperfections of our information and analytic capacity—'what is, what will be and what has formerly been'. (Castoriadis 1985, 39–40)

In the second text mentioned above, Castoriadis also affirms another argument that appears later in Rorty—Marxism isn't anything more than a regression in the history of the socialist movement. For Castoriadis, Marx limits hugely the concerns of the socialist field, when placing the whole emphasis of its theoretical model in subjects related to economic production and classes. Castoriadis reminds us that before Marx, since the beginning of the nineteenth century, the labor movement had adopted the values and the political and social imaginary of the American and French Revolutions and promoted its amplification. Such amplification had a political character, since the socialist idea (of "utopian", "prescientific" socialism) of instituting a "social Republic" was, according to Castoriadis, a remaking of ancient democracy, rediscovered by the Enlightenment. Although he takes these ideals as a starting point, Marx submits them to rationalism, to scientificism, and to theoreticism, and it is in this sense that he restricts and limits the libertarian ideals of the labor movement.

However, in Castoriadis's vision, Marxist's influence on socialist ideas is viewed like a catastrophic thing exactly because *it limits socialism to the equations placed on it by liberalism, that is, what politically articulates the capitalist conception of world*. The political dimension, the need to build a new political institutional frame, is minimized or ignored by Marx, insofar as it appears as dependent on the economy. The political emancipation is not a result of the viewpoint of the institution of a new relation between freedom and equality, but rather is the pure and simple consequence of social revolution, of the violent destruction of the exploiting class and of the appropriation of the "bourgeois" State for armed workers, in the dictatorship of the proletariat. Starting from the equation "oppression + violent revolution = emancipation" Marxism became the most influential reference for socialist movements in many countries. But not, according to Castoriadis, just because of Marx's genius.

The central and sovereign character of production and economy (and the corresponding *reduction* of all social and political problems) is *nothing more* than the organizing themes of the dominant imaginary from that (our) time: the *capitalist* imaginary. As I have been trying to show since 1955 . . ., the 'reception', the penetration of Marxism in the labor movement was, in fact, the re-introduction (or the

resurgence) of the main imaginary social significances of capitalism to this movement, from which it had tried to get away during the preceding period. (Castoriadis 1983, 24)

I believe that these statements characterize my first point. Castoriadis
formulates in the 1970s a global criticism of the essentialism and logocentrism of the Marxist theory of history and of the proletarian revolution
that serves as inspiration for the argument that Rorty will use against
Marx.

The second point that I consider relevant for understanding Rorty's anti-
Marxism is that he pleads in favor of social-democracy against laissez-faire,
signaling the type of liberal utopia that he favors. And this viewpoint serves
as an antidote to the argument mobilized by Marxism against excluding capitalism. In summary, Rorty affirms that liberal democracy has better conditions (it is more effective) to argue against the suffering and the pain than
Marxism. "Why Marx and not Keynes?" asks Rorty of Derrida.

To demonstrate such a thesis, he uses Dewey's heritage, which combines
American national pride and an argument in favor of the economy by Pres-
ident Roosevelt's New Deal, in the context of facing the economic crisis in
the conflicting moment of monopolist capitalism established in the period
between the wars.

Dewey's fundamental argument in regard to this point is exactly the same
as Keynes. Dewey says that the Achilles' heel of liberalism is the notion of
homo oeconomicus. He means the idea that each individual looks out for his
private egoistic interest provides, as a final result, the commonweal. As we
know, one of the pillars of economic liberalism till the great crisis of 1929 was
the myth of the self-adjustable market. The bourgeois idea of freedom corre-
sponded to a practical conception according to which the market economy
should be absolutely free from any State intervention—the Minimum State
concept.

Keynes (1926) in *The End of Laissez-Faire* made a strong criticism of Adam
Smith's "invisible hand." He proposed the distinction between the agenda
and the nonagenda of the State: it would be necessary to verify the moment
in which State regulation over the economy would be necessary, so that capitalism wouldn't become self-destructive.

Dewey was an ardent partisan of this idea. In *Liberalism and Social Action*,
written in 1935, he affirms that some economic planning is necessary to facilitate a social administration for the potentialities of capitalism.

According to Dewey, the original task of liberalism had been the one of
liberating, from the old ways of thinking, habits, and institutions, a group of

individuals that represented the new potentialities of technical development and productivity. After obtaining success in its task of "liberation" of the productive classes from precapitalist conceptions of the world, making use of criticism and the demolition of the ancient order, liberalism came across a new problem. Dewey describes this as the "social organization" of a new order. Although early liberalism had obtained success in destroying the ancient conceptions of the world, in the 1930s it was in crisis because it needed to structure new conceptions and new institutions. The appearance of Nazi-fascism as an alternative to the social disaggregation caused by this crisis seemed to Dewey an authentic tragedy. Before this menace to freedom, it was necessary that liberalism made use of new means to reach its goal: a society founded on freedom. To achieve a free and democratic social order, therefore, it would not be possible any longer without planning to leave the simple search of private individual interests to itself and to entrust competition in the market with providing collective goods and welfare itself. These means were no longer useful to contemporary needs of the liberal order. Organized "social planning," the "social direction" of industry and finance were, in Dewey's vision, the new means.

The competitive social system conceived by laissez-faire liberalism became for the American philosopher a "disguised war." The State was no longer, in its vision, the only agency endowed with coercive power that should be feared by the free market. Power concentrated by the owners of private property and the means of production, Dewey recognizes, was already much larger than the state power. However, unlike Marxism, for Dewey, the "method of the intelligence" and not the "method of the violence" should prevail. Even a blind faith in the Hegelian dialectic could have made Marx think, Dewey affirms, that revolutionary violence on the part of a class could result in a democratic society without classes.

Violence necessarily generates violent reactions and, therefore, it won't be the proper means to reach the desired goal, that is, a free and democratic society. (Notice in Dewey the pragmatic logic of usefulness.) Perhaps the logic of force could obtain results in a country that has never tried freedom and democracy, like Russia in 1917, but in a society with the democratic traditions of United States, with the "genuine democratic spirit" of this country, the use of force would just mean the desire for power on the part of a class. A violent revolution as proposed by Marx would never be acceptable to the American tradition.

According to Deweys diagnosis, American liberalism had to face the social crisis of the 1930s through a radical political reorientation: the substitution of a typically Keynesian social-democratic politics for laissez-faire liberalism. It is a declaration supporting the politics of the social pact of the New Deal, in the expectation that this American initiative could be constituted as a historical alternative to ancient competitive liberalism as well as to the totalitarianism of the left (Soviet communism) and the right (Nazi-fascism).

> The idea that organized social control of economic forces is out of the historical road of liberalism reveals that liberalism is still linked to the residue of its initial phase of *laissez-faire*, with its classical opposition between individual and society. What today turns off the liberal ardor and paralyzes its efforts is the conception that freedom and the development of individuality, as goals, exclude the use of organized social effort, as means. The liberalism of the initial phase considered individuals' isolated and competitive economic action as the middle road for the welfare. Now we should revert the perspective and see that the socialized economy is the middle road for the individual's free development. . . . To reduce the problem of the future to a fight between fascism and communism will be an invitation to catastrophe, that could drag down civilization. A democratic, vivacious and courageous liberalism, will be capable of avoiding a disastrous reduction of the problem. For me, I don't believe that Americans, living under Jefferson's and Lincoln's tradition, will become weak and surrender without a sincere and burning effort to transform democracy into a living reality. (Dewey 1970, 88–90)

It is this vision of what liberalism should be—this mix between social-democracy and nationalism—that Rorty incorporates and takes as a parameter when he declares himself a "post-modern bourgeois liberal." In *Achieving Our Country* this Deweyan matrix becomes explicit along the redescription that Rorty provides of the history of the American left.

Rorty's Anti-Marxism and the "Really Existent Liberalism"

Rorty is among the few contemporary philosophers who are disposed to open dialogue with the social sciences, including themes related to anthropology and political science.

In the two sections above, I presented Rorty's political views related to Marxism, describing them according to his philosophical perspective. That is to say, I tried to unpick the Rortyan antifoundationalist argument. I also tried to identify two sources that I considered important for Rorty's anti-Marxist arguments.

But since Rorty is disposed to a dialogue that extrapolates the limits of its philosophy, it won't be mistaken to weave considerations that have as starting points concerns that are external to strictly philosophical domains.

As a final comment, I will highlight two points that I consider fragile in the Rortyan argument regarding Marx and that indicate respect to the kind of liberalism that Rorty supports:

1. Castoriadis builds a radical philosophical and political criticism of Marx's thought, that has at its heart two related accusations: (a) philosophically, Marx simply reproduces Hegelian epistemology and (b) politically, Marx reintroduces, in the practice of labor movement, the main elements of capitalist's imaginary, that is, of liberal ideology. Rorty, when reading Castoriadis, incorporates into neopragmatism the first part of the criticism and treats the second with disdain. Accordingly, although Marx's foundationalism comes under criticism, his political legacy is given an ambiguous value.

2. Drawing on Dewey to defend national pride and social-democratic institutions, Rorty criticizes "really existent socialism." He affirms that Marx doesn't help us to think of democratic institutions. The prophecy of communist society became the nightmare of totalitarianism. Like Dewey, Rorty argues that liberalism should incorporate the Keynesian program to improve democracy. But if, as Rorty affirms, social theories should be evaluated in terms of their effectiveness, what is the effectiveness of this proposal *today*? What is the character of "really existent liberalism"?

First, Rorty has an ambiguous relationship with Marx's political legacy. In his comment on Derrida's book on Marx, Rorty (1999a) disagrees with the idea that is possible to recover "certain aspects" of the German thinker's work as a source of hope for social change. For him it is not in Marx's work that one can find hope, but in the tradition of the struggles of the labor movement, which was inspired by Marxism.

> Much as I admire . . . the intensity of his [Derrida's] hope for justice, I still am not sure why he thinks that Marx is a particularly notable example of this hope. I am not sure that his loyalty to Marx, and his insistence that everybody else join him in not forgetting Marx, testifies to more than the memory of a significant, but accidental, youthful encounter. (Rorty 1999a, 214)

However, Rorty himself proposes the ransom of certain aspects of Marx's work, as in the text that compares the *Communist Manifesto* to the New Testament. In this text (Rorty 1999b), Marx's work appears as an "invaluable inspirational reading." He stresses once again that the importance of the *Man-*

ifesto is in the inspiration that it provided to the organized workers' social movement. While the *Manifesto* is based upon a mistaken prediction, nevertheless by outlining the promise of an achievable utopia, it provided both inspiration and hope for those who fought against exploitation. The juvenile attachment to Marx, here, doesn't appear as romantic or nostalgic—as it appears in its observation concerning Derrida—but as legitimate motivation for action. For Rorty, Marxism can result in moral gains based upon providing motivation for practical action. *For Rorty, Marx was wrong, but the effects of his political calling provided hope.*

We are inclined to ask, in the first place, hope in what? And, in the second, hope based on what? The answer to the first question, judging by that expressed in the *Communist Manifesto*, can only be hope in a society without exploiters, without private property, without social classes, and without the State. This is the kind of hope that Marx offers. The *Manifesto* doesn't offer any hope for those who put their trust in democracy. On the contrary: Marx denounces it as a pure bourgeois illusion. The answer to the second point can only be that such hope, as offered by the *Manifesto*, is based on a theory of the history of a social revolution capable of giving to its believers a dogmatic certainty in the infallibility of the Marxist prediction, stimulating them to action to make the prophecy come true. This is the kind of foundation of hope that Marx offers, and that Castoriadis and Rorty criticize.

However, given the argument that the philosophy doesn't give foundations to politics, Rorty imagines it to be possible to get the hope provided by Marx's intervention and to discard the theoretical foundationalism by which, in Marxism, it is sustained.

Castoriadis sees Marx's theoreticism and determinism as the source of arguments of State leaders, which transformed hopes for social revolution into a totalitarian nightmare. Communist totalitarianism, Castoriadis notices, is contained, also, in the "glorious hope" announced by the *Communist Manifesto*. The two things cannot be separated. Politics, Rorty admits, can have a "philosophical articulation," although it doesn't possess "philosophical foundations." It is exactly this philosophical articulation among Marx's foundationalism-determinism and the political institutional framework built on its inspiration that Castoriadis notices and Rorty ignores.

The Marxist starting point that there exists a "class being" of the "true" proletariat and that this being is forced to behave historically in certain ways and not in other ways has had a strong political implication in communist states. The totalitarian party became instituted as the only authorized interpreter of the laws of history and the only political spokesperson for scientific knowledge. Only the party, in communist totalitarian states,

> can distinguish between workers that think and act according to 'the essence of its being' and the other ones that are workers just in an empirical and phenomenal sense, and as such they may and shall be reduced to silence (in the best hypothesis, fatherly 'educated'; in the worst, qualified as false workers and sent to a 're-education field' or shot). Being true—that is, according to the Marxian conception, corresponding to the interests and historical role of the proletarian class—the theory (and the Party that embodies it) can run over the heads and the cadavers of empirical workers to incorporate them into the essence of a metaphysical proletariat. (Castoriadis 1983, 27–28)

Foundationalism and totalitarianism, metaphysics and pain, as Castoriadis points out, became in practice two faces of the same coin. One side that we can infer from the passage above is that dialectic materialism should not just be seen as a group of "philosophical answers to philosophical questions" because it became in practice the philosophical justification for political violence. And violence, here, is not simply a tyrannical distortion of somebody that, maliciously, corrupted the teaching and the "glorious hope" transmitted by Marx. It is contained in the priority of theory announced by Marx in texts such as the *Communist Manifesto*.

If we consider this warning, why should we be happy with the possibility that youth read the *Communist Manifesto*—as well as the New Testament? Why should we imagine that youth will be "morally better" if they understand this reading? From the perspective of pragmatism, why and how does a text impregnated by metaphysics, by theoreticism, by rationalism, by logocentrism, by essentialism, and by determinism, help to form "morally better" people, more adapted to democratic coexistence? Is it possible, pragmatically, to say, "Hi, young people, read just those lines of the *Communist Manifesto* in which Marx and Engels describe their hopes for a better world, and close your eyes to the essentialist and logocentric passages"?

I think that this ambiguous way of treating Marx's revolutionary exhortation is simply a reproduction of the communist posture in relation to democracy. For the communists, the democratic Republic (the bourgeois democracy) is a mere passage, a mere moment of accumulation of the forces for that which in a more favorable moment becomes the decisive step—that of the violent revolution. Democracy, for communism, is a simple *instrument* to arrive at the dictatorship of the proletariat. True democracy is what Lenin called the "democratic dictatorship of the proletariat." *Para* Rorty the cultivation of the ideals and values expressed in the *Communist Manifesto* can be good to foment a feeling of solidarity or of hope for a better world in younger generations. But for such hope to be coherent with the democratic-liberal utopia of Rorty, it is possible to infer that it should necessarily be limited to youth, so that it can just be cherished until the moment, with maturity; people understand that capitalism cannot be substituted by a revolution and that the best we can do is to improve liberal democracy.

The second point is that Rorty's liberal-democratic utopia is also, using the same criterion that Rorty used for Marx, a "failed prophecy." What remains to know is: can it still be a "glorious hope"?

As I mentioned above, Dewey affirmed:

> The liberalism of the initial phase considered the individuals' isolated and competitive economic action as the middle road for the welfare, as a goal. Now we should revert to the perspective and see that the socialized economy is the middle road for the individual's free development. (Dewey 1970, 88)

Of course, Dewey doesn't work with the same determinist and fatalistic logic as Marx, but his future perspective in the 1930s was clear: Keynesian capitalism will accomplish the designs of liberalism. It is this perspective that Rorty remakes and reproduces, almost without alteration, sixty years later. During those years, however, history testifies that the Deweyan utopia went bad.

If we use for liberal social theory the same criteria that Rorty proposes for Marxist social theory, will it continue being as useful and effective as Rorty imagines it? Rorty says:

> Contexts provided by theories are tools for effecting change. The theories which provide new contexts are to be evaluated by their efficiency in effecting changes, not (as the logocentrists believed) by their adequacy to an object. Any tool is replaceable as soon as a handier, less clumsy, more easily portable tool is invented. The sheer clumsiness of attempts to use "a problematic coming from the Marxist tradition" when dealing with contemporary problems is the most persuasive reason for doubting Derrida's claim that we must read and reread Marx. (Rorty 1999a, 221)

When referring to the experience of Soviet socialism, Leonid Brezhnev called it "really existent socialism." It is necessary to make a brief comment here about "really existent liberalism" and its relationships with contemporary democracy.

Because in the capitalist periphery, lovers of democracy are now suffering from a bitter sense of emptiness. And it is possible that this is related to the efficiency of liberal social theory in effecting changes.

It is not to say that, in the past twenty years, there haven't been some positive changes. In southern Europe and in Latin America, in the 1980s, so-called democratic transitions brought back civil rights and liberties that the bureaucratic military regimes had taken away. In Russia and in eastern Europe, in the early 1990s, the "democratic revolutions" buried communist totalitarianism. Formally democratic procedures—by fits and starts and with traditional exceptions—started to become part of the political routine of these countries.

And yet, it seems as if we are suffering today from some sort of democratic uneasiness. Those feats we once dreamt democracy would perform—namely, that it would be able to choose more representative leaders, that it would extract from these leaders more political responsibility towards the population, that it would institutionalize open spaces for the systematic participation of organized citizens, and—most importantly—that it would get hold of the economic sphere and submit it to a more egalitarian logic—all this has become sheer fantasy these days. Sand has jammed the democratic set of gears with administration, by the State, of the so-called "market oriented reforms." Such reforms are the contribution that "really existent liberalism" has offered to contemporary democracy.

In the dawn of the modern era, as Norberto Bobbio reminds us, democracy got together with liberalism in a mutually beneficial association: the latter provided the former with the civil guarantees indispensable for actors' freedom and the former would give the latter a method, a procedure, for collective decision making. From this intercourse emerged the liberal-democratic State, which from that moment onwards assumed the concomitant formats of Minimum State and State of Right according to the angle (economic or political) from which we observe it.

As we well know, the emergence of the bourgeois world led to a split between the public and the private, and in turn this produced binary oppositions between equality and liberty, polity and economics, State and market. The concept of State of Right refers to the juridical security necessary to economic and political actors that both enables them to conclude private contracts (the consumption of goods, wage relations, etc.) and to have access to the formal equality presupposed by the public sphere (the free expression of ideas, the organization of partisan groupings, the access to a representation system, etc.). The concept of Minimum State, on the other hand—one of the touchstones of economic liberalism—refers to the ideological dispute over the market's autonomy vis-à-vis the State: insofar as the market now belongs to the universe of private exchange relations, the regulation of this activity by the State structure began to be regarded and repelled as an undue interference, and the very existence of the State was considered a necessary evil.

During the nineteenth century, laissez-faire capitalism, to which the liberal-democratic State attached itself at birth, went through a series of successive crises that culminated with the 1929 crash. The great crisis exposed the myth of a self-regulating market, of Smith's "invisible hand," and created room for a radical change in the relationship between the State and the market. After the Second World War, Keynesianism became the predominant economic policy: mass production and mass consumption would be sustained by full employment and higher real wages.

In association with these changes, the State in central capitalism got rid of the Minimum State's robes and adopted, in particular after 1945, a strong regulatory role, establishing a series of institutions and interclass arrangements geared towards the management of the economy. More than this: higher tax revenues, and the strengthening of the workers' unions, resulted in the gradual achievement of social rights. In the twentieth century, the Welfare State completed the cycle of citizens' rights that had begun in the eighteenth and nineteenth centuries, exactly as described by T. H. Marshall, i.e., the sequential attainment of civil, political, and social rights. Political democracy consolidated itself as the regulating basis on which social and economic democracy would eventually be structured. Bobbio had this in mind when, in his writings, he made a clear distinction between "formal" and "substantive" democracy. The Deweyan "prophecy" seemed to be executed, in much the same way as the first phase of the communist utopia was, that is, "really existent socialism" as a transition phase to communism. If not this perception, the Cold War, understood by Rorty as a battle over democracy, would not make sense.

When, however, the 1970s brought with it the crisis of organized capitalism and of the Welfare State, political democracy was equally threatened. The disorganization of the expansive cycle brought together economic stagnation and increasing inflation. For the new emerging conservatism the problem lay precisely in the institutional provisions of the Welfare State's mass democracy. The "adjustment" policies of the central economies emerged then in response to the crisis of Keynesianism and gained organic unity and public visibility with Thatcher's and Reagan's rise to power. A new ideological construct was being structured—neoliberalism.

The "excess" of social rights was immediately identified by the conservatives as responsible for the State's fiscal crisis and, consequently, the "excess" of social demands started to be pointed at as a source of political instability. This is what Samuel Huntington had in mind when he declared "the crisis of democracy" in the 1970s, in the face of what he considered an imminent risk to "governability." Economic adjustment became synonymous with market deregulation, liberalization of the national economies at the periphery, and the privatization of state companies, all tasks to be carried out by the technocracy that held the corresponding indispensable "technical know-how." The range of the public sphere narrowed. The most crucial decisions about the economy were carefully hidden from the population's scrutiny. In the minds of the conservatives, democracy implied, in Huntington's words, "a certain amount of political apathy."

It was not only the dream of a substantive democracy that was thus buried. Even formal democracy, the historical conquest of the liberal democratic State, is suffering a serious setback. Neoliberalism sought the Minimum State ideology in the liberal tradition and radicalized it, whilst at the same time attempting to make certain premises of the State of Right more relative so as to empty it of its contents in the name of "*raison d'État*" supposedly necessary for the management of its economic policies.

Robert Dahl says that polyarchy (which he regards as a minimum definition of democracy) is a regime that develops institutionalization of procedures and the expansion of citizens' participation simultaneously. Any polyarchical decision-making process must include both the composition of the political agenda (i.e., the decision on which matters will be the object of deliberation) and the decision itself. The decision, in its turn, must be made by those to whom it applies, on equal level with all others. If this definition is reasonable, what name must we then give to those decision-making processes designed to promote the administration of the market-oriented reforms that are currently happening in the countries of the capitalist periphery?

From 1982, when the crisis of the unilateral moratorium of Mexico's foreign debt exploded, the multilateral organizations (the IMF and the World Bank) made of the neoliberal ideological constructs a manual of standard policies for fiscal and financial sanitation as well as for economic openness and deregulation, all to be put into practice in the debtor countries, as compensation for the renegotiation of their debts.

The application of these policies has shown to be viable only if the administration is concentrated in the hands of the State's techno-bureaucracy, if conservative majorities are somehow orchestrated in the parliamentary arena, and if social movements and opposition parties are isolated. Both the agenda composition and the actual decision making are being politically shut in. The logic of legitimacy is losing ground to the logic of efficiency. More and more, economic deregulation has as its consequence the breaking up of democratic institutions and the constriction of the public space.

Those are the democratic institutions that "really existent liberalism" can offer for us today. Of course, this isn't the liberal democracy which Rorty defends. But, what can liberal social theory offer, besides good intentions, to improve that situation? What of its "efficiency in effecting changes"? Rorty says, frequently, that "democracy is the way in which we like to live," without perceiving that, in the contemporary society, the largest menace to this "way of life" doesn't come from communism, which was politically defeated, but from liberalism itself, which in its now dominant version is nondemocratic and similarly antidemocratic.

In *Moral Universalism and Economic Triage* (Rorty 1996), Rorty adopts a realistic point of view, typically liberal, to approach the problem of the utopian construction of a universal moral community. From its viewpoint, democracy has an economic cost and, therefore, there is an interdependence today among the wealth accumulated by a nation and its possibilities of developing democracy. For Rorty, the generalization of liberal democracy depends on the possibility of convincing the rich ones that the priority given to the economy should be avoided.

> The institutions of the rich democracies are now so intertwined with advanced methods of transportation and communication, and more generally with expensive technology, that it is hardly possible to imagine their survival if the rich countries had to reduce their share of the world's resources to a fraction of what they now consume. Democratic institutions in these countries depend on the existence of things like universal literacy, meritocratic social mobility, bureaucratic rationality, and the existence of many competing sources of information about public affairs. Free universities, a free press, incorruptible judges, and unbribable police officers do not come cheap.

And, concluding, he says:

> I can sum up this point as follows: an answer to the question "who are we?" which is to have any moral significance, has to be one which takes money into account. Marx may have overstated when he identified morality with the interests of an economic class, but he had a point. That point is that a politically feasible project of egalitarian redistribution of wealth, requires there to be enough money around to insure that, after the redistribution, the rich will still be able to recognize themselves—will still think their lives worth living. The only way in which the rich can think of themselves as part of the same moral community with the poor is by reference to some scenario which gives hope to the children of the poor without depriving their

own children of hope. . . . In particular, answering the question "who are we?" with "we are members of a moral community which encompasses the human species", depends on an ability to believe that we can avoid economic triage. (Rorty 1996)

But liberal politics of the contemporary world are traveling the exactly inverse road to that which Rorty's utopia points. If the communist utopia of universalization of equality among people was reduced to the dictatorship of one party, the Deweyan liberal-democratic utopia which Rorty defends— which tries to combine the freedom of the search for material wealth with free and socially controlled democratic institutions—is becoming more and more distant. Its appeal, today, is more and more ineffective, because of the "economic triage" promoted by "really existent liberalism."

Bibliography

Castoriadis, C. (1983) *Socialismo ou Barbárie* [*Socialism or Barbarism*]. Translation from French to Portuguese by Milton Meira do Nascimento. São Paulo, Brasiliense.

——— . (1985) *A experiência do movimento operário* [*The Experience of the Labor Movement*]. Translation from French to Portuguese by Carlos Nelson Coutinho. São Paulo, Brasiliense.

Dewey, J. (1970) *Liberalismo, liberdade e cultura* [Brazilian version of *Liberalism and Social Action* and *Freedom and Culture*]. Translation from English to Portuguese by Anísio Teixeira. São Paulo: Editora Nacional/ Editora da USP.

Engels, F. (1974) Discurso ante la tumba de Marx [Speech in Front of Marx's Tomb]. In *Marx y Engels: obras escogidas* [*Marx and Engels: Selected Works*], vol. 3. Moscú, Editorial Progreso.

Festenstein, M. (1999) *Pragmatism and Political Theory: From Dewey to Rorty*. Chicago: University of Chicago Press.

Geras, N. (1995) *Solidarity in the conversation of Humankind: The Ungroundable Liberalism of Richard Rorty*. London: Verso.

Ghiraldelli Jr., P. (1997) Para ler Richard Rorty e sua filosofia da educação [*To Read Richard Rorty and His Philosophy of Education*]. *Filosofia, Sociedade e Educação*. 1, no.1.

——— . (1999) *Richard Rorty: a filosofia do novo mundo em busca de mundos novos*. [*Richard Rorty: The Philosophy of the New World Searching for New Worlds*]. Petrópolis: Editora Vozes.

Melkonian, M. (1999) *Richard Rorty's Politics: Liberalism at the End of the American Century*. New York: Humanity Books.

Rée, J. (1998) Rorty's Nation. *Radical Philosophy* no. 87.

Rorty, R. (1991a) *Objectivity, Relativism, and Truth. Philosophical Papers I*. Cambridge: Cambridge University Press.

——— . (1991b) Feminism and Pragmatism. *Radical Philosophy* no. 59.

——— . (1995) Uma mãozinha para Oliver North. *Novos Estudos Cebra* no. 42.

———. (1996) Moral Universalism and Economic Triage. Paper presented to *UNESCO Philosophy Forum*. Paris.

———. (1997) Back to Class Politics. *Dissent* 44, no. 1.

———. (1998) *Achieving Our Country: Leftist Thought in the Twentieth Century America.* Cambridge, Mass.: Harvard University Press.

———. (1999a) A Spectre Is Haunting the Intellectuals: Derrida on Marx. In *Philosophy and Social Hope.* London: Penguin Books.

———. (1999b) Failed Prophecies, Glorious Hopes. In *Philosophy and Social Hope.* London: Penguin Books.

CHAPTER SEVEN

Richard Rorty's Self-Help Liberalism: A Marxist Critique of America's Most Wanted Ironist

Peter McLaren, Ramin Farahmandpur, and Juha Suoranta

Introduction

The fireworks displays ushering in the new millennium have long subsided, but the smoke has not yet cleared. We haven't noticed that capitalism's 'Goliath' roller-coaster ride has no destination, only repetition. Like a Möbius strip, the exit transforms into the entrance and the ride begins again. In this reengineered era of "no exit" capitalism, the future has already arrived. And to the philosophically inclined, the future is also beginning to look more and more like Richard Rorty playing a toga-clad ambassador from outer space in an early *Star Trek* episode. Presumably the future will take care of itself as long as Americans like Rorty are around to ensure that the universe is run by "liberal gentlefolk" ready and willing to make the necessary incremental efforts to transform the world's globobosses and corporate managers into a fraternity of happy campers determined to "be all that they can be." Precisely at the time when we are witnessing the capitulation of Eastern bloc regimes to the capitalist law of value, attention has waxed with respect to those 'reform' discourses of which Rorty is the liberal academy's prime *animateur*.

While capitalism is becoming more and more like Hal the Computer, and taking on a life of its own, we remain unclear as to whether or not it's programmed to self-terminate or destined to rejuvenate. So far nobody has been able to identify the 'gene' for capitalism in the human species. No doubt that discovery will soon be announced with considerable corporate fanfare. In which case, genetic material from Milton Friedman and Ronald Reagan will likely be carefully sifted from their corpses and put in petri dish displays in a future monument to capitalism—something of a rude counterpoint to Lenin's embalmed flesh in Red Square.

The labor-capital contradiction is today the most fundamental and all-encompassing relation of exploitation—the last of the Russian Matryoshka dolls—in the larger social totality of Western capitalist countries. The more that people are hurt by capitalism, the more frenetically they try to fasten themselves onto the global economic grid. The more that capitalism defeats them, the more they desire to become capitalists. Capitalism no longer requires the tutelage of the state to promote it; it is now self-justificatory. Its internal logic is unassailable. It has insinuated itself into the pores of our psyche; it jumps across our synapses, commanding us to loathe communism and uphold the promise of the American Dream. As Michael Parenti notes, "capitalism is not just an economic system, but a political and cultural one as well, an entire social order" (1997, 133).

Enter philosopher Richard Rorty, a staunch defender of neoliberalism and free-market democracy. Despite the abundance of evidence that capitalist democracies, guided by a neoliberal politics, are condemning the world's laboring class to a life sentence of poverty not only for themselves but for generations to follow, Rorty continues to clings to a Malthusian conviction that the forces that foster equality and political freedom within liberal social democracies far outweigh those that foster inequality and restrict political freedom. True to his staunch and steadfast antiempiricism, Rorty offers no convincing evidence that this is indeed the case.

Rorty the Rebel: The Antiphilosopher's Philosopher

Over the years, Richard Rorty's reputation as one of the most influential philosophers in current literary and philosophical circles has provoked considerable scholarly attention. With an Argus eye on John Dewey's armoire of pragmatist pronouncements on self and society, Rorty's ascentional commentaries on current developments in intellectual and political history are eagerly anticipated by the Left academy and its beleaguered opponents. Rorty's philosophical touchstone has remained his unflinching pragmatism, his fulsome attention to social issues, and his remonstrative opposition to rank-and-file ultra leftists (i.e., Marxists, anarchists).

Richard Rorty is considered one of the most influential, yet controversial, philosophers of our generation. According to John Smith, "Rorty stands out as the most vocal and at the same time the most quixotic" philosophers of the pragmatic school (1992, 5). Rorty has shaken the foundations of the

West's analytic tradition in philosophy so violently that Plato's bones can be heard rattling through the four corners of his cave. In fact, Rorty has participated with delinquent relish in the most urgent moral and political debates of the last twenty years. These debates have ranged from commentaries on contemporary literature to debates on globalization and the future of liberal democracies that are trying to free themselves from the grip of "socially accepted sadism." Rorty can be described as a philosopher-chameleon, an argumentative magician of many rhetorical faces whose epistemological platform sags under the weight of its own contradictory dualism, even as he mightily describes his philosophical view as antidualism. Rorty may also be considered an unrepentant academic outlaw who has sought to destabilize the entire Western tradition of analytic philosophy by accusing it of becoming co-opted by a pragmatically detumescent academic discourse (Von Wright 1992).

We agree with David Hall that it is difficult to criticize Rorty in ways other than participating in an *excursus ad hominem*. This is because Rorty understands that his poetic nominalism is closed to internal critique and that his shifting position on issues is not open to rational analysis. Hall writes that:

> Eschewing historical and rational reconstructions in favor of *geistesgeschichten* permit Rorty, by recourse to a series of strong misreadings, to insulate himself against the standard philosophical criticisms. His quite plausible claim that beliefs change not only rationally, but casually, as well, through recontextualizations stimulated by novel metaphors renders this insulation well-nigh complete. (1994, 169)

Rorty's fellow philosophers are not amused with his immodest claim as the most pristine heir to the Deweyan philosophical and political tradition. In their opinion, Rorty's philosophical pluralism (or what his critics would identify as 'philosophical relativism') has greatly oversimplified Dewey's pragmatism and has discredited pragmatism in general. John Smith (1992) condemns Rorty for reducing the pragmatist tradition to antifoundationalism, engendering what could be called 'post-philosophical culture'. Such reductionism, claims Smith, sorely overlooks contemporary social issues, not to mention all the other disciplinary arenas to which pragmatists have contributed over the course of history: religion, ethics, social and political thought, the history of science, and aesthetics.

Rorty's reinterpretations of the American pragmatist tradition have been criticized by a broad range of pragmatists and philosophers of various stripes (Pihlström 1996). However, much of the criticism against Rorty could be described as disciplinary border skirmishes that concern only the philosophical academic elite. Much of the debate against Rorty from within the philosophy community itself stems from the fact that he has confused things unnecessarily; his detractors continue to hope that he will not make things any more complicated than they already are. That appears to be a terminal case of wishful thinking, given that, throughout his academic career (at least since *Philosophy and the Mirror of Nature*), Rorty has strategically taken cover in counternarratives ranging from the benign to the hostile—while brazenly identifying himself as an antiphilosopher. As Rée puts it: "In the Seventies he curried disfavor with analytic philosophers by accusing them of blinkered vanity; in the Eighties he leveled the same accusation at philosophers in general; and during the Nineties he has extended it to his allies on the cultural left" (1998, 11). While Rorty confesses that he is not amused, it is difficult to fathom the extent to which—if any—he is actually affected by the intemperate comments and irremovable objections of his fellow philosophers. Cryptically, he states:

> I am sometimes told, by critics from both ends of the political spectrum, that my views are so weird as to be merely frivolous. They suspect that I will say anything to get a gasp, that I am just amusing myself by contradicting everybody else. This hurts. (1999, 5)

The Foundations of Rorty's Antifoundationalism

Although Rorty's *Philosophy and the Mirror of Nature* (1979) is accepted as a modern classic in philosophy, many philosophers have failed to understand the logic behind Rorty's work. It could be said that his book has effectively exploded the contemporary frames of analytic philosophy. While *Philosophy and the Mirror of Nature* was not warmly received by most of Rorty's fellow philosophers, its ideas were unflaggingly supported by many social scientists and educational theorists. Its success was, in part, due to the fact that it provided some answers to seemingly eternal problems with respect to the relationship between scientific explanation and humanistic understanding, between the natural sciences and the humanities.

Social and educational scientists took Rorty's basic message seriously: that the researcher's task is not so much to explain social phenomena as to facilitate 'edifying conversations' of various kinds. Rorty states: "I shall use 'edification' to stand for this project of finding new, better, more interesting, more fruitful ways of speaking" (1980, 360). Relying on Gadamer's *Truth and Method*, Rorty draws a dividing line between the desire for edification and the desire for truth. In Rorty's interpretation, the former is more interesting and needed to understand and cope with the world as well as to reach for a decent society in which institutions do not humiliate: "From the educational, as opposed to the epistemological or the technological, point of view, the way things are said is more important than the possession of truths" (Rorty 1980, 359).

Rorty learned two important lessons from the enthusiastic reception of *Philosophy and the Mirror of Nature*. On one hand, it gave him the self-confidence he had previously lacked. On the other hand, it taught him that there was no point in reaching for his youthful dream of a single vision which would keep both the explanation of reality and the fundamentals of justice together. Keeping epistemological and ontological questions separated from moral ones, he has turned more and more towards Darwinism. For Rorty, there is no criterion, either for growth or for education. Requesting such a criterion "is like asking a dinosaur to specify what would make for a good mammal or asking a fourth-century Athenian to propose forms of life for the citizens of a twentieth-century industrial democracy" (Rorty 1999, 120). Thus, education is always a type of experiment, a choice of nature.

As human beings, we can, of course, hope "that the future will be unspecifiably different from, and unspecifiably freer than, the past" (Rorty 1999, 120). And if hoping does not help, we can, claims Rorty, give natural growth a helping hand. When reflecting on the larger-than-life question that will save us from ecological, economic, and social destruction, Rorty—representing us 'Northern gentlefolk'—offers the following meditation on education:

> The only things we know of which might help are top-down techno-bureaucratic initiatives like the cruel Chinese only-one-child-per-family policy (or, literalizing the top-down metaphor and pushing things one monstrous step further, spraying villages from the air with sterilizing chemicals). If there is a happy solution to the dilemma created by the need of very poor Brazilians to find work and the need of the rest of us for the oxygen produced by the Amazonian rain forest, it is going to be the result of some as yet unimagined bureaucratic-technological initiative, not of revolution in 'values'. (Rorty 1999, 227–28)

Although Rorty identifies himself as an antifoundationalist, Rockmore proclaims that "the terms 'antifoundationalism' and 'foundationalism' are not natural, but normative, there is no one way to draw the distinction between them" (1992, 4). We should also note that different types of antifoundationalisms abound. For instance, metaphysical antifoundationalism refers to the denial of ultimate reality or a fundamental kind of being. Epistemological antifoundationalism, for its part, refers to the view that there are no secure foundations for knowledge. Thus, antifoundationalism is not a philosophical miracle invented by Rorty, but one discursive position out of several others (intutionalism and foundationalism) that makes philosophical and methodological discussion possible.

Rockmore reminds us that Rorty did not coin the term "antifoundationalism," although he sometimes seems to credit himself (1992, 3). The debate over the foundations of knowledge, including the antifoundationalist point of view, can be traced as far back as early Greek thought. Furthermore, Rorty's use of the term "antifoundationalism" is uncharacteristic because he limits its use to criticize an analytic approach to epistemology and thus mistakenly equates the analytic approach with a theory of knowledge. Rorty's philosophical worldview is impressively captured in the words of Carey:

> Reality must be repaired for it consistently breaks down: people get lost physically and spiritually, experiments fail, evidence counter to the representation is produced, mental derangement sets in—threats all to our models of and for reality that lead to intense repair work. Finally, we must, often with fear and regret, toss away our authoritative representations of reality and begin to build the world anew. (1975, 16–17)

Rorty is mainly interested in the question which has captured the imagination of philosophers throughout history: how to begin to repair and build the world anew. Rorty's epistemological antifoundationalism casts aside representations as more or less accurate pictures of the world. He also wants to do away with scientific and ideological authorities—but only some of them—in his metaphysical antifoundationalism. Both Jesus and Marx, claims Rorty, should be relegated to the rag-and-bone shop of passé perspectives, while Darwin and Dewey deserve canonization in the liberal think tanks (whose intellectual capital Rorty celebrates). In other words, not everyone is invited to dinner; history's banquet is, for Rorty, reserved for the select few. So much for Rorty's pluralism.

Darwin and Dewey are among those who purposefully follow Rorty's extremely naïve and idealistic methodological imperative: "the habits of relying on persuasion rather than force, of respect for the opinions of colleagues, of curiosity and eagerness for new data and ideas, are the *only* virtues which scientists have" (Rorty 1991, 39). It is as if Rorty did not know that, from time to time, academic life is nasty, messy, not to mention Machiavellian.

Rorty's effort in revitalizing America's national pride parallels his dream of keeping the academy squeaky clean while ignoring the "multicultural" voices from outside. Here Rorty's thinking is internally contradictory and thus self-defeating. On one hand, Rorty proclaims that:

> All the universities worthy of the name have always been centers of social protest. If American universities ever cease to be such centers, they will lose both their self-respect and the respect of the learned world. It is doubtful whether the current critics of the universities who are called 'conservative intellectuals' deserve this description. For intellectuals are supposed to be aware of, and speak to, issues of social justice. (1998, 82)

On the other hand, Rorty wishes to quarantine political movements outside the campus lest they infect academia. According to Rorty, these movements state nothing original; what they do is to "simply add further concreteness to sketches of the good old egalitarian utopia" (Rorty 1999, 235).

However, nagging questions surrounding Rorty's politics remain unanswered: What are the criteria, beyond "growth itself" in Rorty's Dewey-laden vocabulary, to decide who will be inside or outside of the academy? Who, in the end, collects the social and economic capital?

Rorty's Antirevolution

Achieving Our Country (1998) is Rorty's latest—and most—ambitious project in the field of political philosophy. He begins the book with the following conviction: "National pride is to countries what self-respect is to individuals: a necessary condition for self-improvement" (3). He is eager to set forth the essential ingredients of national pride. Rorty begins his narrative by claiming that almost all 'American' stories are written and told "in tones either of self-mockery or of self-disgust" (4). Some cultural heroes are urgently needed to change the current tone. Self-evidently, Rorty wants to be recognized as one of the 'chosen'.

In Rorty's narrative of salvation, there are several key distinctions. The main one is between the "good" old reformist Left and the "bad" new cultural Left. For the old reformists, "American patriotism, redistributionist economics, anti-communism, and Deweyan pragmatism went together easily and naturally" (Rorty 1998, 61). At one time leftist politics was associated with antimilitarism, and with a need for laws and bureaucratic initiatives in order to redistribute the wealth produced by the capitalist mode of production. In Rorty's opinion, those days are long gone. Rorty has a warm heart for the reformist Left. They never doubted "that America was a great, noble, progressive country in which justice would eventually triumph" (59).

On the other hand, there is the current cultural Left, whom Rorty believes is guilty of two cardinal sins. First, the current cultural Left does not participate in the struggle for a just society (Rorty 1998). Even worse, it privileges the theoretical over the practical and is guilty of possessing a 'spectator' point of view. Rorty suggests that the cultural Left needs to grind their fancy theories to a halt and instead try to figure out "what remains of our pride in being Americans" (1998, 92). Rorty criticizes the new cultural Left's search for its one-size-fits-all standard for truth. The Left seek such a standard, Rorty claims, in the spirit of "eschatologies like Hegel's and Marx's, inverted eschatologies like Heidegger's, and the rationalizations of hopelessness like Foucault's and Lacan" in order to "satisfy the urges that theology used to satisfy" (1998, 38).

Although Rorty is more than willing to criticize the radical Left for its Hegelian-Marxian eschatology, his utopian lexicon lacks a social and political agenda and offers little in the way of meaningful commentary on social change. In his recent work, Rorty fails to map out strategies for working towards economic and social justice.

Rorty's philosopher-hero is basically an intellectual historian who perceptively documents ways of living and thinking and how the self-portraits of individuals change in the course of time (Kunelius 1999). Rorty believes that without the speculation of Hegel, Heidegger, Marx, or Dewey, humankind would be much poorer than it is now. On the other hand, this kind of critical storytelling is not something in which Rorty considers himself genuinely competent: "Although I think that historical narrative and utopian speculation are the best sort of background for political deliberation, I have no special expertise at constructing such narratives and speculations" (Rorty 1999, 234).

However, despite the unguarded naivetes and bellicose expostulations of Rorty's political philosophy, his latest texts may well turn out to be, as Rée suggests, "signs of a long-delayed breaking of the ice in socialist politics following the end of the Cold War" (1998, 9). In his latest volumes, Rorty (1998; 1999) offers a standard critique of global capitalism. Yet he ends up supporting the political foundations that make such a capitalism possible.

Rorty on Marxism

Rorty continues to cast a vituperative eye on political theory—Marxism especially—and banishes it from the Holy Liberal Empire where he enjoys a refunctioned mandarin status as the ruling elite's *Chico Malo* "Bad Boy". Rorty trawls superficially through the works of Marx, Lenin, and Trotsky. The cover story in all of this is, of course, that "leftist theory is not necessary." He does not believe leftists need deep theories or cause-and-effect relationships and in this sense indulging in Marxist theory is simply an excuse for not involving oneself in the pressing daily tasks of ameliorating suffering (Melkonian 1999).

It is difficult to take Rorty's criticism of Marxism seriously, especially when he so disdainfully rejects the politics of those who write about the dilemmas surrounding life in a white male Anglo-Saxon heterosexist culture, a culture, by the way, that he feels doesn't exist. The pathetic nature of his 'angry white man on the left position' is deftly summarized by Alan Johnson, who asserts: "His failure to distinguish the spectorial academic left from the more general phenomenon of the new social movements; his tendency to counterpose economics to culture, and trade unions to groups organized on the basis of their identity, his implicit blaming of the desperate state of the left on identity politics, makes for a blunderbuss of a polemic which, as Martin Duberman has pointed out, sends the message 'Shut Up!' to a wider group of people" (2000, 105).

Rorty suggests that since there are no foundations to human knowledge, Marxist concepts such as 'ideology' along with its 'reality-appearance' distinction, is useless. Rorty believes that communities of people understand the social world by using vocabularies. However, Rorty warns us that the vocabularies we use are incommensurable because each community uses different vocabularies.

In addition, Rorty's antiessentialism refutes claims that there exists a human nature or a "true self" since there are no singular traits or characteristics that can be identified as 'human' (Melkonian 1999). He acknowledges that the self is fundamentally provisional; it consists of a constellation of beliefs, attitudes, and values accumulated through the arduous process of socialization. He insists that individuals are socialized to act and behave in certain ways while lacking 'essential' human traits. Rorty also claims that since there is no "true self," concepts such as 'alienation' have little or no utility. He argues that "[t]here is only the shaping of an animal into a human being by a process of socialization, followed (with luck) by the self-individualization and self-creation of that human being through his or her own later revolt against that very same process" (Rorty 1999, 118). It is hardly surprising that Rorty would reject universal human rights since, in his opinion, there are no objective truths. Instead, he proposes that human rights should be based on localized consensual agreements.

Rorty (1999) believes that democracy is a "promising experiment" grounded in a "shared knowledge" of a community of individuals. He believes that theories that have not been substantiated using his pragmatic criteria should be summarily abandoned. As an antiphilosophy philosopher, Rorty (1999) believes that theory should serve practical purposes. He suggests that the reduction of practice into theory (as with Marxism) leads to empty promises. Thus, Rorty (1998) recommends that Marxists abandon their dependence on theory and philosophy, reexamine the work of Whitman, Dewey, and Lincoln, and ask themselves how the country that they prognosticated can be built.

Rorty (1999) draws a bold line between knowledge and hope. He explains that hope is grounded in prediction while knowledge is grounded in experience. Claiming that Marxists' fixation on hope constitutes a philosophy of "false predictions" and "failed prophecies," he likens Marxism more to a religion than to a vehicle for social transformation. In his comparison of the *Communist Manifesto* to the New Testament, Rorty claims that both documents are premised on the hope of creating a better world by claiming to have access to "superior knowledge." Both documents merely possess "inspirational value" for Rorty. We Marxists, by contrast, appreciate the social and analytical content of the *Communist Manifesto*, including Marx's notion that "all that is solid melts into air"—a brilliant rendering of the experience of modernity in our view.

Rorty fails to recognize that most Marxists deny that progress is firmly secured by the iron laws of historical materialism (Sünker 1997). Marxism is not equipped with 'cruise-control' mechanisms that will automatically transport civilization towards a socialist utopia. Marxists, however, hypothesize that under certain social conditions in which the working class succeeds in recognizing itself not only as a class for itself but a class in itself, the working class can transform itself into a revolutionary class capable of ending the exploitative relations of power under capitalism.

Rorty (1998) believes that the struggle for a classless society is neither natural or rational since society is a collection of social experiments lacking a teleological destination. He maintains that the effort in creating a Marxian classless society, although desirable in itself, remains only a detached and whimsical notion since there exists no empirical evidence supporting it. It comes as no surprise when Rorty recommends that the "Left vs. liberal" distinction be abandoned since the old Left (meaning classical Marxists) now constitute the reformist Left. In the end, Rorty's pragmatic politics remains firmly in support of social reformism, since social revolution is no longer a viable option for him.

Finally, Rorty (1998) distinguishes between "spectatorship" and "agency" and identifies Marxists as 'spectators' that have merely criticized and not transformed what is wrong with America. Rorty proposes that the Marxists transform themselves to "agents" by participating in a constructive political discourse: in short, a pragmatic Rortyan-style politics.

A Marxist Critique of Rorty's Politics

Rorty's resilient attempt to bury Marxism has unwittingly provided the grounds for rejecting his own liberal democratic politics. A recent comment by Michael Burawoy is apposite when he warns: "Before hastening to the funeral parlor, one should remember that although Marxism may have been a specter that haunted the twentieth century, by the same token it also inspired some of the century's greatest and most creative thinking—for and against Marxism—in philosophy, history, economics, and politics, not to mention sociology. Intellectuals who celebrate the end of Marxism may be digging their own graves, too" (2000, 151). Marx's ghost, hovering high above its grave site in London, continues to observe crimes routinely committed against millions of innocent men, women, and children on behalf of a New World Order with the United States at the helm.

The Nature of Human Nature

A Marxist approach to the question of human nature has some points in common with Rorty and some that are in bold distinction. Rorty believes that human nature is a myth, that it is really a process of socialization devoid of distinguishing characteristics that can be identified as singularly 'human'. Marxists believe that human nature is neither fixed nor predetermined. They reject the claims of Social Darwinists that human nature is biologically determined and the metaphysical position that human existence depends on some form of spiritual essence. Marxists fundamentally posit a dialectical relation between biology and human agency. We agree with C. J. Arthur who asserts: "There is . . . a dialectically conceived relation between his [sic] nature as determined by the conditions of his life, and the practical transformations of those conditions. The link between the two is labor" (1995, 21).

We espouse a Marxian notion of human nature that is grounded within the social relations of production (Geras, 1983). In our view, human beings share a set of common traits such as the ability to produce their means of subsistence. In his *Philosophical Manuscripts*, Marx makes a case in support of human nature by writing that: "A being which does not have its nature outside of itself is not a natural being and does not play no part in the system of nature. A being which has no object outside itself is not an objective being. A being which is not itself an object for a third being has no being for its object, i.e. it has no objective relationships and its existence is not objective" (1975, 390).

Marx views human nature processually, as a type of flux shaped by human beings acting externally on the world at the same time as it shapes human beings. Human needs are decidedly not transhistorical; rather, they are relative insofar as they are shaped by social forces in different ways at different historical moments. Rorty seems to accept this position when he says that people are "children of their time and place, without any significant metaphysical or biological limits on their plasticity" (cited in Sayers 1998, 150). Yet he makes the gross claim that there is no such thing as human nature. True, one cannot step outside of the social, or beyond socialization. Nevertheless, it is important to understand the dynamic relation between the social and the biological, otherwise one is left with the untenable notion that human beings exist as some kind of tabula rasa. We engage in productive activity in order to satisfy our needs, but as historical beings we create new needs in the process. The social relations out of which these needs are created are shaped by the development of new forms of productive activity and productive powers.

We defend the social and historical character of human nature against Rorty's antiessentialism. We need to oppose the false antimony he postulates between the social and human nature. Human will and desire are still intertwined biosocially, even if the specific character of social life is determined in the last instance by the development of the level of productive forces.

As Marxist educators, we believe that Rorty's antifoundational views are inherently flawed and misleading. In the absence of universal principles, there is no injustice, since there would be a multitude of definitions of justice and injustice by different communities (Geras 1995). Thus, an absence of an agreement on universal human rights leans towards social, cultural, and political relativism. We maintain that without any form of objectivity, anything goes.

Rorty's invitation for celebrating the achievements of Western liberal democracies is exceptionally plagued with problems. Referring to liberal democracy in the United States, Rorty proudly claims that it "slowly and painfully, threw off a foreign yoke, freed its slaves, enfranchised its women, restrained Robber Barons and licensed its trade unions, liberalized its religious practices, broadened its religious and moral tolerance" (1999, 121). However, Rorty suffers from classic Reaganesque amnesia, leaving unmolested dominant arrangements of power and privilege. He appears to have forgotten that the robber barons of yesterday have now been replaced by the global carpetbaggers of today; that white supremacy is alive and well throughout the United States; and that violence against women, gays, and lesbians remains widespread (particularly in the military). One of the more glaring lacunae in Rorty's corpus of works is his failure to link racism to wider capitalist social relations, those very social relations that he feels have liberated the United States from tyranny and hatred. In contrast to Rorty's decapitation of racism from political economy, Marxists stress its indissoluble link. Parenti writes:

> Marxists further maintain that racism involves not just personal attitude but institutional structure and systematic power. They point out that racist organizations and sentiments are often propagated by well-financed reactionary forces seeking to divide the working populace against itself, fracturing it into antagonistic ethnic enclaves. (1997, 133–34)

We agree with David Sidorsky (2000) who argues that Rorty fails to criticize right-wing politics primarily by focusing on the retreat of the Left. While Rorty claims that Marxists have failed to fulfil their dreams of a classless society, he neglects to discuss the emergence of right-wing and conservative politics in the 1980s and 1990s which took the offensive by attacking welfare programs, affirmative action, and bilingual education. Rorty fails to adequately distinguish between right-wing and left-wing politics. While the Right has avidly defended the interests of the private sector and transnational corporations, Marxists, on the other hand, have supported working-class struggles. Finally, Sidorsky points out that Rorty fails to propose an alternative economic model to neoliberalism. In short, Rorty's pragmatism is actually little more than pluralism in disguise: a tolerance of diverse opinions and views that we believe signals an ongoing *individualisierangsprozess.*

We believe that Rorty's pragmatism retains its class character as a liberal extension of bourgeois ideology. Rorty's biased advocacy of democratic consensus implies that the democratization of capitalism remains a possibility. He claims that regardless of class antagonisms and class interests, communities of people divided along racial, gendered, and class lines can work side by side in an ever-expanding democracy.

However, we find that advancing democratic ideals, while at the same time ignoring class interests, amount to little more than a reactionary form of populism. Rorty's pragmatism glaringly sidesteps issues related to class, the exploitation of labor, and capital. He fails to address with either verve or vision the politics of property relations, the globalization of capital, neoliberalism and the new global imperialism, and the class character of American society.

As a consequence, he fails to recognize that the inhuman face of socialism and the human face of capitalism are the obverse of each other.

We wonder what Rorty thinks of the recent revelations—first by the European press followed by the North American press—that PSYOPS (Psychological Operations) specialists from the U.S. Army had worked as interns at CNN's Atlanta news headquarters and at National Public Radio. PSYOPS is a division of the U.S. Army that has been created to develop propaganda that lowers the morale of 'enemy forces' and is designed to "build support among the civil population" in other countries for U.S. objectives (Ackerman 2000, 1). Its illegal domestic operations were first exposed during the Iran-Contra scandal when the now defunct Office of Public Diplomacy (formerly part of the National Security Council) was operated by the 4th Army PSYOPS Group stationed at Fort Bragg. This group—that successfully demonized Nicaragua's Sandinista government—is the same group that later produced the CNN and NPR interns. A high-ranking PSYOPS officer recently "called for greater cooperation between the armed forces and media giants" (Ackerman 2000, 1). Is this an example of Rorty's liberal democracy in action?

Rorty has replaced God with "democratic consensus," thereby substituting good, old-fashioned, issues-oriented politics for the scholarly exegesis of Marx, Engels, Trotsky, Lukacs, and Lenin. In other words, he wants to banish the church in favor of tobacco-chewing veranda conversations for ragtag members of the polis, and sherry-sipping, cigar-puffing dialogue among the literati.

Rorty evades debating political economy not only by failing to undress his own bourgeois assumptions about capital, but also by barricading himself within the very impenetrable walls of academic philosophy that he himself has criticized. Were we to take Rorty's pragmatism seriously, we would have to question whether it provides the best explanatory framework not only for understanding neoliberalism, but also for strategically reducing the immense social, economic, and political inequalities under global capitalism. We believe that Rorty's pragmatism fails to provide a convincing argument against the widening disparities between the rich and the poor.

Finally, we disagree with Rorty's claim that "Marxism was not only a catastrophe for all the countries in which Marxists took power, but a disaster for the reformist Left in all countries in which they did not" (1998, 41). Although socialism has been temporarily set back in the former Soviet Union and Eastern European socialist countries, these countries succeeded in making some substantial strides towards social and economic equality. In addition, Rorty cannot simply ignore achievements made by socialist Cuba during the last forty years, especially in the areas of health care, literacy, and employment. The struggle for socialism is far from over. In fact, we may be witnessing a new beginning.

Our position is grounded in the premise that surplus extraction within capitalist exchange practices are all-pervasive within capitalist economies and mediate the production of the constitutive structures of the "lifeworld" in profound and politically defining ways. It is only by recognizing the all-pervasive influence of capitalist exchange and by culturally producing catalytic agency through subjectivities able and willing to work collectively in order to resist and transform capitalist accumulation, that a pedagogy of liberation can be formed. Terry Eagleton argues that "it is possible for certain forms of social life to drive a wedge between these two dimensions of the self, individual and communal, and this, in effect, is what the young Marx means by *alienation*" (1999, 27). Here Marx is referring to a particularly profound form of alienation, especially when you consider the ontological position taken by Marx on the issue of the productive powers and capacities that human beings possess—powers and capacities that enable them to transform the world. Eagleton summarizes Marx's position thus: "My product is my existence for the other, and presupposes the other's existence for me" (1999, 27).

Our naturally productive species-being is constrained by the "minority of the opulent" who own and control the means of production so that the production of the masses becomes instrumental to the self-development of the elite capitalist class. We do not simply mean "production" in the economic sense, but also in the cultural/symbolic sense. This is consistent with Marx's position on the unfolding of an individual's productive powers. According to Eagleton:

> We are free when, like artists, we produce without the goad of physical necessity; and it is this nature which for Marx is the essence of all individuals. In developing my own individual personality through fashioning a world, I am also realizing what it is that I have most deeply in common with others, so that individual and species being are ultimately one. My product is my existence for the other, and presupposes the other's existence for me. This for Marx is an ontological truth. (1999, 97)

We do not have time to rehearse this notion of self-development except by way of brief description. According to David Bernans, class exploitation within capitalist societies occupies a strategic centrality in organizing those very activities that make us human. Bernans follows Volosinov in maintaining that speech genres themselves are determined by production relations and sociopolitical order. This is an important assertion especially in view of the fact that the market system is being applied to democracy itself, where democracy is seen as occurring at the sites that market intervention occurs the least, where abstract law overrides concrete determinations and abstracts real existence into nothingness, where distributive principles overrule concrete struggles for new freedoms, where a successful democracy is defined in terms of its ability to become self-legitimating and self-justificatory, where the market is permitted to remain impersonal and omnipresent and is encouraged and facilitated in its efforts to totalize the field of social relations in which it has become a central force (McMurtry 1998). Speech genres and language games facilitate the interdictions and injunctions of the Big Other so that their authorial voice remains invisible so that interdictions against regulating the 'natural' and 'free' market seem freestanding (McMurtry 1998; 1999).

Bernans is correct in maintaining that surplus extraction occurs through processes that are dialogical and simultaneously economic, political, and ideological. We agree with him that these are not ontologically privileged processes but rather become central in the way that they organize the constitutive processes of everyday life. In other words, class struggle is also a language game, perhaps the most fundamental game in town. It is not just a piece in an autonomous chain of equivalence but rather a language game that organizes all the other language games. All language games are accented by class power. Bernans makes the important point that, by virtue of their organizing function, dialogical processes of surplus extraction have a certain primacy with respect to other forms of social interaction. As part of the constitutive activities that make up social life, the dialogical processes of surplus extraction factor forcefully and foundationally. Not only are they central in organizing other dialogical forms, but they also play a major part in imposing material limitations on human social interaction. In fact, Bernans argues that because the dialogical processes of surplus extraction organize speakers and addressees in particular ways, a radical transformation of all social hierarchies (i.e., those of race, class, gender, sexuality) demands the continual affirmation of a working-class struggle against capital (1999, 30). Following Volosinov, Bernans maintains that the sign becomes the very arena of class struggle because the continual accumulation of capital can only continue through an exchange that favors one partner while the other is reduced to "mere survival." Of course, capital accumulation is also functionally integrated with nonclass hierarchies such as racism and sexism since it is obvious that white male workers derive material benefits from sexist and racist exploitation even while they are exploited themselves. It is at this point that we welcome Carspecken's materialist understanding of cultural production that he derived from the work of Paul Willis (1977). For Carspecken, cultural production is constitutive of praxis in that it serves as both the medium and the outcome of action and constitutes the "action conditions" or "structures" for self-production through work. Praxis also includes the social-communicative preconditions for the emergence of a self and the motivational structures that are created along with these preconditions.

Bradley Macdonald looks to the practices of the self from the perspective of a historical materialist conception of desire. According to Macdonald's prescient observations, Marx relates desire to "the totality of ways in which sensuous beings attempt to engage and objectify their world, in the process aspiring towards plenitude and singularity" (1999, 32). Such desires and pleasures are diverted from their full potential because of seemingly insuperable constraints of diverse kinds resulting from capital accumulation. As Macdonald puts it, desire exists as an ontological horizon but is taken up in specific historical formations; its ontology does not exist outside of history but is wrapped up in it through its embodiment in the sensuous materiality and potentialities of pain and joy, suffering and well-being.

As Sayers notes, there exists a dialectic of needs and productive powers; each develops in relation to each other (1998, 152). Capitalism is to be condemned not just for failing to satisfy universal biological needs but the needs that it itself has created (134). Needs—be they biological or psychological—are always modified by certain social conditions. Needs are always social—even the need for food—because satisfaction and the quest for satisfaction take on specific cultural, historical, and social forms within certain contexts. Socially modified needs are the only needs that exist concretely—the rest, notes Sayers, are abstractions. True needs are those that are necessary for a minimum standard of social life and happiness. But it would be a mistake to designate all new needs as 'false' because, as our powers and capacities change, as they develop in and through history, new needs and desires emerge. Human potentialities are not unchanging. As Sayers notes, even alienation, in certain contexts, can help to increase self-development and lead to a new stage of individuation (137). Thus, capitalism has both a positive and a negative aspect to it. In the movement of historical reality, we look beyond capitalism, and indeed, beyond capital itself.

We want to be clear here that we are not trying to limit or reverse economic development but to control such developments in the interests of workers. We object to the fact that the human potentialities under capitalism can be realized only by a small number of the world population. Our conception of economic justice is not based on transhistorical principles that are externally self-evident or to a universal standard of reason. Justice, admittedly, is always held hostage to lived historical experience. Justice cannot be realized in relation to the logic of ideas themselves, but only in terms of the social formations that give rise to these ideas and that emerge historically out of human struggle. We are arguing for the formation of what we call 'revolutionary subjectivity' that works the fissures of the self, that connects across the private spaces of splintered political agency and the public spaces of collective struggle.

We believe that the fact that we are not fully transparent to ourselves suggests that we become conscious of our own embeddedness in the theoretical assumptions that guide our everyday praxis. We do this as a means of providing a better guide in our attempts to make warrantable choices in how we act in, on, and through the world. We do this as a way of identifying and surmounting the historical continuities and discontinuities that constrain our efforts at promoting social justice. This runs counter to Rorty's position that there exists no theoretical defense for one's actions other than how they relate to existing political and moral traditions of public life. In the final analysis, Rorty appears to be supporting Nietzsche's 'Eternal Recurrence of the Same' when he advocates for a form of liberalism that returns the same set of hierarchical discourses and social practices—only shrouded by the empty promise of an ever-renewed 'Otherness'. It is in this sense that Rorty lapses into a fibrillating hopelessness. Alan Johnson writes that "when the tensions in his thought—between his acceptance of the free market and his revolt against its results, his hatred of the bosses and his despair about the workers, his attention to protectionism and its honor at its implications—overwhelm Rorty, he slips into hopelessness" (2000, 115).

While he accuses Marxists of being part of a state religion, denigrates the history of social movements, and vehemently exercises contempt of Marxist leaders such as Lenin for, among other things, his stress on political analysis, Rorty views class struggle itself as simply a drama orchestrated by leftists who want to feel they are part of some world-historical drama. Rorty believes that people, regardless of their class interests, can work together for the common welfare, and his unrestricted relativism and particularism denies the importance of any general laws of development. Rorty is disinclined to relegate class to an important part of his project, nor does he pay attention to the means by which the forces of production (means of production and human labor), and their level of development, impact social, cultural, and institutional formations. Instead, he takes an unreserved stance in protecting bourgeois liberal interests. Melkonian (1999) notes that Rorty "cannot accommodate the suggestion that liberal institutions be recast within the context of working-class state power . . . he is committed . . . to the institutions of large market economies." "Large market economies," he believes, constitute the "economic determinants" of liberal democracies (1999, 174).

In the face of Rorty's reformist and redistributionist politics and his eschewal of ontologies of each and every stripe, we support an unblushingly Marxist ontology, grounded in a scientific understanding of the social totality, a realistic analysis of capitalist society, and the view that the interests between labor and capital are essentially incompatible.

Rorty finds the acme of liberal autonomy in a box of metaphors to be used in the process of self-fashioning; how this academic game of performative Scrabble helps campesinos craft a collective agency capable of preventing their skulls from being crushed under the jackboots of paramilitary death squads is quite another matter. Rorty's project of metaphoric self-fashioning does little to address the fact that liberal democracies have been engaged since their inception in degrading acts of imperialist violence and oppression.

Rorty's dream of self-creation through recursively articulated descriptions and redescriptions set against the conventions of mainstream social discourse turns on his belief that socialization will be superceded by edification and an opportunity to privately redescribe oneself at will. In our view, such an antidialectical and antidialogical approach to knowledge is delusional. His sheltered and favored position in the academy—what Johnson refers to as "a bold-as-brass elitism" (2000, 114)—appears to have erected a partition between him and the masses that has disabled his ability to experience the contradictions inherent in the capitalist enterprise itself. If we are seeking guardians of democracy in this current era of late capitalism, then it is less likely that we will find them in university seminar rooms and more likely that they will be found among the struggling masses in the streets.

While Rorty may see himself as luxurious champion of the Left—as he urges academic leftists to embrace pluralism, move beyond their bovine leftism as immaculate spectators in the safe precincts of the seminar room where the culture wars are fought, and give up their pretentious claims to objectivity and truth—we see him caught in an assiduous avoidance of substantive engagements with political economy in favor of grazing in the lush fields of literary conceit, or musing with fellow cognoscenti along the philosopher's ivy-covered walkway. And while his call for homelessness studies and economic redistribution in *Achieving Our Country* (1998) is a step in the right direction, we believe that his larger struggle—to redirect professional irony to the cause of public activism as 'Americans' rather than as human beings— is misguided. We believe the main game is to rethink the nature of capital as a social relation within the larger capital-labor antagonism.

In mounting his oppositional politics, Rorty appears to bear his opponents little open rancor. Why should he? His is comfortably ensconced in the salons of the bourgeois academy where he thrives capriciously on the succulence of the discourses of consensus and manipulates his nihilism as an alibi for a groundless defense of human freedom. David Hall writes that: "Like Nietzsche, Rorty is a Benign Nihilist. And that nihilism expresses itself directly in Rorty's provincialism, ethnocentrism, and heroism. It also shapes his attitudes towards poetry and prophecy—issues central to his narrativist posture" (1994, 170).

Rorty's notion of the decentered subject that emerges from his expostulations about antifoundationalism, in our view, corresponds nicely with the desiring subject produced by capitalism. His antifoundationalist agent itself remains embedded in an economic matrix. In denying alternative possibilities of subject-formation in opposition to capitalism, he participates in a reconditioning of the subject so that it becomes functionally advantageous for the reproduction of the capitalist class. In fact, he does more than this; he instaurates a new elitism, a neoaristocratic wing of the academy that exhibits pretenses towards social transformation yet leaves unmolested current capitalist relations of exploitation. Rorty's procapitalist and neoliberal politics offers little more than a mild countervailing force to the conservative mainstream and a conceptual dalliance with Left liberalism. As such it enfeebles anticapitalist struggle and pauperizes the educational Left. Melkonian (1999) notes that Rorty

> cannot accommodate the suggestion that liberal institutions be recast within the context of working-class state power . . . [because] he is committed not merely to . . . several liberal institutions . . . but also to "the institutions of large market economies." "Large market economies," he believes, constitute the "economic determinants" of liberal democracies: The North Atlantic has achieved its measure of decency and equality by relying on "a free market in capital and on compromises between pressure groups." In this respect, he is once again backing away from Dewey's New Liberalism to a position closer to that of the English classical liberals who associated liberty with laissez-faire economic policies. (143)

As an effete advocate of Left reformism, a pragmatist panjandrum whose raised fist carries inside of it the condensed power of Walt Whitman and John Dewey, Rorty stumbles into an enfeebling vortex of relativism. We need more than Rorty's white-knuckled promise for a petit-bourgeois revitalization of democracy but rather the permanent revolution of which Trotsky spoke. In this respect, the words of Geoff Waite are apposite:

world communism has always come into being at moments of counterrevolution and defeat (as exemplified by the USSR and by Gramsci's Italy of the early twenties). Born in defeat, communism never guarantees victory, only ongoing struggle. As such, it may be the most realistic counter-movement against Capital Triumphant in postcontemporary times. (1996, 3)

Conclusion: The Renewed Importance of Marx

Out of the bloody tumult of capitalist social relations and the wounds of political disappointment, Marxism has cancelled democracy's promissory note, replacing it with the demand that it effect a political breach with capitalism and a move towards socialism. Yet most Americans recoil at the mere mental touch of Marx, giving Marxism little compass today. As the United States waves its wand of instant rebuttal, capitalism is embraced, sustaining a promise of democracy that entails its denial. As Marxism attempts to put some spine into the politics of the Left, postmodernists and conservatives alike decry its stress on class struggle. The effect of such a denunciation advances a conciliatory spirit towards the established order and acts in unreflective accord with ruling-class interests. According to Aijaz Ahmad:

> Theoretically, the *possibility* of socialism arises from within the contradictions of capitalism. Morally, opposition to capitalism is its own justification since capitalism is poisoning human survival itself, let alone human happiness. In the present circumstances, the resolve to overturn this globally dominant system does not indeed involve what Ernest Bloch once called 'utopian surplus'; but the Utopian aspect of the communist imagination need not translate itself into 'the messianic'. (1999, 95)

We need to rethink the nature of capital as a social form; we need to transform both the mediatory forms (property relations and class formations) and their essential determinants. The abolition of private property is not an end in itself but rather a step towards the transformation of the labor process. It is fruitless to call for the abolition of private property without the abolition of the value-form of labor. Marx's underlying dialectic of negativity makes this clear. The major issue is not the abolition of private property but to abolish capital itself, through the creation of freely associated labor (Hudis 2000). The first negation is the negation of the external forms (private property). The negation of the negation that follows is the negation of external barriers to self-movement towards a transcendence of alienation. The second negation is absolute negativity or self-reflected negativity that pervades the positive transcendence of alienation, and positive humanism beginning from itself (Hudis 2000). This is what brings about a permanent revolution.

One promising sign on the horizon is that the political fade-out of Marx has been temporary; the old bearded devil is coming back with a vengeance, having been summoned by those who both recognize and rage against the fact that "the inexorable march of privatization [is] leading England (and a good part of the Western world) forward to the social hierarchy of the 17th century" (Morris 2000, 67).

While Marx might not have anticipated the specific trajectory capitalism would take at this particular moment in history, his work was most certainly premonitory of the current crisis of capitalism. What is so significant about Marx's analysis is that it stresses above all the underlying systemic dynamics of capitalism in all of its capillary detail. No doubt Marx would have recognized the current crisis of capitalism as implicated in the global capitalist economy as a whole, inextricably tied to the laws of motion of capital and the ways in which capital and wage-labor reproduces itself (McNally 1999). While it fails to offer ready-to-wear strategies for social struggle in the arena of critical education, Marxist theory is congruent with left multiculturalists and bilingual educators who recognize the relationship between the exploitation of human labor and systems of classification and mythologies linked to the demonization of certain groups on the basis of race, ethnicity, phenotype, etc. (McLaren 1997). It is also helpful in efforts by multiculturalists to tease out the labyrinthine complexities that scaffold race, class, gender, and sexual antagonisms and their co-constitutivity (McLaren and Farahmandpur 1999b).

Even in moments of defeat, Marxism has never ceased undermining capitalism's unrelenting logic of profiteerism, with unparalleled tenacity, revitalizing itself in the space of its own isolation, drawing nourishment from its own marginalization and abandonment. Marxists acknowledge that the best substitute for not having "pragmatic" solutions to the pressing problems of our planet is to acquire a deep understanding and intimate and robust relationship with the questions while developing an informed grasp of the frame in which such questions are asked.

Critical pedagogy cries out for a critical Marxist consciousness, one that moves beyond a scenario where Rorty's Athenian polis meets redistributive socialism. The critical pedagogy that we seek is driven more by a larger project of socialist democracy linked to the abolition of capital and to revolutionary movements than to the uncorked effervescence of Rorty's Jacuzzi populism (McLaren and Farahmandpur 2000; 1999a; 1999b). We believe that philosophy can play a part in the project of critical pedagogy. We are joined in solidarity with Adorno when he writes that:

The only philosophy which can be responsibly practiced in face of despair is the attempt to contemplate all things as they would present themselves from the standpoint of redemption: all else is reconstruction, mere technique. (1951, 247)

Note

For a description of what distinguishes our approach to critical pedagogy from its more liberal, domesticated variants, see Peter McLaren (2000), *Che Guevara, Paulo Freire, and the pedagogy of revolution*. Boulder, Colo.: Rowman & Littlefield.

Bibliography

Ackerman, S. (2000, June) PSYOPS in the newsroom. EXTRA! *Update*, 1.

Adorno, T. (1951) *Minima Moralia*. London: Verso.

Ahmad, A. (1999) Reconciling Derrida: 'Spectres of Marx' and deconstructive politics. In M. Sprinker (ed.), *Ghostly demarcations: A symposium on Jacques Derrida's Specters of Marx* (88–109). London: Verso.

Arthur, C. J. (ed.) (1995) Introduction. *The German Ideology*. New York: International Publishers.

Bernans, D. (1999) Historical materialism and ordinary language: Grammatical peculiarities of the class struggle "language game." *Rethinking Marxism* 11(2), 18–37.

Burawoy, M. (2000) Marxism after Communism. *Theory and Society* 29(2), 151–174.

Carey, J. (1975) A cultural approach to communication. *Communication* 2 (1), 1–22.

Carspecken, (1999) *Four scenes for posing the question of meaning and other explorations in critical philosophy and critical methodology*. New York: Peter Lang.

Eagleton, T. (1999) *Marx*. New York: Routledge.

Feyerabend, P. (1993) *Against method*. Third Edition. London: Verso.

Geras, N. (1983) *Marx and human nature: refutation of a legend*. London: Verso.

———. (1995) *Solidarity in the conversation of humankind: The ungroundable liberalism of Richard Rorty*. London: Verso.

Hall, D. L. (1994) *Richard Rorty: Prophet and poet of the new pragmatism*. Albany: State University of New York Press.

Hudis, P. (2000) The dialectical structure of Marx's concept of 'revolution in permanence'. *Capital and Class* 70, 127–43.

Johnson, A. (2000) The politics of Richard Rorty. *New Politics* 8(1), 103–21.

Kunelius, R. (1999) Philosophy today: waiting for the revolution. Richard Rorty's interview. niin & näin—*Finnish Philosophical Journal* 6(2), 22–27. (Original in Finnish.)

MacDonald, B. (1999) Marx and the figure of desire. *Rethinking Marxism* 11(4), 21–37.

Marx, K. (1975) *Early writings* (R. Livingstone and G. Benton, trans.). New York: Vintage Books.

McLaren, P. and R. Farahmandpur. (1999a) Critical pedagogy, postmodernism, and the retreat from class: Towards a contraband pedagogy. *Theoria* 93, 83–115.

———. (1999b) Critical multiculturalism and globalization: Some implications for a politics of resistance. *Journal of Curriculum Theorizing* 15(3), 27–46.

———. (2000) Reconsidering Marx in Post-Marxist Times: A Requiem for Postmodernism? *Educational Researcher*, 29(3), 25–33.

McLaren, P. (2000) *Che Guevara, Paulo Freire, and the pedagogy of revolution.* Boulder, Colo.: Rowman & Littlefield.

McMurtry, J. (1998) *Unequal freedoms: The global market as an ethical system.* West Hartford, Conn.: Kumarian.

———. (1999) *The cancer stage of capitalism.* London: Pluto Press.

McNally, D. (1999) The present as history: Thoughts on capitalism at the Millennium. *Monthly Review* 51(3), 135–45.

Melkonian, M. (1999). *Richard Rorty's politics: Liberalism at the end of the American century.* New York: Humanity Books.

Morris, S. L. (2000) Boys R Us. *LA Weekly.* March 17–23, 67.

Parenti, M. (1997) *Blackshirts and Reds: Rational fascism and the overthrow of communism.* San Francisco: City Lights.

Pihlström, S. (1996) Structuring the world: The issue of realism and the nature of ontological problems in classical and contemporary pragmatism. *Acta Philosophica Fennica* 59. Helsinki: The Philosophical Society of Finland.

Rée, J. (1998) Strenuous unbelief. *London Review of Books* (20), 7–11.

Rockmore, T. (1992) Introduction. In *Antifoundationalism old and new.* T. Rockmore and B. Singer, eds., 1–12. Philadelphia: Temple University Press.

Rorty, R. (1980) *Philosophy and the mirror of nature.* Princeton N.J.: Princeton University Press.

———. (1989) *Contingency, irony, and solidarity.* Cambridge: Cambridge University Press.

———. (1991) *Objectivity, relativism, and truth.* Philosophical papers, vol. 1. Cambridge: Cambridge University Press.

———. (1998) *Achieving our country: Leftist thought in the twentieth-century America.* Cambridge, Mass.: Harvard University Press.

———. (1999) *Philosophy and social hope.* London: Penguin Books.

Sayers, S. (1998) *Marxism and human nature.* London: Routledge.

Sidorsky, D. (2000) Does the left have the power to speak? *Partisan Review* 67(1), 122–30.

Smith, J. (1992) *America's philosophical vision.* Chicago: University of Chicago Press.

Sünker, H. (1997) Heydorn's bildungs theory and content as social analysis. In R. F. Farnen and H. Sünker, eds., *The politics, sociology, and economics of education: Interdisciplinary and comparative perspectives,* (113–28). New York: St. Martin's Press.

von Wright, G. H. (1992) *The Owl of Minerva.* Keuruu: Otava. (Original in Finnish.)

Waite, G. (1996) *Nietzsche's corpse/e: Aesthetics, politics, prophesy, or, the spectacular technoculture of everyday life.* Durham: Duke University Press.

Willis, P. (1977) *Learning to labor: How working class kids get working class jobs.* Westmead, U.K.: Gower.

CHAPTER EIGHT

Richard Rorty and the End of Philosophy of Education

Kenneth Wain

Provocations

Some years back, replying to earlier articles by Rene Arcilla (1990) and Carol Nicholson (1989) that were positive about the potential of his philosophy to open new avenues in education, Richard Rorty made a statement that startled me at the time. Namely, that philosophy has nothing to say to education just as it has nothing to say to politics (Rorty 1990a, 41). This is not the first time I have referred to this piece of writing, having already done so previously in an article I wrote about Rorty and education. There I tried to show that his claim to be a follower of Dewey in his thinking about philosophy, politics, and education failed to hold up to critical examination no matter how often he repeated it (Wain 1995). Since then I have often thought of responding to his provocation as one who has for many years regarded himself as a philosopher engaged with education even though I have always found it awkward to describe myself as a philosopher of education. More seriously, one who has taught student teachers a subject named philosophy of education in their B.Ed. course at the University of Malta. On the grounds of this statement Rorty himself denied, against what Arcilla and Nicholson had suggested, that his philosophy could be made any relevant use of in tackling issues in education. Elsewhere he went even further describing the intrusion of philosophy in education and politics not just as irrelevant but as downright harmful to both enterprises also, clouding practical issues and concerns and rendering them completely intractable. In "Education without Dogma" (Rorty 1990b) he referred to what he described as the major issue dividing the political Right and Left on education for years, often escalating, he said, into a bitter quarrel between them, over the proper relationship between 'truth' and 'freedom' or enculturation and individuation, turning a perfectly straightforward matter resolvable through concrete politics into a protracted and unfruitful philosophical polemic about the 'true nature' and the 'true interests' of the learner. Such issues, he argued in the article, are not resolved through doing philosophy better but through down-to-earth, practical bargaining between the contesting parties. In this particular case all that was required was a practical political compromise between the two sides. This, he contended, would quickly follow were they to realize that the 'truth' (or enculturation) is better served in 'lower' education or schooling, while 'freedom' (or individuation) should be the province of nonvocational 'higher' education at the university in the form of 'edification'. And that the quarrel between them is, therefore, pointless.

There is, of course, a quick way of reacting to these declarations, namely, by dismissing them as all part of the postmodernist fun and games and not to be taken seriously. Except that Rorty himself spent a substantial part of the same article expressing his distaste for 'postmodernism', dismissing Lyotard's *The Postmodern Condition* (1979) as "a collection of dubious *obiter dicta* about recent scientific and technological changes" (1990a, 43), and criticizing the French 'postmodernists' in general for writing in "terms infected by what seems to me a repellent Parisian world-weariness and hopelessness, as well as with leftover Marxist cynicism about gradual, non-revolutionary reform" (1990a, 44), and that I have a great deal of respect for him as a philosopher besides. Statements of this kind suggest that, like a lot of people, *he* doesn't take 'postmodernism' very seriously himself. But this would be a too hasty conclusion also. His relationship with 'postmodernism' and the French 'postmodernists' is not so straightforward. As is well known, it was not always the case that he rejected 'postmodernism' so dismissively and categorically. Indeed there was a time when he was describing himself as a 'liberal bourgeois postmodernist' (Rorty 1983). He obviously doesn't do so anymore, and there are several places and occasions where he has explained this retraction since. His fundamental bone of contention with Derrida, and more especially with Foucault (he seems more and more to have ignored Lyotard over the years), as the statement I quoted earlier indicates, is political. He came to perceive, after a number of his critics who featured in *Reading Rorty* (1990) and elsewhere had pointed out to him, that being 'postmodernist' is politically incompatible with being liberal.

Indeed, though in his 'reply' to Arcilla and Nicholson Rorty showed himself to be out of sympathy with practically every other aspect of his characterization of the contemporary 'postmodern' world (especially that it is in some sort of crisis), he supported Lyotard's view that people today have grown skeptical toward the grand narratives of progress in science and of emancipation in politics that marked the project of modernity and that Lyotard defined as postmodern (1990a, 43), and acknowledged his support for a "project of postmodernism" if it is simply intended as "a new name" for the much milder "idea of breaking the crust of convention and thereby helping the weak against the strong," found in Dewey already (1990a, 44). His attitude towards the French 'postmodernists' is perfectly summarized in "Trotsky and the Wild Orchids" (1992) and in the reply to Arcilla and Nicholson itself where he describes them as "philosophically right though politically silly" (1990a, 43). An attitude echoed by others who are similarly sympathetic to the philosophical work of Derrida, Foucault, and the writers who have been lumped under this name but regard their politics as, at best, incoherent, at worst dangerous. I am putting the word 'postmodernism' in scare quotes because I am unhappy myself with referring to Lyotard, Derrida, and Foucault as 'postmodernists' in any way other than that in which Rorty acknowledges himself to be a 'postmodernist'. Namely, as one sensitive to the problem with sustaining the modernist project and the modernist vocabulary of the Enlightenment in our times. Otherwise, I am happier referring to their philosophy as poststructuralist, and sustaining the differences between them in the way they approach politics (a difference Rorty himself acknowledges in his later writing). The reason why I take Rorty's conclusions about philosophy and education so seriously is because I think that poststructuralism is philosophically right also. What I shall show in this chapter is that his remark that there is no more a relationship between philosophy and education than there is between philosophy and politics is a consequence of his general rejection of the politics of the French poststructuralists. And of his own problems with harmonizing the liberal and postmodernist elements in his thinking. Moreover, that over the years he has changed his view over the matter and has come to recognize a link between philosophy and politics and, by extension, education, of a particular kind. Which draws upon Dewey in certain respects and leads him to a kind of writing about education and politics which is in tune with his continuing rejection of 'philosophy of education' as a discipline.

Rorty's political troubles with poststructuralism began with *Philosophy and the Mirror of Nature* (1980, henceforth *PMN*), the book which first launched him into prominence as a philosopher. There he tried to bring analytic philosophy, the school within which he was raised and had hitherto worked, to terms with American pragmatism and continental philosophy, something nobody else had attempted before. So that, in effect, the book was written as an attempt to redefine his own understanding of philosophy at the time in terms of these influences. Wittgenstein, Dewey, and Heidegger were the philosophers whom he described as its heroes, with Heidegger being, of course, his link with 'poststructuralism'. But the influence of Lyotard was also more than apparent in the book, as was undoubtedly that of Gadamer. In the process of redefining his views on philosophy the book set about undermining what he described as the hegemonic politics of the dominant philosophic tradition going back to Plato, which claims for philosophy the role of guardian of knowledge and underwriter of science and culture. What he wanted was to replace its epistemological foundationalism with a nonhegemonic hermeneutic outlook, which has no ambitions to be a "successor subject" to epistemology. Indeed, which shows that no such subject is needed (1980, 315). And which renounces representing itself as a discipline or *fach* and regards itself, much more modestly, instead as a strand in "the conversation of mankind." He also defined education in the book on Gadamerian lines as "edification" achieved through conversation. And it was this definition that Arcilla, Nicholson, and others regarded as promising (1980, 360).

Two years after *PMN*, Rorty published another book, *Consequences of Pragmatism* (1982, henceforth *CP*), a collection of articles, many of which discussed the current state of philosophy in the United States and in general. Again, there was this unhappiness with the idea of philosophy as a discipline. *CP* covered his work between 1972 and 1980 and was, therefore, coterminous with *PMN*. In its introduction, Rorty sketched out a utopian culture which he significantly referred to as "postphilosophical". A culture with no ruling principle, as he described it, no center or structure, or respect for hard fact—no standard of what is "adequate" in languages and life (1982, xl). In which experts are replaced by all-purpose intellectuals "ready to offer a view on pretty much everything, in the hope of making it hang with everything else." Who have no special 'problem' to solve, 'method' to work with, or disciplinary standards to abide by, and no collective 'professional' self-image to uphold. No dream of immortality or permanence to sustain, and find no discomfort with the idea that their work is "doomed to be outdated" (1982, xl), and that they are leaving nothing permanent behind (1982, xli). Like the lives of the inhabitants of Snow's 'literary culture' their "highest hope is to grasp their time in thought" (1982, xli). Intellectuals, in short, whose task is twofold. *Hermeneutic*, showing "how the other side looks from our own point of view . . . how the odd or paradoxical or offensive things they say hang together with the rest of what they want to say, and how what they say looks when put in our own alternative idiom" (1980, 364–65). And *therapeutic*, breaking the crust of convention, as Dewey taught us to do in the name of a more humane society, through the 'poetic' inverse of hermeneutics; "the attempt to reinterpret our familiar surroundings in the unfamiliar terms of our new inventions" (1980, 360). These thoughts, transferred to education, are already radical. They deny the need for 'experts' in education and suggest that we should stop regarding philosophy of education as a discipline and characterizing ourselves as philosophers of education. They suggest that education should be regarded, at best, as just another subject all-purpose intellectuals perceive the need to engage with when the crust hardens on the policies and practices pursued in its name; when these become dogmatic, or when some new idea, concept, narrative, discourse, solution, etc., invades our conventional discourse suddenly rendering it problematic.

These two intellectual activities, hermeneutic and therapeutic, each the inverse of the other, described so sketchily in *CP*, were elaborated in great detail by Rorty in *PMN*. Where, taking his cue from Thomas Kuhn's distinction of ordinary from revolutionary science, he distinguished two general kinds of discourse. 'Normal', which is 'rational' or rule-directed, "conducted within an agreed-upon set of conventions about what counts as a relevant contribution, what counts as answering a question, what counts as having a good argument for that answer or a good criticism of it." And 'abnormal', which has the contrary characteristics and comes into play "when someone joins in the discourse who is ignorant of these conventions or who sets them aside." The character of normal discourse is that it is 'disciplined' and works within conventions; abnormal discourse, to the contrary, operates outside all conventions. There is no discipline for it "any more than there is a discipline devoted to the study of the unpredictable, or of 'creativity'." It may produce anything from nonsense to intellectual revolution (1980, 320). At the same time as he distinguished these two kinds of discourse, Rorty distinguished two corresponding kinds of thinkers: 'constructive' and 'reactive' or 'therapeutic'. The former are writers with a view to present, theories to offer and justify (in short, they are orthodox philosophers). The latter are the opposite; they "decry the very notion of having a view, while avoiding having a view about having views" (which is what saves them from getting caught in the paradox of relativism) (1980, 371). They "are abnormal at this meta-level" also (1980, 370). They are skeptical "primarily about systematic philosophy, and the whole project of universal commensuration" that underpins epistemological foundationalism, supporting the project of edification instead. Dewey, Wittgenstein, and Heidegger are outstanding examples of philosophers of this kind, he says in *PMN* (1980, 368). They are not to be confused with revolutionary philosophers who are not all of the edifying kind since some have been systematic. The two intellectual activities, hermeneutic and therapeutic, are subdivisions of reactive thinking. Rorty contrasts them with the systematic thinking of the constructive philosopher who engages in what philosophy has been thought to be about since Plato, namely, constructing theories and justifying positions with arguments. The reactive thinker is interested neither in theories nor in arguments.

It is important to be clear about the relationship Rorty drew between normal and abnormal discourse; abnormal discourse, he insisted, is always parasitical on normal discourse; it cannot exist without it, just as edification or education is parasitic on enculturation. "Even the education of the revolutionary or the prophet," he says in *PMN*, has to start from there, from one's culture (1980, 365). In the same way the reactive philosophers of today are parasitic on the constructive philosophers of old, they cannot exist without them. Corresponding dualisms to that between the normal and abnormal come to define his approaches to politics and education in his later work. In his politics Rorty comes to make a radical distinction between the realm of the public and that of the private, both distinguished in terms of different kinds of discourse and activity. In education, as I pointed out earlier, he came to distinguish between 'lower' and 'higher' education with truth inhabiting the realm of the former and freedom that of the latter. But this is jumping the gun a bit.

Strong Textualism and Politics

Even as Rorty was describing his postphilosophical utopia and stating his support for a reactive therapeutic philosophy of this dual kind, hermeneutic and poetic, he had already undermined the first of these approaches in a significant article he published in *CP*. An article that often passes unnoticed but actually signalled an important shift in his thinking; namely, his break with hermeneutics, with 'weak textualists', as he now called Gadamer and his followers, because they think that "epistemology still looks classy," (1982b, 156) aligning himself instead with the 'great new figures', with Nietzsche, James, and Dewey who "have tried to show what our lives might be like if we had no hope of what Nietzsche called 'metaphysical comfort'" (1982b, 150). Hermeneutics, as a seeker of such comfort, about which he had written so much in *PMN*, he now accused of showing "loss of nerve," and expressed his admiration for the 'strong textualism' of Derrida instead (1982b). Like Derrida, he had wanted to see philosophy absorbed within the general current of an undifferentiated literary textuality rather than represented as a discipline, and had begun to speak of literary critics as the intellectuals of the postphilosophical age. Now he pronounced himself for Derrida's critique of

Gadamerian hermeneutics, namely, that it is assimilative of the other. Strong textualism requires us to "try to work ourselves out of our jobs by conscientiously blurring the literature-philosophy distinction and promoting the idea of a seamless, undifferentiated 'general text'" (1984, 3). It is poetic rather than hermeneutic in nature. Hermeneutics is serious business. Derrida, on the other hand, is the perfect example of the 'strong poet', of the philosopher who does not take himself seriously, who makes "philosophy ever more impure—more unprofessional, funnier, more allusive, sexier, and above all more 'written'" (1982a, 93). Wittgenstein and Heidegger were not now on the list of 'great figures'. They were replaced on it by Nietzsche and James. The only name that survived from his list in *PMN* was Dewey's.

This shift in his thinking about hermeneutics, which left him acknowledging only the poetic, clearly marked a crucial turning point in his work. Meanwhile, while he was struggling with his philosophical orientations, he came increasingly under pressure from his liberal political critics. The general criticism against his post-*PMN* work, exemplified in *Reading Rorty* in particular, as I indicated earlier, was that his romantic postmodernism and his liberal politics did not gel. His immediate reaction was to make strong, explicit statements about his liberal political affiliations in different places. In "Thugs and Theorists, a Reply to Bernstein," for instance, he responded to the criticism that his views are "likely to give aid and comfort to the wrong people," (1987, 564) by describing his 'political credo' (1987, 565) in eight 'theses' about social democracy, which broadly represented the political outlook of the West in the time of the Cold War. These were theses, he contended, that several of his liberal critics "who might not mind describing themselves as 'social democrats'," would readily accept and comply with (1987, 567). So that, he argued, there was abundant 'overlapping consensus' with them for cooperation with them on concrete political projects to be possible, while permitting continuing disagreement with them on some of these projects' aspects. Political consensus, he argued in his article, does not rule out continuing differences in philosophical tastes either (1987, 573). The point he was driving at was that the key difference between himself and his social democrat critics was not over substantial political beliefs but over how to do philosophy; specifically over the utility of writing political theory as such. He has, since then, continued to concern himself with articulating his views about the political future of social democracy, his most sustained piece of writing in this respect being his book *Achieving Our Country* (1998). But more importantly for the purposes of this chapter, in "Thugs and Theorists," while contending that doing theory serves no use "in thinking about the present political situation," he went on to say that it can, however, serve us in "thinking through our utopian visions" (1987, 569). This, the writing of utopia, was how he believed one can write politics poetically, and this is how he wrote his next book, *Contingency, Irony, and Solidarity* (1989, hence-forth *CIS*), where he described his liberal utopia and responded to the criti-cism in *Reading Rorty*.

In *CIS*, Rorty returned to his fundamental bifurcation of discourse in *PMN* into normal and abnormal. Only this time he recast it as a bifurcation between private and public discourse. 'Postmodernism', as I said earlier, he now proclaimed as politically silly, something of value only to our private in-dividual self-construction. Meanwhile, very significantly in my view, he abandoned the expression 'post-philosophical utopia' which he had used in *CP* and referred to his liberal utopia as 'post-metaphysical' instead. The lib-eral ironist is the hero of this utopia he envisages. Rorty contrasts her with the metaphysicist who believes in the possibility of a noncontingent final vo-cabulary and refers her discourse to established truths of different kinds, ac-cusing the ironist of being a 'relativist'. He also contrasts her with the com-monsensist who, on her part, is completely insensitive to the intellectual concerns that produce the ironist, who has no worries that her vocabulary must always be uncertain because she simply takes the world around her for granted, including the world constructed for her by the metaphysicist. The ironist tries to demonstrate the contingency of our beliefs, thereby defeating the metaphysician and undermining the confidence of the commonsensist whose final vocabulary she shows up with all its limitations and delusions. Rorty, who identifies liberalism in the book with an intolerance towards cru-elty in general, accepts the predictable criticism that this kind of exposure is humiliating and, thereby, cruel, but condones it on the grounds that it is an inevitable feature of intellectual debate. What makes the redescription of the metaphysicist attractive to many people, he contends, is that it is presented as 'education', as the uncovering of one's true self and interests, and con-nected with freedom and authenticity. The ironist does not offer any of the assurance of the metaphysician. In fact, Rorty argues, what she is really blamed for "is not an inclination to humiliate but an inability to empower" (1989, 91). Having already rejected the metaphysician's definition of educa-tion before, Rorty now relates it not to edification and the practice of hermeneutics but to irony and the practice of strong poetry.

The significant thing about *CIS* in this respect is that in it Rorty insists that irony must be kept out of the realm of politics, the public realm, where the discourse should be pragmatic and set to the agenda of liberal reform in-stead. He judges it as he judges Derridean deconstruction and Foucauldian genealogy, as "invaluable in our attempt to form a private self-image but pretty much useless when it comes to politics" (1989, 87). In the book, he goes on to contrast ironist writers, like Kierkegaard, Nietzsche, Baudelaire, Proust, Heidegger, and Nabokov, "in whom the desire for self-creation, for private autonomy, dominates," and who are useful only as private 'exemplars', with 'historicist', 'public', writers like Marx, Mill, Dewey, Habermas, and Rawls. Who write as our "fellow citizens," (1989, xiii) and who are "engaged in a shared, social effort" with their "fellow citizens" to "make our institutions and practices more just and less cruel," i.e., more liberal (1989, xiv). This they do, however, not by inventing their own personal utopias but by articulating the utopian aspirations of the weak and oppressed, the voiceless; the "victims of cruelty, people who are suffering [and] who do not have much in the way of language" (1989, 94). The notion of the 'voice of the oppressed' he dismisses as a pure fiction; there is, he says, no 'voice of the oppressed' since the oppressed have no voice. They are silent. Indeed, being 'voiceless' is characteristic of their condition, a symptom of their oppression. They, therefore, need someone to speak for them, not only to voice their suffering and humiliation, but also their aspirations for a better world. And this is the public task of the liberal intellectual who possesses the tools, the imagination and resources of language for the purpose.

One notes here, in *CIS*, a radical shift from the way Rorty envisaged the public role of intellectuals in *PMN* and *CP*, where they were engaged with the therapeutic task of helping "their readers or society as a whole, break free from outworn vocabularies and attitudes," and with the hermeneutic of helping them see how the strange and unusual, what belongs to an alien culture or language game, hangs within their horizon of language and understanding. Now, in *CIS*, their task is different. It is to reveal the cruelties in their midst through novels like Orwell's and Nabokov's and to articulate the hopes of the weak by engaging themselves in utopian writing. At the same time as he says this, Rorty declares his sympathy with the political approach of the later Rawls for, as he expresses it, putting "democratic politics first and philosophy second" (1991, 191). Rawls shows us that "social policy needs no more authority than successful accommodation among individuals, individuals who find themselves heir to the same historical traditions and faced with the same problems" (1991, 184). What liberal societies need to ensure is a pragmatic, reflective, equilibrium between the interests and demands of its citizens (1991, 184). But Rorty goes on to identify another instance where political writing is legitimate as a 'method' (the scare quotes are his own). This is when a contest develops "between an entrenched vocabulary which has become a nuisance and a half-formed new vocabulary which vaguely promises great things" (1989, 9). This 'method' is illustrated in his own writing of *CIS* which seeks not so much to articulate the voice of the weak as to articulate the emerging vocabulary of a new liberal utopia in the West. 'Our' task, he says in CIS is "to replace a human self-image which has been made obsolete by social and cultural change with a new self-image, a self-image better adapted to the results of those changes" (1989, 198). The way this is done is by "redescrib(ing) lots and lots of things in new ways, until you have created a pattern of linguistic behaviour which will tempt the rising generations to adopt it, thereby causing them to look for appropriate new forms of nonlinguistic behaviour, for example the adoption of new scientific equipment or new social institutions" (1989, 9).

"We philosophers," he says more recently, "have to give up the priority of contemplation over action." Like Marx we have to look to the future rather than to the past. We should resemble engineers and lawyers in this respect who "find out what their clients need" and respond to it, rather than priests and sages who set their own agendas (1995, 198). Now, the man who was proposing the death of philosophy and the advent of a postphilosophical society in CP says that "philosophy cannot possibly end until social and cultural change end," which is logical given that the task he now assigns it is precisely that of articulating this change. "Only a society without politics," he continues, "—that is to say, a society run by tyrants who prevent social and cultural change from occurring—would no longer require philosophers. In such societies, where there are no politics, philosophers can only be priests in the service of a state religion. In free societies, there will always be a need for their services, for such societies never stop changing, and hence never stop making old vocabularies obsolete" (1995, 198). In short, 'philosophers', he now argues, are required by free societies to help them redescribe themselves in emerging vocabularies that respond to the changes they are experiencing. By enabling these societies to articulate their emerging self-image they adapt themselves better to the future. His own writing of CIS is consistent with this conclusion as a self-conscious contribution of this kind. A redescription, akin, he claims, to Rawls', of an emerging liberal vocabulary. His object is not, in the way of constructive philosophers, to offer arguments against the metaphysical vocabularies in our societies that are, he believes, becoming obsolete in the process of change, but to "try to make the vocabulary I favour look attractive by showing how it may be used to describe a variety of topics," namely, language, conscience, the self, and intellectual and moral progress (1989, 9). The "I favour" is very significant here. Rorty's philosopher no longer ascribes to herself the right to speak for or on behalf of humanity at large. When she speaks it is either for herself from her own ethnocentric viewpoint or for the voiceless, with whose pain and suffering she engages imaginatively.

Rejecting the Discipline

What emerges forcefully from this rough account of his thinking about philosophy and politics over the last twenty years is his constant reassessment of both over the years since he wrote *PMN*. From advocating a strong textualism and promoting a 'post-philosophical' hermeneutic culture served by all-purpose intellectuals writing like literary critics, and thereby giving the impression of wanting to do away with it completely, he has moved gradually towards rehabilitating philosophy. Moreover, he has also rehabilitated politics as a legitimate subject of interest for philosophers, and, by extension, education also. He now affirms himself as a philosopher with both a private task of ironic self-creation and a public one of utopian writing, on the lines of Marx, Mill, Dewey, and Rawls. What he continues to reject is not philosophy as such but 'metaphysics'. Only a society run by tyrants and therefore uninterested in social change and reform, he now says, can dispense with philosophy. Philosophy as utopian writing, he says, is important in helping societies redescribe their political and, one could add, educational, aspirations in the light of change, and in redescribing those aspirations, more specifically, from the point of view of the oppressed within the societies it serves. This is clearly a retraction from his statements in his "Reply to Arcilla and Nicholson" with which I began. What he is now proposing is not so much the abandonment of philosophy in politics but an inversion of the traditional role it has always held since Plato. An inversion which, as he correctly says, Dewey also favored: that of putting philosophy at the service of democracy, not the other way round, using it to determine democracy's epistemological foundations. How can this be done? Dewey himself tried to show us in writing *Democracy and Education* (1966), a piece of utopian writing in Rorty's sense of the word, if there is one, where he articulates his aspirations for education in a democracy. A significant criticism against Dewey himself for many years was that he could not be taken seriously either as a general philosopher or as a philosopher of education, in particular, precisely because he did not write philosophy as though it were a discipline. Rorty is credited with having played a large part in Dewey's rehabilitation as an important philosopher in the Anglo-Saxon world over these past twenty years or so, and a large contribution to this rehabilitation has been Rorty's poststructuralist attack on the writing of philosophy as a discipline.

But opposition to the casting of philosophy in general as a discipline means, by extension, opposition to having a discipline called philosophy of education. The important distinction needs to be made here between writing about education philosophically and having this discipline called philosophy of education. The most recent Rorty, in fact, seems to have resolved his problems with the former but retained his problems with the latter. And this is one aspect of his thinking, as I said in the previous paragraph, concordant with Dewey where education is concerned. Dewey, in fact, explicitly argued against writing philosophy of education as a discipline and tried to show us how we could write about education differently. This way of writing about it differently is not, however, usually one of the things that is weighed or considered by his critics and pronounced upon on its own merits. This is because the view that it must be written as a discipline prevailed for many years and, as Walter Feinberg recently reminded Maxine Greene in responding to her views about the future of philosophy of education, still continues to do so (1995). Indeed, he took *her* to task for not having carved out the space for the discipline we call philosophy of education in her projections about the future of philosophy and education. For having, in her projections, reflected on how a 'postmodern' (as D. C. Phillips refers to it, 1995) approach to philosophy could open onto education in general and nothing else. Greene, referring to Lyotard, described the tension opened by the postmodern condition of Western culture between wanting to hold on to the modernist ideals of freedom, social justice, equality, human rights, the self, and so on, while recognizing the loss of legitimation of the discourse that originally framed them and gave them their credibility (1995). In this situation she suggested two principal activities for philosophers of education today. To "expose the inadequacies (and the racism, and the sexism)" of so much of that discourse without disposing of the political and educational texts that contained it (those by Rousseau, Kant, Jefferson, Mill, Dewey, Greene, Hirst and Peters, Freire, etc.) (1995, 6). And to help people "relearn how to look at the world" (in Merleu-Ponty's expression) (1995, 11). She had proposed deconstruction as the way of doing this, conceived of as Derrida described it as a practice of '*overturning*' the hegemonic binary oppositions that are built into Western culture holding us is their thrall: black/white, male/female, cognitive/affective, etc. A program Rorty would obviously only support in part, the part about helping people "relearn how to look at the world," since he disapproves of using deconstruction for political purposes. In this latter respect, in fact, Greene is more in tune with the French poststructuralists than Rorty.

The advantage of a discipline, for Feinberg, is that it focuses one's enterprise. In effect, he praises Greene for doing that, for locating the philosophical interest in education "within an intergenerational context," "within institutions and practices that are explicitly intended to educate," for these institutions and practices, those of schooing, are indeed, he says, the specific subject matter and concern of "Philosophers of Education." Without them "the profession of Philosophy of Education as we know it today would not exist" (1995, 26). The problem with "the discourse Greene describes," however, the discourse about freedom, social justice etc., "need not constitute Philosophy of Education, at least as presently conceived," at all (1995). Philosophy of Education is distinct by having its own specific school-related discourse. This is precisely what, it was claimed by its early pioneers in the Anglo-Saxon world, justified its claim to an identity as a discipline in its own right. Once it loses this focus it loses this justification. One problem with Dewey in this respect was precisely that he refused to accept that focus, practically identifying education with life itself and insisting that we should be looking at other kinds of learning. Not just the 'explicitly intended' outcomes of formal teaching but the unintended outcomes of informal learning that occur through interaction with an environment. Indeed, he went so far as to hold that "We never educate directly, but indirectly by means of the environment" (1966, 19). Dewey saw no problem with defining the relationship between the way education is theorized and its practice, which, to the contrary, dogged Philosophy of Education from the start. To his mind, the concerns of philosophy were quite simply those of practice, the social practices concerning learning. He, therefore, did not need to worry that what he was doing was 'truly philosophy' also, as did, and continue to do, many Philosophers of Education. Foreseeing the later difficulty of Philosophy of Education to get itself accepted by practitioners, he argued that when they cast philosophy as a discipline "philosophers become a specialized class which uses a technical language. Unlike the vocabulary in which the direct difficulties are stated," it becomes a language of professors, of "professionals," as Feinberg calls them (1995, 328).

Dewey traced the first philosophical interest in education to the sophists for whom "the problems of philosophy originate in the conflicts and difficulties of social life" and stem from the experiences of ordinary people. They are, as Greene suggests, about such things as the relations of mind and matter; body and soul; humanity and physical nature; the individual and the social; theory (or knowing) and practice (or doing). What philosophy does is bring "to explicit consciousness what men have come to think, in virtue of the quality of their current experience, about nature, themselves, and the reality they conceive to include or to govern both." What it seeks is "a wisdom which would influence the conduct of life" (1966, 324). It is, thus, Dewey argues like Rorty, reactive not foundational, about thinking not about knowing. It is about "thinking what the known demands of us—what responsive attitude it exacts" (1966, 326). Thus, what occasions it is 'an unsettlement', or problem. It is essentially, as Rorty put it at the time of *PMN* and *CP*, therapeutic; "it

aims at overcoming disturbance," (1966, 326) a "reconstruction of experience" (1966, 80) aimed at creating a new settlement. It requires "the disposi-
tion to penetrate to deeper levels of meaning—to go below the surface and
find out the connections of any event or object, and to keep at it." And is
"averse to taking anything as isolated; it tries to place an act in its context—
which constitutes its significance" (1966, 326). Dewey, thus, explicitly rejected the premise about the relationship between theory and practice that
underpinned the birth of Philosophy of Education as a discipline (analytic
philosophy of education): "'Philosophy of Education,'" he said, "is not an
eternal application of ready made ideas to a system of practice having a radically different origin and purpose" (1966, 331). To the contrary it may be defined "*as the general theory of education*" (1966, 328), while the world of learning is "the laboratory in which philosophic distinctions become concrete and
are tested" (1966, 329).

In this sense, it is, like education itself, about recovering continuity of experience, about the readaptation of experience needed to keep action alive
and growing. In short, it is reconstructive as well as being reactive; it also "in-
creases ability to direct the course of subsequent experience" (1966, 76) by
creating a settlement. Tying this purpose in with the importance Dewey ascribes to need for 'communication' or conversation to create it, one can identify the hermeneutic purposes in his understanding of philosophy that the
early Rorty identified with it. The problems it addresses are those, as Greene
and, of course ultimately Derrida, suggests, that spring from the barriers to
our thought set by the 'dualisms' in which we have been inured to think since
the time of the Greeks and that make for an "absence of fluent and free intercourse" (1966, 333). Dewey thought, like Derrida, that the object of philosophy of education is to address these 'dualisms' in order to bring this flu-
ency and freedom about. He varies from Derrida, however, in the crucial
respect that the latter did not understand philosophy as reconstructive, or
hermeneutic, at all. So that the later, 'strong textualist', Derridean Rorty criticized him for the fact that he also "*wanted* to write a metaphysical system."
Rorty's problem with Dewey is that "throughout his life, he wavered between
a therapeutic stance toward philosophy and another, quite different,
stance—one in which philosophy was to become 'scientific' and 'empirical'
and to do something serious, systematic, important, and constructive"
(1982c, 72). In this respect, as well as in his predeliction for community,
Richard Peters repeatedly observed, he remained under the spell of his early
Hegelianism (1977).

Peters criticized Dewey for not having resolved the various dualisms he addressed in his works, for having failed in his enterprise to effect a satisfactory

synthesis. Rorty argues, as would Derrida, that it was the project of effecting a synthesis that was mistaken to begin with. Thus, to take the philosophy-practice issue that interests us, the object is not to undertake a synthesis of the two together, which, in his view is a futile exercise unless you turn to metaphysics for help, but to recognize that they each belong to a different realm of activity or discourse, the first that of the philosophers, the second of the practitioners, and to keep them apart. There is, in other words, no closing the theory-practice 'gap' that has been worrying philosophers since the time analytic philosophy fell out of favor with some sort of synthesis. To the contrary, we should ensure that that gap stays open, that we recognize each of the elements of the dualism for what it is, and consign each to different activities, different realms of discourse, the one of the philosopher, the other of the practitioner. These were the grounds on which, in his reply to Arcilla and Nicholson, he denied any relevance for philosophy in either politics or education. As I have shown, he has since retracted on his view that it has nothing to say to politics, and has come to hold that it can be engaged not in speculation but in the articulation of the political aspirations of one's society and, more especially, those of its weakest members: the voiceless. This concurs with one part of what Greene says about the role of philosophy: that it should help people "relearn how to look at the world" but conflicts with the other where she says that it should aim at exposing the political inadequacy of much of our contemporary discourse. The latter is in tune with the intentions of the French poststructuralists, with the 'unmasking' of our institutional discourses and 'games of truth', which they believed should be the object of genealogy and deconstruction, an indispensable part of 'the work of freedom'. But Rorty has attacked these intentions consistently over the years just as he has attacked critical theory in its form as ideology critique. The difference, as he says, is really down to the purposes to which one wants to put philosophy. And those purposes are different for Rorty and for the French poststructuralists who, unlike him, worry about utopian writing in general, are especially skeptical about the idea of representing a liberal utopia, and are opposed, in Foucault's case at least, to speaking on behalf of anyone.

Bibliography

Arcilla, R. V. (1990) Edification, Conversation, and Narrative: Rortyan Motifs for Philosophy of Education, *Educational Theory* 40, no. 1, Winter (35–39).

Dewey, J. (1966) *Democracy and Education*. London: Collier Macmillan.

Feinberg, W. (1995) The Discourse of Philosophy of Education, in Wendy Kohli, ed., *Critical Conversations in Philosophy of Education*. New York: Routledge.

Greene, M. (1995) What Counts as Philosophy of Education? In Wendy Kohli, ed., *Critical Conversations in Philosophy of Education*. New York: Routledge.

Lyotard, J.-F. (1979) *The Postmodern Condition: A Report on Knowledge*. Minneapolis: University of Minnesota Press.

Malachowski, A. (ed.) (1990) *Reading Rorty*. Oxford: Basil Blackwell.

Nicholson, C. (1989) Postmodernism, Feminism, and Education: the Need for Solidarity, *Educational Theory* 39, no. 3, Summer (197–205).

Peters, R. S. (1977) John Dewey's Philosophy of Education, in R. S. Peters, ed., *John Dewey Reconsidered*, London: Routledge and Kegan Paul.

Philips, D. C. (1995) Counting Down to the Millennium. In Wendy Kohli, ed., *Critical Conversations in Philosophy of Education*. New York: Routledge.

Rorty, R. (1980) *Philosophy and the Mirror of Nature*. Oxford: Basil Blackwell.

———. (1982) *Consequences of Pragmatism*, Brighton: The Harvester Press.

———. (1982a) Philosophy as a Kind of Writing: An Essay on Derrida, in *Consequences of Pragmatism*. Brighton: Harvester Press.

———. (1982b) Nineteenth Century Idealism and Twentieth-Century Textualism. In R. Rorty, *Consequences of Pragmatism*. Brighton: Harvester Press.

———. (1982c) Dewey's Metaphysics. In R. Rorty, *Consequences of Pragmatism*. Brighton: Harvester Press.

———. (1983) Postmodernist Bourgeois Liberalism, *Journal of Philosophy* 80, October (583–89).

———. (1984) Deconstruction and Circumvention, *Critical Inquiry* 11, September (1–23).

———. (1987) Thugs and Theorists, a Reply to Bernstein, *Political Theory* 15, no. 4, November (564–80).

———. (1989) *Contingency, Irony, and Solidarity*. Cambridge: Cambridge University Press.

———. (1990a) The Dangers of Over-Philosophication-Reply to Arcilla and Nicholson, *Educational Theory* 40, no. 1, Winter (41–44).

———. (1990b) Education Without Dogma, *Dialogue* 2 (44–47).

———. (1991) Priority of Democracy to Philosophy, in *Objectivity, Relativism, and Truth, Philosophical Papers, Volume 1*. Cambridge: Cambridge University Press.

———. (1992) Trotsky and the Wild Orchids, *Common Knowledge* 1, no. 3 (140–53).

———. (1995) Philosophy and the Future. In Herman J. Saatkamp Jr., ed., *Rorty and Pragmatism: The Philosopher Replies to His Critics*. Nashville: Vanderbilt University Press.

———. (1998) *Achieving Our Country: Leftist Thought in Twentieth-Century America*. Cambridge, Mass.: Harvard University Press.

Wain, K. (1995) Richard Rorty, Education, and Politics, *Educational Theory* 45, no. 3, Summer, 395–409.

∽

CHAPTER NINE

Achieving America: Postmodernism and Rorty's Critique of the Cultural Left

Michael A. Peters

Stories about what a nation has been and should try to be are not attempts at accurate representation, but rather attempts to forge a moral identity.

—Richard Rorty, *Achieving Our Country: Leftist Thought in Twentieth-Century America*

The idea of a Western democratic conversation between friends has never produced a single concept.

—Gilles Deleuze and Félix Guattari, *What Is Philosophy?* trans. Hugh Tomlinson and Graham Burchell

Introduction

There is a not-so-subtle irony in the title and an obvious playfulness carried by the phrase "The End of Postmodernism?" The question mark acts to recoil upon a set of discourses and cultural phenomena that, at least in the popular imaginary, proclaims in apocalyptic tones "the end": the end of modernism, the end of metaphysics, the end of humanism, the end of Man. It resonates with its modernist Hegelian sibling discourses, both rightist and leftist, that still carry some theoretical weight: the end of ideology, the end of history, the end of the welfare state, the end of communism or capitalism. And, at the same time, it shares the same kind of popular expectation of something that follows "the end": whether it be "the new," "the beginning," or "a return," historically speaking. In one sense these eschatological narratives of endings (and beginnings) are endemic to Western culture and help define both its cultural specificity and its sources of renewal. "Post-modernism," like a host of other similar terms christened with the same pre-fix, such as "Post-Impressionism" and "Post-Expressionism," employs a re-active rhetorical device or strategy, betraying what I call a "naming anxiety." Reading the signs of exhaustion—an end or completion—the users of this device, following many precedents, lacked the confidence to name "the new" and fell back upon the strategy of naming what it is not. This process of negative definition is, intellectually, both less risky and less ambitious. Charles Jencks (1996, 14–15) has recorded seventy such related uses, including "post-industrial," "postminimalism," "post-Marxism," and "post-liberal era," and charted a genealogy of "postmodernism" in terms of its pre-history (1870–1950), its positive definition (1950–1980), and its fi-nal phase characterized by attacks upon it and its anthologization.

I don't think there is anything exceptional in this narratological tactic and, culturally speaking, as good modernists we ought not to be surprised at the enormous and seemingly interminable debate about the term "postmod-ernism." Indeed, different scholars have suggested that once the meanings of the term have been fixed and stabilized, the life will have been drained from it and the debate will be over. We ought not to be surprised also that the term "postmodernism" should eventually face its own linguistic limit—its own narrative endgame. Indeed, if we take Jean-François Lyotard's (1984, 79) original insight that postmodernism is "not modernism at its end but in its nascent state and that state is constant," then, culturally speaking, we should expect it. As you will remember, Lyotard raises the question of "the post-modern" in his discussion of the Kantian sublime and the attempt to present the unpresentable that he considers as a characterization of the history of successive avant-gardes, whose impulse is now exhausted. I think his obser-vation is worthy of repeating here.

> What, then, is the postmodern? What place does it or does it not occupy in the vertiginous work of the questions hurled at the rules of image and narration? It is undoubtedly a part of the modern. All that has been received, if only yester-day (modo, modo, Petronious used to say), must be suspected. What space does Cézanne challenge? The Impressionists'. What object do Picasso and Braque at-tack? Cézanne's. What presupposition does Duchamp break with in 1912? That which says one must make a painting, be it cubist. And Buren questions that other presupposition which he believes had survived untouched by the work of Duchamp: the place of presentation of the work. In an amazing acceleration, the generations precipitate themselves. A work can become modern only if it is first postmodern. (Lyotard 1984, 79)

In the last few years, there have been a number of conferences that have taken up similar themes to "The End of Postmodernism?" For example, the 1997 University of Chicago Conference on "After Postmodernism," the "Civic Values from an After Postmodern Perspective" to have been held in Bulgaria in 1999, and the ICA 1996 "Reconsidering Postmodernism." The Chicago conference advertised itself in terms of the following question: "If we absorb postmodernism, if we recognize the variety and ungroundedness of grounds, but do not want to stop in arbitrariness, relativism, or aphoria, *what comes after postmodernism?*" The "post" considered as an indicator of "what comes after" is a classic modernist trope that, historically, has come to define philosophy after Kant: a break or "rupture" with the past that is "in fact a way of forgetting or repressing the past, that is to say, repeating it and not surpassing it" (Lyotard 1992, 90). Yet in respect of art, literature, philosophy, and politics,

> the "post" of "postmodern" does not signify a movement of *comeback, flashback* or *feedback*, that is, not a movement of repetition but a procedure in "ana-": a procedure of analysis, anamnesis, anagogy and anamorphosis which elaborates an "initial forgetting." (Lyotard 1992, 93)

Surely, Wittgenstein's understanding of his own philosophy demonstrates this tendency? When he suggests in the preface to the *Tractatus* that his "truths" are both unassailable and definitive and that he has found "the final solutions of the problems" facing modern philosophy he is at one and the same time exemplifying "how little is achieved when these problems are solved" (Wittgenstein 1922, 4). Rorty routinely uses this strategy himself in talk of "post-Kantianian culture," "post-Nietzscheanism," or "post-analytic philosophy."

Interpreting the "post" as one concerning the ability to cope with Nietzsche's legacy, Gary Madison (1997) at the Chicago conference characterizes Rorty as "a carefree, happy-go-lucky nihilist" who has been, perhaps, the least bothered by "the demise of truth" and the most assured of what to do after "the end of Philosophy." This gloss on Rorty's work does neither justice to either the complexity of his views on the notions of Truth or "postmodernism" nor the degree to which his position has changed over time. Yet Madison has got something also right here. I think it is true to say that of contemporary philosophers Rorty seems to be the one most comfortable with Nietzsche's legacy and what Madison calls "the burden of nihilism." While Madison has pinpointed correctly something about Rorty's post-philosophical attitude—its "carefreeness," its (unbearable?) lightness, and its politically utopian quality (though Madison does not mention this feature)—he does not explain why Rorty is less burdened than other post-Nietzscheans.

Quite simply, I shall maintain that Rorty must be viewed in his native context as someone who engages the philosophical tradition from the perspective of an American living at the end of the millennium—one who views Nietzsche as a European pragmatist, as "the most eminent disciple of Emerson" (1991b, 61). Like Nietzsche, he wants to drop the cognitivism that has dominated Western intellectual life since Plato, but, unlike Nietzsche and under the utopian influence of Dewey, he wishes "to do so in the interests of an egalitarian society rather than in the interests of a defiant and lonely individualism" (1991b). This is the difference between the last philosophy of the old (European) world, bespeaking "the end of metaphysics" that focuses upon the question of European nihilism and imminent cultural disintegration, and the confident, self-assured, utopian philosophy of the New World, which, in its youthful confidence, has never experienced itself as a culture in an organic sense nor felt the crushing import of Nietzsche's question.

It is a New World pragmatist utopian philosophy that is able, like European Nietzscheanism, to reject the Enlightenment's metaphysical baggage of foundationalism and representationalism, and yet unlike its European older cousin, it does not jettison the promise of the Enlightenment's political project. It does, however, substitute a local, historical, and contingent sense of self for the transhistorical metaphysical subject of philosophical liberalism. Indeed, Rorty sees no connection between the philosophical and political strands of the Enlightenment. The success of the "American experiment of self-creation" (Rorty 1998, 23), unlike its European counterparts, does depend upon or require any philosophical assurance or justification; philosophy, like poetry, is to be regarded simply as another means of self-expression. On this view, it is up to intellectuals and artists to tell inspiring stories and to create symbols of greatness about the nation's past as the means of competing for political leadership. Narratives of national self-creation ought to be oriented to what the nation can try to become rather than how it has come to be. And, perhaps, this is the crucial difference of culture and style between Rorty and the European post-Nietzscheans: he believes in the narrative celebration of his nation's past as the best means to inspire hope about its future, rather than a "working through" of its troublesome or shameful episodes. It is exemplified in the difference between what Nietzsche in the *Untimely Meditations* calls a "monumental history" that venerates and memorializes the past, and the critical use of history, which Nietzsche also criticizes in the name of genealogy, as offering a critique of past injustices based on the "truths" held in the present. Where the European post-Nietzscheans are historically disenchanted and weighted down by the past—by the pogroms, the Holocaust, the World Wars, and postwar policies of ethnic cleansing—

Rortyans can dissociate American patriotism from the genocide of indigenous Americans, the southern Amero-African slave economy, the bombing of Hiroshima and Nagasaki, and the Vietnam War, to concentrate on uplifting stories designed to engender national hope and encourage concerted political action aimed at specific reforms.

"Postmodernism" and Rorty's Narrative Turn

Richard Rorty (1980), claiming Wittgenstein, Heidegger, and Dewey as his heroes, emerged at the end of the 1970s as one of the leading philosophers in the English-speaking world to inquire into the status and role of his discipline after the collapse of the Kantian enterprise. His antirepresentationalism, based upon readings of Sellars, Quine, and Davidson, led him to a radical historicizing of philosophy. If there is no distinction between the necessary and the contingent, or between scheme and content, then, he argued, it is no longer clear what counts as "analysis" nor what role analytic philosophy can serve.

Rorty's antirepresentationalism puts natural science on a par with the rest of culture: knowledge is not a matter of getting reality right; rather it is a matter of acquiring the appropriate habits of action for *coping* with reality. Rorty wants to rescue us from a set of pseudoproblems generated by the realist intuition that true statements stand in a representational relation to the world. Antirepresentationalists think that the realist-idealist and skepticism-antiskepticism controversies have been both pointless and undesirable, if only because they see no way of formulating an independent test of accuracy of representation. The notion of such a test implies a standpoint outside our own conceptual scheme for purposes of analyzing and comparing the "correspondence" of representations with nonlinguistic entities.

Rorty embraces the work of Donald Davidson as that which lets the fly out of the fly-bottle. If we take Davidson's recommendation seriously and we reject the scheme-content distinction, we shall no longer be worried about relativism. If we accept that there is no vantage point for comparison outside our own conceptual scheme, we will no longer think of natural science, or physics, as that privileged part of culture either that can provide us with a sky-hook for escaping our culturally saturated beliefs or provide us with an independent standpoint from which we can view clearly the relations of those beliefs to reality. On this view, there are no interesting epistemological differences between natural science, and physics, and the rest of culture. The end of metaphysics is "the final stage in the secularisation of culture" (Rorty in Borradori 1994, 106) and philosophy, radically detranscendentized and deprofessionalized, becomes just one form of "cultural criticism" among others. Deprived of any privileged status or definitive vocabulary, philosophy must operate with historical and socially contextual criteria in the same way as the humanities and the social sciences. Rorty's hope at the beginning of this decade was that "English-speaking philosophy in the twenty-first century will have put the representational problematic behind it, as most French- or German-speaking philosophy already has" (1991a, 12).

In developing an alternative role for philosophy in post-Kantian culture, Rorty rejected philosophy-as-epistemology to embrace philosophy-as-hermeneutics—philosophy as an edifying conversation. In doing so he was among the first to bridge the gap between Anglo-American analytic philosophy and its Continental counterpart, forging something of an uneasy neopragmatist alliance with poststructuralism.

A decade later, Rorty suggested that in his imagination Dewey had come to eclipse both Wittgenstein and Heidegger, and in his later writings he self-consciously styled himself as a defender of what he calls Deweyan liberalism. The full political consequences of his brand of liberalism became evident in a series of papers on "democracy," "cosmopolitanism," and "liberalism"—a position, at one point, he flippantly called "Postmodernist Bourgeois Liberalism" (Rorty 1991a). It is a position that openly espoused a kind of ethnocentrism as an inescapable condition of liberal culture (see Peters and Marshall 1999). In the early nineties, many critics and commentators took Rorty's position as the most fully fledged and deliberate attempt to work through the consequences of pragmatism and to link an antifoundational and antirationalist liberalism with "postmodernism."

Yet the term "postmodernist" is a problematic label to apply to Rorty for a number of reasons, not least because he has suggested subsequently on a number of occasions that it has no consistent meaning. He began to distance himself from his previous uses of the term in the introduction to *Essays on Heidegger* in ways that distinctly foreshadow his present argument. There he wrote:

I have sometimes used 'postmodern' myself, in the rather narrow sense defined by Lyotard as 'distrust of metanarratives'. But I wish that I had not. The term has been so over-used that it is causing more trouble than it is worth. I have given up on the attempt to find something common to Michael Graves' buildings, Pynchon's and Rushdie's novels, Ashbery's poems, various sorts of popular music, and the writings of Heidegger and Derrida. I have become more hesitant about attempts to periodise culture . . . it seems safer and more useful to periodise and dramatise each discipline or genre separately, rather than trying to think of them all as swept up together in massive sea changes. (Rorty 1991b, 1)

Rorty's political liberalism came in for a great deal of criticism for what was perceived as his misuse of a colonizing, imperialistic, and encompassing liberal "we."[1] While Rorty in the early 1990s was dismissive of Marx and the neo-Marxist critics who attacked him, his real quarry seemed to be "postmodern political theory." He was scathing about what he called the "Foucauldian left," which he maintained had given up on the idea of democratic politics. The "Foucauldian left" is mired in critique and unable to deliver an alternative utopian vision. The best parts of what Rorty called "the post-Nietzschean tradition of Franco-German thought" (1991b, 1), by which he means the thought of Heidegger and Derrida, are those parts which "help us see how things look under nonrepresentationalist, nonlogocentrist descriptions" (1991b, 5). The worst parts are those parts that engage politics. Rorty's criticism is that post-Nietzschean politics is obsessed with "radical critique" and infected with a despair and general sense of cultural pessimism.

By contrast, a Deweyan vision of the modern world is dominated by social hope and it is directed to actual problems of contemporary democratic societies, which it addresses in a reformist and pragmatic spirit. With the exception of Dewey and possibly Weber, "Our political imagination has not been enlarged by the philosophy of our century" (1991b, 26) and, in any case, our social democratic vocabulary is all right as it is and does not require any further sophistication by philosophers.

Rorty thinks that the crucial difference between Nietzsche and the American pragmatists

> is that Nietzsche, like Heidegger, saw his personal adventure of self-over-coming as linked to the West, as having world-historical importance. Nietzsche and Heidegger were unable to resist thinking of their own achievements as having broken into a clearing, one which no previous thinker had previously entered. James and Dewey, by contrast, were free of world-historical ambitions themselves. The only such ambition they had was for their country, which they saw as the likeliest place for a social democratic, egalitarian, romantically hopeful society to emerge. (Rorty 1991b, 62)

By contrast with Nietzsche, the American pragmatists saw no relation between the Platonic positing of an inner, essential, and moral nature of human beings as a Truth discoverable as an aspect of a permanent reality and the worth of democracy as a political system somehow founded upon this intuition.

Rorty divides liberal social theory into "Kantians" and "Hegelians," where the latter understand "humanity" as a biological rather than a moral notion and dignity as something that is conferred by a community. He calls the

"Hegelian" defense of American democracy "postmodernist bourgeois liberalism," a term that only sounds oxymoronic because of an inherited but optional political vocabulary used to justify bourgeois liberal institutions and the fact the most "of those who think of themselves as beyond metaphysics and metanarratives also think of themselves as having opted out of the bourgeoisie" (Rorty 1991a, 199). "Bourgeois liberalism"—a set of cultural practices and institutions prevailing under certain economic and historical conditions—is contrasted with "philosophical liberalism"—a set of Kantian principles. "Postmodernist" is used simply to mean "distrust of metanarratives" and while Rorty attributes his use of the term to Lyotard, it really reflects Rorty's naturalization of Hegel and his Wittgensteinian antifoundationalism. The crucial point, on Rorty's view, is that the moral self is redescribed in Quinean terms "as a network of beliefs, desires, and emotions with nothing behind it."

Rorty's "postmodernist bourgeois liberalism" and, in particular, his use of the term "ethnocentrism" has engendered an outpouring of criticism from the Left. Rorty's response is to admit a "misleading ambiguity" in his original use of the term which, he says, made him appear as though he was attempting "a transcendental deduction of democratic politics from antirepresentationalism premises" (Rorty 1991a, 15). He then proceeds to distinguish between ethnocentrism "as an inescapable condition," synonymous with "human finitude" on the one hand, and "as a reference to a particular *ethnos*" on the other; that is, as loyalty to the sociopolitical culture of liberalism. While his critics, he says, are willing to accept the antirepresentationalism, they see themselves as standing outside the culture of liberalism. Rorty, however, does not see them as outsiders but rather as playing a role within this culture for they have neither developed an alternative culture nor have they a utopian vision to offer. Their rage at the slow extension of freedom to marginal groups is understandable, but the "over-theoretical and over-philosophized" form that it takes is of no practical or political use. This seems to be Rorty's most trenchant criticism of the contemporary post-Marxist Left: ideology-critique or 'deconstruction' of existing social practices or liberal institutions have no point unless they point to alternative practices or a new utopia. He writes: "My doubts about the contemporary Foucauldian left concern its failure to offer such visions and such suggestions" (Rorty 1991a, 16).

Rorty doubts whether there is an identifiable phenomenon called "postmodernism" because he sees no sharp break in Western political or cultural life since the time of the French Revolution, although he does acknowledge there is "increasingly less respect for the Enlightenment divisions between spheres of culture," a process beginning with Hegel and completed in Dewey. Poststructuralism, to him, is simply "the latest moment of a historicization of philosophy which has been going on continuously since Hegel" (Rorty 1990, 43).

Yet, even so, Rorty is somewhat ambiguous in his rejection of the term "postmodernism." In *Truth, Politics, and "Post-Modernism"* (Rorty 1997), Rorty is more self-conscious about the term 'post-modernist' applied to his own work. His strategy is to put 'post-modernism' in scare quotes and to distance himself from it as a term of self-description. He writes: "sometimes I am called 'post-modernist' because of my pragmatist views about truth and rationality" (35) and yet, he indicates, the term is also used in another sense to refer to an attitude of political hopelessness, an attitude that, since 1968, seems to Rorty to signal both a distrust of liberal humanism and "a retreat from real politics into academic politics" (35).

In the lecture "Is 'post-modernism' relevant to politics?" Rorty thinks we should "abandon the last vestiges of eighteenth-century rationalism in favour of twentieth-century pragmatism" (Rorty 1997, 36). He believes that "abandoning western rationalism has no discouraging political implications" (36) and casts doubt upon the relations between the "vocabularies of intellectuals" and sociopolitical changes. In particular, he suggests that: "The urge to periodize has led intellectuals to think that the rejection of what Derrida calls the 'metaphysics of presence' just *must* have political implications."

Rorty wants to make room for two stories: one about intellectual "progress" and the other about political "progress." The former story concerns the "intellectuals' search for wider, richer, more adequate world views" (39) and is a story that Rorty shares with post-Nietzscheans: Rortyans and post-Nietzscheans give up the distinction between appearance and reality "in favour of a distinction between less useful descriptions and more useful descriptions" (41). The latter story, that narrates "human history as the story of increasing freedom" (40), is based upon a palpable sense of progress not detectable by establishing "Truth" but through a kind of hindsight or retrospection. To the question "Has humanity experienced increased freedom and decreased cruelty?" Rorty answers unequivocally in the affirmative.

Achieving America

In *Achieving Our Country* Richard Rorty (1998) continues the campaign against the "cultural left" he initiated earlier in the decade at roughly the same point that he began to have doubts about the meaning of the term "postmodernism." The "cultural left" (rather than "postmodernists") is now the term Rorty prefers to use to describe the constellation of left academics who have chosen to embrace "apocalyptic French and German philosophy"—Nietzsche, Heidegger, Foucault, and Derrida. Based upon this "resigned," "pessimistic," "spectatorial," "abstract," "over-theorized" and "over-philosophized" system-critique, the cultural left allegedly has substituted philosophy for political economy, sadism (Freud) for selfishness (Marx), Otherness for economic inequality, and collaborated with the Right in replacing real politics with cultural politics. The result, according to Rorty, is that the academic left no longer participates in the "American experiment of self-creation" (23): it has "no vision of a country to be achieved by building a consensus on the need for specific reforms" (15) and it has no program that can deal effectively with the immiseration produced by the globalization of the labor market. In short, the cultural left by focusing upon issues of race, ethnicity, and gender has steered towards identity politics and away from economic politics, thus fragmenting the left and destroying the possibility of a progressive alliance.

By contrast to both the "cultural left," who should learn to "kick its philosophy habit" (91), and the Marxist left, who should give up the term "late capitalism" and restyle themselves as nonsentimental left liberals, Rorty champions a Deweyan progressivism in politics, at once utopian, active, and secular. If the Left was to follow Rorty's Whitmanesque Dewey, then it could get "back into the business of piecemeal reform within the framework of a market economy" (105), settle upon which laws have to be changed to make constitutional democracy respectable again.

Good poststructuralists might applaud Richard Rorty for helping to dismantle truth as correspondence, a project he began as a pragmatist of the certain sort shortly after the publication of *The Linguistic Turn* (1967). They might also feel a little astonished (as children do when they first witness a magician making something disappear) that Rorty manages to demolish all criteria—analytic, disciplinary, historico-political—and yet still somehow retain a standard of judgment or position that allows him to project the rich Atlantic liberal democracies, and particularly the United States as the culture of inclusiveness, as the apex of human historical development to date. They might also display a kind of incomprehension at the way Rorty tells this story of nationhood and patriotism in ways that seem to defy the common-sense of world geopolitics: the growing unequal distribution of world resources; the increasing gap between the North and South, involving novel kinds of labor and capital exploitation; an Americanization of world culture; the eco-privileges of "clean" superpowers that consign environmentally damaging industries to the Third World.

They may also want to contest the way in which his narrative turn seems to underlie his capacity to build an unvarnished utopian politics aimed at specific reforms. If I have correctly interpreted Rorty, then his postmodern pragmatism—specifically, his turn away from the appearance/reality distinction in favor of narrative and the distinction of more or less useful descriptions—seems to underlie his politics and to license his ability to offer narrative accounts of recent political history. This would seem to suggest that there is a relation of sorts between the two stories of the Enlightenment that he wants to tell.

Others also have picked up on Rorty's seemingly equivocal stance in relation to the ontological status of language. He presents a picture of Western culture as moving away from a scientific worldview to a more literary form of life where the only constraints upon inquiry are conversational ones and he describes his own philosophical strategy as a movement "against theory and toward narrative" (Rorty 1982, xvi). Yet, following Davidson, he breaks with the idea that language is a medium of either representation or expression. Language is also not a *thing*, nor is it a substitute for a represented reality as in the reified accounts of language provided by Heidegger, Foucault, or Derrida. There are, for Rorty, no interesting differences between language and things and they do not involve different kinds of rationality. There is only use, and language becomes one more tool for coping with reality. The strong critic or philosopher is one who introduces new vocabularies into the community that provokes new questions and leads to conceptual change. The pragmatist philosophy turns to narrative to tell stories about his favorite texts and new and suggestive stories about the history of philosophy that challenge our prevailing self-descriptions. The problem is that we are offered no clear criterion for deciding which is the best or most satisfactory vocabulary among a range of competing new ones. To say that the best story concerning our present and future action is the one that makes most sense of our past life, or the one that fits best with the story of nation-building seems only to beg the question. How is the criterion of "coherence with the past" here to be judged when "the past" is that which is actively constituted through narrative?

Ankersmit (1997) locates some tensions in Rorty's account of narrative when he pinpoints the influence upon him of Davidson's antihistoricist philosophy of language. Davidson and Rorty distinguish between use and meaning and approach the notion of metaphor from the perspective of use only. On this Tarskian-inspired account of language little room is left for metaphor. Yet, on Hayden White's (1973) influential account, metaphor has been considered the single most important trope for organizing and invigorating the historical text. As Ankersmit (1997, 57) points out, Rorty tends to work with metaphor and irony as the two most important figurative dimensions of his philosophical narrative (as against White's four tropes of metaphor, synecdote, metonymy, and irony), though he lacks a systematic account of how they are related. For Rorty, it is the creativity of metaphor that is responsible for new vocabularies or changes in an existing one. But then, how does this resolve the question about what criteria or means we can choose between competing metaphors? How is it possible to make consistent judgments concerning historical narratives on the basis of best metaphors?

Post-Nietzscheans also may be a little surprised that to see the amount of "political" work that Rorty's dualisms do: two stories of the Enlightenment—political and intellectual; two selves or two "cultures"—public and private; two politics and two Lefts—academic versus activist, utopian versus dystopian, real versus cultural. It is not clear to me on what theoretical basis these dualisms are established. Is each of them based upon irreconcilable or incommensurable vocabularies? One of the effects of these dualisms is to artificially separate identity from economic politics, belying the way in which identity is economically reproduced, as well as being socially and culturally reproduced, at a variety of sites (see Palumbo-Liu 46, n. 9). Judith Butler considers a similar kind of claim made by Marxists against the 'merely cultural'. Her position here I think is relevant and instructive. She writes: "The nostalgia for a false and exclusionary unity is linked to the disparagement of the cultural, and with a renewed sexual and social conservatism on the left" (Butler 1998, 38). She continues:

> The neoconservatism within the left that seeks to discount the cultural can only always be another cultural intervention, whatever else it is. And yet the tactical manipulation of the distinction between cultural and economic to reinstitute the discreditied notion of secondary oppression will only provoke the resistance to the imposition of unity, strengthening the suspicion that unity is only purchased through violent excision. Indeed, I would add that the understanding of this violence has compelled the affiliation with poststructuralism on the Left, that is, a way of reading that lets us understand what must be cut out from a concept of unity in order for it to gain the appearance of necessity and coherence, and to insist that difference remain constitutive of any struggle. (Butler 1998, 44)

To conclude, let me raise briefly three criticisms of Rorty's conception of a liberal utopia. The first concerns his understanding of conflict and its role in the political process; the second revolves around his reification of the notion of "our country" and the implicit assumption that world moral and political progress is dependent upon the universalization of the liberal democratic model; the third concerns Rorty's use of the public/private distinction.

First, for Rorty democratic politics is a matter of an ever-expanding social inclusiveness, of increasing the number of people included in the conversational "we." Chantal Mouffe (1996b, 5) raises the problem with Rorty's account of democratic politics as follows:

> Like his hero, John Dewey, Rorty's understanding of social conflict is limited because he is unable to come to terms with the implications of value pluralism and accept that conflict between fundamental values can never be resolved.

If Mouffe is right, if this is indeed the case, then the faith that Rorty puts in persuasion and economic progress seems misplaced. Economic equality, while both a desired and necessary end, will not of itself solve the problem of value difference. If the dimension of antagonism or conflict is central to the political process and there are diverse and irreconcilable conceptions of the good, then it would seem dangerous and naïve to think that we can limit our involvement in politics simply to pressing for specific reforms or to changes to the law.

Second, it seems to me that there is a structural parallel between Rorty's claims concerning difference and identity at the level of the nation, and his claims, perhaps, only implied, concerning value difference and identity, at the international level. The first part of this structural homology can be established by reference to a passage from David Palumbo-Liu (1999, 47), who writes:

> Rorty wants to jettison notions of a "common humanity" yet his aesthetics are precisely that which confirm the content of a transcendental "human being." And this is where literature comes into play so forcefully. Rorty seeks a transcendental form to mediate and anchor his "pragmatics": it will be the narrative form of the nation. This prereflexive, intuited "shudder" is nothing less than a sublime, unexaminable, objective, but invisible thing out there called "our country."

The second part of the homology I shall express as a worry I have, as I am not sure I can for the moment express it in the form of an argument. It is the anxiety that the same attitude Rorty exhibits to the cultural and gender difference and to the question of value pluralism at the level of the nation, will be repeated by Rortyans at the international level. It is an anxiety about the force of his patriotism, about the reification of the term "our country": in short his Amero-centrism. My fear as a citizen of a very small country (New Zealand) on the periphery of the world system is that Rorty's faith in consensus and in the smooth world evolution of liberal democracy, will ride over ethnic and cultural differences and not be able to recognize when those differences constitute an active challenge to the Amero-pragmatist interpretation of liberal democracy. In short, my fear is that the dualism of self and other—of "we" liberals and the rest—will structurally repeat itself at the level of the world system.

Third, a set of criticisms concerning the distinction between the public and the private: these criticisms were first raised in the discussions Rorty had with Critchley, Laclau, and Derrida at the College International de Philosophie in 1993, and subsequently published as *Deconstruction and Pragmatism* in 1996. I raise them in truncated form again here because Rorty never got an opportunity to answer them at the time of the seminar and because I am unaware that he has specifically addressed them elsewhere in his work subsequently.

First, Rorty's position on the public/private distinction, especially in relation to categorizing Derrida's work. In *Contingency, Irony, and Solidarity*, Rorty (1989) proposes the distinction between "private ironist" and "public liberal," consigning Derrida to the former category and arguing that his work has no political consequences. As he writes in *Deconstruction and Pragmatism*:

> I divide philosophers, rather crudely, into those (like Mill, Dewey and Rawls) whose work fulfils primarily public purposes, and those whose work fulfils primarily private purposes. I think of the Nietzsche-Heidegger-Derrida assault on metaphysics as producing private satisfactions to people who are deeply involved with philosophy (and therefore, necessarily, with metaphysics) but not as politically consequential, *except in a very indirect and long-term way.* (my emphasis, Rorty 1996, 16)

While I have some inkling, I would very much like to know what Rorty means by the last clause.

While Rorty (1998, 138) acknowledges that he considers Derrida to be a "romantic utopian"—a label that Derrida rejects in favor of the "messianic"—he also suggests that "a revival of ineffability" is linked to a "principled, theorized, philosophical hopelessness" of the Left (37). His answer is to relegate Derrida to private life insofar as he offers "a quasi-religious form of spiritual pathos" (96).

Derrida, himself, in response to Rorty—while accepting much else of Rorty's description of his work—rejects Rorty's public/private distinction as applying to his work by suggesting that his more literary texts "are not evidence of a retreat towards the private, they are performative problematizations of the public/private distinction" (Derrida 1996, 79). Literature in the way Derrida studies or practices it, he suggests, is "the complete opposite of the expression of private life." "Literature," he continues "is a public institution of recent invention," defined in terms of its European history by "the principled authorization that anything can be said publicly" (Derrida 1996, 80).

This is now "old hat" and part of the history of the debate, but to summarize let me quote Chantal Mouffe once more:

> It is Rorty's over-rigid distinction between the public and the private which blinds him to the complexity of the weaving between two spheres, and which leads him to denounce any attempt to articulate the quest for individual autonomy with the question of social justice. (Mouffe 1996b, 3)

She suggests that when Rorty divides up the desire for self-creation and the desire for community into "two irreconcilable and final vocabularies," he also "deprives us of the rich critical potential opened up by public ironists like Nietzsche and Foucault" (Mouffe 1996b, 3).

Rorty must defend his distinction against these criticisms and, in addition, show that contingently speaking, or in practice, the distinction is not mediated by redefinitions of the private in terms of the "personal" or the "domestic." If we accept that the private sphere is a historical development dependent upon the emergence of certain institutions (not least "literature" and the "reading public"), then I would have thought that one aspect of the very cultural politics Rorty dismisses—that of gender—would provide important and substantial criticisms of the way in which this distinction has been drawn in the past with the economic consequence of masking the gendered division of labor in the household and rendering women's unpaid work invisible.[2]

Notes

This paper was presented at the conference "The End of Postmodernism?" a Colloquium to Host Richard Rorty, Humanities Research Center, Australian National University, August 21–22, 1999.

1. For examples of these left wing criticisms see, for example, Bernstein (1987), Burrows (1990), Fraser (1990). In reply see Rorty (1987), his introduction to *Objectivity, Relativism, and Truth* (1991a) and in the essay "De Man and the American Cultural Left," in *Essays on Heidegger and Others* (1991b).

2. For an account that attempts to rethink cultural politics, challenging the political dogma from both Right and Left, see Giroux (2000).

Bibliography

Ankersmit, F. R. (1997) Between Language and History: Rorty's Promised Land, *Common Knowledge*, 6 (1): 44–78.

Borradori, G. (1994) *The American Philosopher*, trans. R. Crocitto. Chicago: University of Chicago Press.

Bernstein, R. (1987) One Step Forward, Two Steps Back, *Political Theory* 15 (4): 539–63.

Burrows, J. (1990) Conversational Politics: Rorty's Pragmatist Apology for Liberalism. In A. Malachowsky (ed.). *Reading Rorty*, Oxford: Basil Blackwell.

Butler, J. (1998) Merely Cultural, *New Left Review*: 33–44.

Derrida, J. (1996) Remarks on Deconstruction and Pragmatism. In Chantal Mouffe (ed.), *Deconstruction and Pragmatism*. London: Routledge, 77–88.

Fraser, N. (1990) Solidarity or Singularity? In A. Malachowsky (ed.), *Reading Rorty*. Oxford: Basil Blackwell, 303–21.

Fritzman, J. M. (1993) Thinking with Fraser about Rorty, Feminism, and Pragmatism, *Praxis International* 13 (2): 113–25.

Haber, H. (1994) *Beyond Postmodern Politics: Lyotard, Rorty, Foucault*. New York: Routledge.

Hendley, S. (1995) Putting Ourselves Up for Question: A Postmodern Critique of Richard Rorty's Postmodernist Bourgeois Liberalism, *Journal of Value Inquiry* 29: 241–53.

Giroux, H. A. (2000) Rethinking Cultural Politics: Challenging Political Dogmatism from Right to Left. In *Impure Acts: The Practical Politics of Cultural Studies*. New York: Routledge.

Jencks, C. (1996) *What Is Post-Modernism?* 4th ed. London: Academy Editions.

Lyotard, J.-F. (1984) *The Postmodern Condition: A Report on Knowledge*, trans. G. Bennington and Brian Massumi, foreword by F. Jameson. Minneapolis: University of Minnesota Press.

———. (1989) Universal History and Cultural Differences. In A. Benjamin (ed.), *The Lyotard Reader*. Oxford: Basil Blackwell.

———. (1992) *The Postmodern Explained to Children, Correspondence 1982–1985*. Sydney: Power Publications.

———. (1993) *Political Writings*, trans. B. Readings and K. Geiman. Minneapolis: University of Minnesota Press.

Lyotard, J.-F., with J. L. Thébaud (1985) *Just Gaming*, trans. W. Godzich. Minneapolis: University of Minnesota Press.

Madison, G. (1997) Coping with Nietzsche's Legacy: Rorty, Derrida, Gadamer. Paper presented at "After Postmodernism," University of Chicago, available at www.focusing.org/madison2.html.

Mouffe, C. (1996a) (ed.) *Deconstruction and Pragmatism*. London: Routledge.

———. (1996b) Deconstruction, Pragmatism, and the Politics of Democracy. In Chantal Mouffe (ed.), *Deconstruction and Pragmatism*. London: Routledge, 1–12.

Palumbo-Liu, D. (1999) Awful Patriotism: Richard Rorty and the Politics of Knowing, *Diacritics* 29 (1) 37–56.

Peters, M. A. and J. D. Marshall (1999) Rorty, Wittgenstein, and Postmodernism: Neopragmatism and the Politics of the *Ethnos*, in *Wittgenstein, Philosophy, Postmodernism, Pedagogy*. Westport, Conn.: Bergin & Garvey.

Rorty, R. (1967) (ed.) *The Linguistic Turn: Recent Essays in Philosophical Method*. Chicago: Chicago University Press.

——. (1980) *Philosophy and the Mirror of Nature*. Oxford: Blackwell.

——. (1982) *Consequences of Pragmatism: Essays 1972–1980*. Brighton: Harvester.

——. (1989) *Contingency, Irony, and Solidarity*. Cambridge: Cambridge University Press.

——. (1990) The Dangers of Over-Philosophication—Reply to Arcilla and Nicholson, *Educational Theory* 40 (1): 41–44.

——. (1991a) *Objectivity, Relativism, and Truth, Philosophical Papers*, Vol. 1. Cambridge: Cambridge University Press.

——. (1991b) *Essays on Heidegger and Others: Philosophical Papers*, Vol. 2. Cambridge: Cambridge University Press.

——. (1996) Remarks on Deconstruction and Pragmatism. In Chantal Mouffe (ed.), *Deconstruction and Pragmatism*, London and New York: Routledge, 13–18.

——. (1997) *Truth, Politics, and "Postmodernism": The 1997 Spinoza Lectures*. Amsterdam: Van Gorcum.

——. (1998) *Achieving our Country: Leftist thought in twentieth-century America*. Cambridge, Mass.: Harvard University Press.

White, H. (1973) *Metahistory: The Historical Imagination in Nineteenth-Century Europe*. Baltimore: Johns Hopkins University Press.

Wittgenstein, L. (1922) *Tractatus Logico-Philosophicus*, trans. D. F. Pears and B. F. McGuiness, introduction by B. Russell. London: Routledge and Kegan Paul.

Index

About the Contributors

Steven Best received his Ph.D. in philosophy at the University of Texas, Austin. He is currently associate professor of philosophy at the University of Texas at El Paso. With Douglas Kellner, he coauthored *Postmodern Theory: Critical Interrogations* and *The Postmodern Turn*, as well as *The Politics of Historical Vision*.

Ramin Farahmandpur is a doctoral candidate at the Graduate School of Education and Information Studies at the University of California, Los Angeles. A former middle school teacher in Los Angeles, he is now a lecturer at the Charter School of Education at California State University, Los Angeles. Farahmandpur has coauthored a number of articles with Peter McLaren on a variety of topics ranging from globalization, neoliberalism, critical pedagogy, and critical multiculturalism in scholarly journals such as *Educational Researcher*, *Journal of Teacher Education*, *Multicultural Education*, *Educational Policy*, *Journal of Curriculum Theorizing*, and *Theoria: A Journal of Social and Political Theory*. Farahmandpur also works with UCLA's teacher education program. Currently he is working on a coauthored book (with Peter McLaren) entitled, *Globalization and the New Imperialism: Toward a Revolutionary Pedagogy* (forthcoming).

Jim Garrison is professor of philosophy of education at Virginia Tech in Blacksburg, Virginia. His research and teaching interests center on pragmatism and the philosophy of John Dewey, especially as it applies to teacher education. His recent books are an edited work, *The New Scholarship on Dewey* (1995), and *Dewey and Eros* (1997). His most recent book is *William James and Education*, coedited with Ronald L. Podeschi and Eric Bredo, forthcoming. He wrote the chapter on education for the companion volume to *The Collected Works of John Dewey*, edited by Larry Hickman, director of the Dewey Center, and was an invited participant at the World Congress of Philosophy in 1998 where he spoke on Dewey's theory of philosophical criticism. He was, until recently, editor in chief of *Studies in Philosophy and Education*, an international journal of philosophy and education affiliated with the International Network of Philosophers of Education.

Paulo Ghiraldelli Jr. is professor of contemporary philosophy and philosophy of education at the Universidade Estadual Paulista at Marília, São Paulo. His research interests center on neomarxism, Frankfurt School, and neopragmatism. Among his several books are: *Richard Rorty—a filosofia do Novo Mundo em busca de mundos novos* and *O que você precisa saber sobre Filosofia da Educação*. He is general editor of "Portal Brasileiro da Filosofia e Filosofia da Educação" (www.filosofia.pro.br) and the coordinator of the Pragmatism Work Group of the Association of National Post-Graduates in Philosophy (Brazil).

Douglas Kellner received his Ph.D. in philosophy from Columbia University and for many years was a professor of philosophy at the University of Texas, Austin. He is currently George F. Kneller Chair in the Philosophy of Education at UCLA and is author of many books on social theory, politics, history, and culture, including *Camera Politica: The Politics and Ideology of Contemporary Hollywood Film*, coauthored with Michael Ryan; *Critical Theory, Marxism, and Modernity; Jean Baudrillard: From Marxism to Postmodernism and Beyond; Postmodern Theory: Critical Interrogations* (with Steven Best); *Television and the Crisis of Democracy; The Persian Gulf TV War; Media Culture;* and *The Postmodern Turn* (with Steven Best).

James D. Marshall, professor of education (former dean) at the University of Auckland, New Zealand, has interests in educational philosophy and French poststructuralism, especially Michel Foucault. He has contributed to a number of edited collections and has published widely in international journals in educational philosophy, education, social theory, and policy. Recent books and monographs include *Michel Foucault: Personal Autonomy and Education* (1996), *Discipline and Punishment in New Zealand Education* (with son Dominique, 1997), *Wittgenstein: Philosophy, Postmodernism, Pedagogy* (1999), *Education Policy* (1999) (the last two with Michael Peters), and *Nietzsche's*

Legacy for Education: Past and Present Values (2000, coedited with Michael Peters and Paul Smeyers).

Peter McLaren is formerly renowned scholar-in-residence at the School of Education and Allied Professions, Miami University of Ohio, where he also served as director of the Center for Education and Cultural Studies. Peter McLaren is professor at the Graduate School of Education and Information Studies, University of California, Los Angeles. Active as a critical social theorist and in local, national, and international political reform efforts, Professor McLaren has published over thirty books and monographs in a variety of fields, including anthropology, cultural studies, critical literacy, sociology, critical pedagogy, and multicultural education. His books and articles have been translated into thirteen languages. Professor McLaren lectures worldwide on the politics of liberation. His most recent books include *Critical Pedagogy and Predatory Culture, Revolutionary Multiculturalism, Schooling as a Ritual Performance* (3d edition, Rowman & Littlefield), *Life in Schools* (3d edition), and *Che Guevara.*

Michael A. Peters holds a joint post as professor of education at the Universities of Auckland, New Zealand, and Glasgow, United Kingdom. He has research interests in educational theory and policy, and in contemporary philosophy, especially Continental philosophy. He has published a number of books in these fields, including *Wittgenstein: Philosophy, Postmodernism, Pedagogy* (1999) with James Marshall; *Curriculum in the Postmodern Condition* (2000) with Alicia de Alba, Edgar González-Gaudiano, and Colin Lankshear; *University Futures and the Politics of Reform* (1999) with Peter Roberts; *Poststructuralism, Politics, and Education* (1996); *Individualism and Community: Education and Social Policy in the Postmodern Condition* (1996) with James Marshall; and *Counternarratives* (1996) with Henry A. Giroux, Colin Lankshear, and Peter McLaren. He has also edited a number of collections, including *Nietzsche's Legacy for Education: Past and Present Values* (2001), edited with James Marshall and Paul Smeyers; *Virtual Technologies in Tertiary Education* (1998) with Peter Roberts; *Cultural Politics and the University* (1997); *Naming the Multiple: Poststructuralism and Education* (1998); *Critical Theory, Poststructuralism, and the Social Context* (1996); and *Education and the Postmodern Condition* (1995/1997). Peters is executive editor of *Educational Philosophy and Theory* (Carfax) and is coeditor of the on-line Encyclopedia of Philosophy of Education at http://www.educacao.pro.br/.

Bjørn Torgrim Ramberg is professor of philosophy at the University of Oslo, Norway. He did his Ph.D. at Queen's University at Kingston, Ontario

(1988), and was a member of the philosophy department at Simon Fraser University, British Columbia, from 1991 until 2000. His book, *Donald Davidson's Philosophy of Language: An Introduction*, was published in 1989. His writings on Rorty include a contribution to the volume *Rorty and His Critics* (Robert Brandom, ed., 2000), and the entry on Rorty in the Stanford Encyclopedia of Philosophy (http://plato.stanford.edu/entries/rorty/).

Alberto Tosi Rodrigues has a Ph.D. from State University of Campinas, São Paulo, Brazil, in social sciences focusing on the area of state and government policies. He teaches at the Department of Social Sciences, Political Studies Laboratory, Federal University of Espírito Santo, Vitória, Espírito Santo, Brazil, and has recently published *O Brasil de Fernando a Fernando; neoliberalismo corrupção e protesto na política brasileira de 1989 a 1994 (Brazil, from Fernando to Fernando: Neoliberalism, Corruption, and Protest in Brazilian Politics, from 1989 to 1994*, 2000).

Juha Suoranta has a Ph.D. in education and is professor of education in the Faculty of Education, University of Lapland, Finland. He is the author of *Integrated Media Machine*.

Kenneth Wain is professor of education at the University of Malta where besides teaching philosophy of education in the education faculty he also teaches philosophy courses in the arts faculty. Professor Wain is also an ex-dean of the education faculty, involved in teacher education, and has formed part of, and sometimes chaired, a number of government commissions on different aspects of education, most recently on the national curriculum. His publications include articles in *Educational Theory, Journal of Philosophy of Education, Studies in Philosophy and Education, Educational Philosophy and Theory*, and other journals. His published books are *Philosophy of Lifelong Education* (1987), *The Maltese National Minimum Curriculum* (1990), *Theories of Teaching* (1992), and *The Value Crisis* (1995). He has been working for the last seven years on a book about the learning society in a postmodern age.